THE
UNAUTHORIZED

Anne Rice
Companion

Kat Frazier

Statue in New Orleans cemetery

Other Andrews and McMeel books

by George Beahm

———————◆———————

The Stephen King Companion (1989)

The Stephen King Story

War of Words: The Censorship Debate

Michael Jordan: A Shooting Star

The Stephen King Companion
(Revised Edition, 1995)

THE
UNAUTHORIZED
Anne Rice
Companion

edited by
George Beahm

Andrews and McMeel

A Universal Press Syndicate Company
Kansas City

Library of Congress Cataloging-in-Publication Data

The unauthorized Anne Rice companion / edited by George Beahm.—1st ed.
p.   cm.
Includes bibliographical references (p.   ).
ISBN 0-8362-1036-0
1. Rice, Anne, 1941–   —Criticism and interpretation.
2. Women and literature—United States—History—
20th century.   3. Horror tales, American—History and
criticism.   4. Gothic revival (Literature)—United States.
5. New Orleans (La.)—In literature.   6. Rice, Anne,
1941–   —Interviews.   7. Witchcraft in literature.
8. Vampires in literature.   I. Beahm, George W.
PS3568.I265Z55   1996
813'.54—dc20   95–4507
CIP

See page 243 for continuation of copyright notice

Cover photography by Lee Crum/Outline
Book design: Hillside Studio, Inc.
Typography: Connell Zeko Type and Graphics

First edition

———————————◆———————————

TO DONNA MARTIN

with friendship well seasoned over the years

Oblique view of the Rice residence on First Street

Contents

PART THREE

On Anne Rice

◆ RICE THE WRITER ◆

PART FOUR
Chiaroscuro—Anne Rice and the Cinema

◆ INTERVIEW WITH THE VAMPIRE ◆

◆ MISCELLANY ◆

Appendices

George Beahm

Close-up of detail on a headstone at the
Lafayette Cemetery in New Orleans

The great instrument of

moral good is the imagination.

Shelley

Foreword

by Colleen Doran

The vampire is everything we love about sex and the night and
the dark dream-side of ourselves: adventure on the edge of pain,
the thrill to be had from breaking taboos.

Poppy Z. Brite, from introduction to
her anthology, *Love in Vein*

◆

Ever since *Interview with the Vampire*, the world of Anne Rice with its dark,
dream edge and its sweet, subversive sensuality has fascinated millions of
readers. The story of a young vampire with a conscience, his amoral maker,
and their haunting, child-vampire companion, *Interview with the Vampire* is a
visceral, shadowed romance, disturbing and beautiful and horrific. The angst-
ridden Louis, at war with his vampire nature, reflects our own resistance to
our dark side, while the beguilingly wicked Lestat mirrors that part of ourselves that revels in the sensual, the seductive, the shadowed edge.

My first introduction to the work of Anne Rice was *The Vampire Lestat*.
I sat down one evening for a one-chapter read and didn't stop until I finished about three o'clock the next morning. *Interview* came next, and since
then I have devoured each of Anne Rice's offerings, from her immensely
popular Vampire Chronicles series to her intricate portraits of the Mayfair
witches, from her erotica to her period novels, *Cry to Heaven* and *The Feast
of All Saints*.

I was eventually commissioned to illustrate a dream assignment—an
adaptation of Rice's short story "The Master of Rampling Gate." As an artist,
I am fascinated with the immortal beauty and sensual allure of Rice's world—
its dark emotions and her singular literary voice, southern Gothic and dripping
with the atmosphere of her beloved home, New Orleans.

New Orleans's unique beauty, its dangerous shadows, and its bright streets
washed in a haze of steamy southern summer mirror the chiaroscuro world
of the writings of Anne Rice: dark and light hand in hand, allure and evil,
decadence in the delicate filigree of the pristine, white wrought iron work, like

lace fans shielding the secrets behind the dark window-eyes of the ancient, gorgeous houses.

The life of Anne Rice has been chronicled by Katherine Ramsland in her fascinating book *Prism of the Night*. The complex facets of Rice's turbulent world are given further study in the book you now hold, *The Unauthorized Anne Rice Companion*.

George Beahm has previously chronicled the life and work of Stephen King in *The Stephen King Companion, The Stephen King Story*, and *Demon-Driven: Stephen King and the Art of Writing*. Although Anne Rice has often been referred to as "the female Stephen King," their work—except for the fact that they have both written about vampires—has little in common. Stephen King's simple, direct literary voice, as no-nonsense as his New England roots, is a world away from the gothic and erotic Rice.

George Beahm has provided Anne Rice fans with an invaluable resource, a true literary companion, the first of its kind. This book is a resource and reference guide, with rare interviews, articles, profiles, commentary by both critics and contemporaries, and an invaluable appendix of the many editions of Rice's work in all its forms.

George has dedicated months of research to this project, and his respect for the author and her work shows. And as one of Anne Rice's millions of fans, I am grateful.

Colleen Doran

Introduction

Produce, produce, produce . . . for the night is coming.

Matthew Arnold

◆

In *Masters of Darkness*, an anthology of horror fiction, the writers who contributed were asked to select among their own works a personal favorite. Stephen King—one of the most prolific writers in our time—chose "The Woman in the Room," an autobiographical piece that told of the relationship between a son and his dying mother.

In the afterword to his story, King wrote that fiction is traditionally cathartic for the reader, but this story was cathartic for the writer as well. It was, he noted, healing fiction. In the process of writing that story, King worked through the range of emotions that had swept over him like a dark storm when he saw his mother succumb, slowly and inevitably, to an illness that they both knew was fatal.

"The Woman in the Room" is, simply, one of the best stories King has written.

In Anne Rice's life, the darkest period began in 1972. As Rice told Millie Ball of the New Orleans *Times-Picayune* years later, "I lost my daughter, Michele, with leukemia right before her sixth birthday . . . and I finished *Interview with the Vampire* early in 1974. . . . When I wrote *Interview*, I wasn't conscious that I made little Claudia look like Michele. She's a little girl who becomes a vampire and never grows up. I can tell you now that the book was written out of grief, but I certainly didn't think about it at the time." Anne Rice turned to the typewriter and wrote the seminal vampire novel of our time, *Interview with the Vampire*.

Breaking with literary tradition, *Interview with the Vampire* was no horror genre novel, written for a quick buck. For people alienated from society, especially teenagers, the novel had autobiographical overtones. It's okay to be an outsider, the novel reassures us; dare to be different and come out of the darkness!

Since that first book, Anne Rice has consistently broken taboos, writing supernatural fiction that opened up new, mainstream boundaries, as well as erotic fiction (historical and contemporary). Clearly, Rice refuses to be pigeonholed, opting to write whatever moves her, without regard to market considerations.

In her foreword to this book, Colleen Doran—artist, writer, and self-publisher—points out that Rice's appeal is her uniquely "gothic and erotic" perspective, which characterizes her best work. Colleen's also on the mark in observing that Stephen King's fiction, while excellent, lacks the erotic edge that defines Rice's fiction. There is, she notes, a world of difference. It is all the difference in the world, and if you want to read her work, there's only one place in the known universe that you will find it: in New Orleans, where— far from the admiring fans that write and phone her, far from the long lines of booksellers who, with books in hand, await their turn for an autograph at a book signing; in short, far from the madding crowd—Anne Rice shuts herself off for several months and does what every true writer must do: write for oneself.

If Rice's fiction lacked substance, there would not be several books written about her work; there would not be critical articles discussing her work in scholarly journals; there would not be long lines of fans standing outside bookstores for hours, waiting to get her autograph; and there would not be commitments from Hollywood, anxious to tap the dark, rich vein that runs like black gold through her best work, waiting to be visually mined for a larger audience.

Now, about this book. If you've seen my earlier companion-style book, *The Stephen King Companion*, you'll know what to expect. As Colleen remarks, I've assembled a wealth of diverse material on Rice: profiles and interviews and commentary that shed light on Rice as an individual as well as on her work. This, to me, is the real value of the book—it provides an overview to Rice's life and work through multiple perspectives, over the last two decades.

If you are a new reader of Anne Rice's fiction, I envy you. There are worlds the like of which you can't imagine—vampires and witches and ghosts, erotic worlds awash in sensuality and carnality, and period novels that transport you to another time, another place. Rice's fiction will do what all good fiction *must*: take you away, mentally, and let you see her books through the lens of your own imagination.

If you are already familiar with Rice's fiction, there's little I need to say, except that I hope this book will tell you some things that you didn't know before, illuminating the writer or her work.

One more thing. This book focuses on the supernatural world of Anne Rice—the ghosts and witches and vampires and mummies and other creatures that go bump in the night. This book does not cover her erotic fiction, a deliberate choice since I did not want to duplicate what Katherine Ramsland has done with *The Roquelaure Reader*. Similarly, because Katherine Ramsland's *Prism of the Night* and Bette B. Roberts's *Anne Rice* provide detailed examinations of each Rice novel, I have avoided rehashing that material the third time around; instead, I've elected to reprint selected reviews from book trade journals like *Publishers Weekly* and *Library Journal*.

Now, it's time to board the train. It'll be pulling out of the station soon, and some of the terrain we'll be passing through will look familiar . . . but some of it will look pretty strange. So keep those window shades up, because what will unfold before you will be like nothing you've ever seen—Anne Rice country, where anything can and *will* happen.

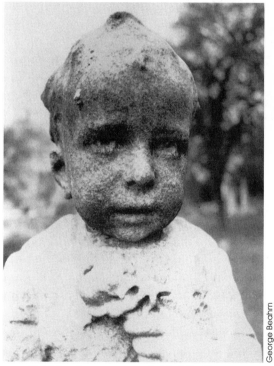

Child figurine at cemetery in Norfolk, Virginia

PART ONE

The Real World of Anne Rice

> Life seems at times to be almost unbearable, just almost unbearable—
> it's just one inch from horrible; the amount of pain, the amount of
> waste, the amount of loss, the amount of destruction, the chaos—
> everything. And I think that's like a vision that's always right near
> me; and I write, and I see my family, and I follow my obsessions, and
> I explore what I have to explore to fight that.

Anne Rice, from Lifetime profile, "Anne Rice: Birth of the Vampire"

◆

Thomas Wolfe was wrong. You *can* go home again, and nobody knows that better than Anne Rice, who grew up as a child in New Orleans, moved to Texas, then to Southern California, and finally returned to New Orleans, completing the circle. A celebrated literary figure who has put her literary stamp on the city, just as John Grisham has claimed Oxford, Mississippi, and Stephen King, Bangor, Maine, Anne Rice has made New Orleans an unholy mecca for her fans. The Rice residence on First Street is a well-known tourist attraction to locals as well as out-of-towners who come, not for the conventions or Mardi Gras or the jazz festival, but to revel in the otherworldly fiction of Rice and frequent the local haunts that are an integral part of her fiction.

In this section, we also see Anne Rice in the real world: as a literary figure profiled, which provides an overview of her life and published work. We also tour her famous residences in New Orleans, a city that has haunted her since childhood.

In recent years, except for book tours, Rice has deliberately kept a lower profile: fewer signings at bookstores, fewer public appearances, and fewer contacts with the media, wherein she has been attacked, provoked, and misquoted by journalists seeking not the truth but increased circulation through controversy, the hallmark of tabloid journalism. Consequently, she has preferred to control publication of news about herself through her own newsletter, a local fan club with its authorized newsletter, local releases, and ads—forums that allow her to speak her mind without fear of being misquoted, or her words taken out of context.

Though her fiction is marked with imaginative flights of fantasy, her real world is grounded in reality: the need to have security around the house, to keep well-intentioned but prying fans at arm's length; the need to control carefully her public appearances, because the lines have grown too long; and the need to put down roots and gather family around her in an attempt to preserve what she can of a life that has, of late, become increasingly less private, more demanding, and considerably more stressed in her role as a local celebrity, a bestselling author, and an internationally known figure.

Anne Rice talks to the media on the occasion of the world premiere of *Interview with the Vampire* in New Orleans.

Chronology

Note: The chronology that follows is abbreviated, focusing on key personal moments and professional publications. For those wishing a more detailed chronology, see *Prism of the Night* by Katherine Ramsland.

◆

1941   Howard Allen O'Brien (Anne Rice) born on October 4 in New Orleans.

1957   Family moves from New Orleans to Richardson, Texas.

Meets husband-to-be, Stan Rice, in high school.

1959   Graduates from high school.

1961   Marries Stan Rice.

1964   The Rices move to San Francisco, at the height of the hippie movement.

1966   The Rices have their first child, Michele.

1969   The Rices move to Berkeley.

1972   Michele dies of leukemia.

1973   Anne writes novel, *Interview with the Vampire*.

1974   Meets literary agent Phyllis Seidel at a writers' conference; Seidel subsequently sells the novel to Knopf.

1976   Anne publishes *Interview with the Vampire*. It is the first in a series of the Vampire Chronicles.

1978   The Rices have their second child, Christopher.

1979   Anne publishes a historical novel, *The Feast of All Saints*,
        at Simon & Schuster.

1982   Anne publishes a second historical novel, *Cry to Heaven*.

        A short story, "Master of Rampling Gate," is published in
        Redbook magazine.

1983   Anne publishes *The Claiming of Sleeping Beauty*, the first in an
        erotic trilogy, under the pen name A. N. Roquelaure.

1984   Publishes *Beauty's Punishment*, the second in the trilogy, under
        the pen name A. N. Roquelaure.

1985   Publishes a contemporary erotic novel, *Exit to Eden*, under the
        pen name Anne Rampling.

        Publishes *Beauty's Release*, the third in the trilogy, under the
        pen name A. N. Roquelaure.

        Publishes *The Vampire Lestat*.

1986   Anne publishes another contemporary erotic novel, *Belinda*,
        under the pen name Anne Rampling.

1988   Publishes *The Queen of the Damned*.

        The Rices move to New Orleans.

1989   Anne publishes *The Mummy, or Ramses the Damned*.

1990   Publishes *The Witching Hour*, the first in the Lives of the
        Mayfair Witches.

        The first book about Anne Rice, *Prism of the Night* by
        Katherine Ramsland, is published.

1992   Anne publishes *The Tale of the Body Thief*.

1993   Publishes *Lasher*.

The Rices purchase St. Elizabeth's in New Orleans.

1994   Anne publishes *Taltos*.

The motion picture *Exit to Eden* is released in October.

The motion picture *Interview with the Vampire* is released in November.

1995   Anne publishes *Memnoch the Devil*.

Hosts the Memnoch Ball, under the auspices of The Vampire Lestat Fan Club.

1996   Anne to publish *The Servant of the Bones*.

Figure in cemetery in New Orleans

Anne Rice:
The Literary Queen of the Damned

I'm like most fantasy writers: This is the way I write about reality.
When I step into [and] become a vampire or a witch, I'm able to
write about good and evil, guilt and pain, life and death in a way
that I can't when I'm trying to write realistically.

I tried for years to write realism, but it was very artificial to me.
And when I happened onto this idea of interviewing a vampire and
letting him speak, my whole world opened up.

Anne Rice, on "The Larry King Show" (November 11, 1994)

◆

The antique hearse carrying Anne Rice's black casket made its way through
the streets of New Orleans. The hearse did not stop at Lafayette Cemetery,
but continued on its way, trailed by jazz musicians who brought up the
rear—Anne Rice had always wanted a jazz funeral, and now her wish had
come true.

The hearse arrived at its final resting stop: not a cemetery but the Garden
District Book Shop at the Rink, at the intersection of Prytania Street and
Washington Avenue, adjacent to Lafayette Cemetery, which found its fic-
tional way into the Vampire Chronicles and the Lives of the Mayfair Witches
as well. Pallbearers removed the casket and brought it carefully inside.
Outside, Rice fans formed a line two city blocks long, trailing down the street
like a long cape; they had waited patiently for this rare opportunity to see
Anne Rice.

The casket, when opened, revealed its human cargo: Rice dressed in a
vintage wedding gown. Understandably, for this important event, she wanted
to look her best. But because it was hot, she had held in her hands a small
battery-operated fan that cooled her during the procession from her house
to the cemetery and finally to the bookstore.

Then, with a helping hand, she got out of the casket and took a seat at
Britton E. Trice's bookstore, the first stop on her book tour to promote *Memnoch the Devil*. She then signed books for hours.

Clearly, she had a hell of a good time. It was pure Anne Rice, and she loved every minute of it. It was, as she explained, "wonderfully weird."

Welcome to the wonderfully weird world of Anne Rice.

Transcending the Genre

Like Stephen King's, Anne Rice's roots can be found in the horror and supernatural field; and, like King, Rice transcended the narrow confines of the genre and went mainstream.

The approach to the subject matter, Rice learned, was everything; she took the material seriously, with what King termed "honest intent . . . that has to stand at the base of any writing career." Rice decided that to tell her stories, she could not write the kind of Protestant fiction that dealt with the angst of middle-class white Americans. Instead, immortals—the things that went bump in the night—would be her fictional instruments of instruction, destruction, and deconstruction: witches, mummies, ghosts, and . . . vampires.

Traditionally treated in popular culture as toothless terrors, vampires had lost their bite, their ability to scare, to terrify. Stephen King changed that with *'Salem's Lot*, considered to be a classic book in the field, but it was Anne Rice who transformed the very nature of vampires—most notably Lestat—from feeders to existentialists who pondered the questions surrounding life and death in all its cosmic mystery.

"I think the vampire is one of the most flexible and deeply romantic figures you can use in pop culture," Rice said to Larry King during a TV interview on November 11, 1994. "As everybody knows, really fine vampire stories and movies tend to be much larger than their parts. . . . Larry, if [*Interview with the Vampire*] wasn't about something bigger than that, we wouldn't be talking. The novel's been around for eighteen years. It's easy to write a throwaway vampire novel—anybody can do that."

Rice is right. The horror genre is rife with inexpensive paperbacks that are consumed as mind candy, useful only for temporary diversion. No wonder Dean R. Koontz, a founding father of the Horror Writers of America, speaking of the level of craft in the horror genre, concluded that "we are overwhelmed with trash."

Though Rice has been well known in the book community for nearly two decades, she has only recently seen her works make it to the silver screen: *Exit to Eden*, starring Dan Aykroyd and Rosie O'Donnell, and *Interview with the Vampire*. The former movie was more a farce than a force, but the latter was among the top ten grossing—and gross-out—movies of the year. More than a moneymaker, the movie also tapped a new vein; new Rice fans haunted the bookstores, wanting to know what happened in *The Vampire Lestat.*

Why are Rice's novels so popular? As with any bestselling author, there are several obvious reasons. She produces on average a new novel every year, which over a period of time builds an audience that is willing to pay the extra bucks for the hardback instead of waiting for the paperback. She writes commercial fiction, primarily supernatural tales of ghosts and witches and vampires and mummies, though she has also written historical novels and, by her admission, pornography. But most of all, her novels appeal to both sexes and all ages, with a large female readership that finds the gothic eroticism irresistible, and young people in their teens and twenties who, like her characters, feel alienated from society, excluded not by choice but by circumstance.

How popular is Rice? *Memnoch the Devil* went to press with 750,000 copies, in hardback, at $25. (For the well heeled, a signed, limited edition from Britton E. Trice Publishing costs $150 for the least expensive edition; the more expensive editions, costing $250 and $375, sold out shortly after publication.)

Her marathon book-signing sessions attract record crowds—typically many hundreds—recalling the appeal of rock stars and other celebrities, not book authors who traditionally stay at home and write and stay out of the limelight.

The compensation, of course, is that a Rice signing is not merely a book signing but, carefully orchestrated by her publisher, a Publishing Event, complete with live entertainment to keep you distracted from the snail-like pace of the line itself, inching its way to Rice's table.

It wasn't always so. Rice, like all writers, had to find herself and her fictional voice, a search that would take nearly four decades: her first novel was not published until 1976.

The Early Years

Howard Allen O'Brien (Anne Rice's name at birth) was the second daughter of Howard and Katherine (Allen) O'Brien. Born in New Orleans on October 4, 1941, she grew up in the Irish Channel section of the city.

Before entering first grade at Redemptorist School, she chose to change her name to Anne. Her parents, who encouraged self-expression and individuality, went along; from that point on, she was Anne, not Howard.

Brought up in a family of storytellers—her mother was creative and imaginative, her father was an aspiring writer—Anne and her sisters (Alice, Karen, and Tamara) told each other stories, too.

Though Anne wanted to fit in and be a good little Catholic girl at Redemptorist like her classmates, she realized early on that she was the proverbial square peg trying to fit into the round hole. She *was* different, and it was a difference that even the nuns at school noticed, especially her growing interest in the otherworldly, an interest heightened by the admittedly haunted history of New Orleans itself. "We were very weird," she once said. "And we felt very set apart."

At an early age, Rice knew what it was to be an outsider. On one hand, she wanted very much to be liked and admired for her own individuality, encouraged by her parents; and on the other, she found herself irresistibly drawn to the local haunts in New Orleans, especially the cemeteries with their above-ground mausoleums, the movie house with flickering films of mummies and monsters, and the local library where she devoured tales of the supernatural.

An outsider at school, Anne was also—depending on her mother's mood—an outsider at home, at times. Her mother, an alcoholic, took comfort herself in spirits. Not quite fifteen years old, Anne saw her mother prematurely die in 1956. It was the end of her innocence.

Turning to her faith for solace at a time of personal angst and confusion, she found Catholicism lacking in answers. She had embraced the religion as a matter of faith but, increasingly, in the years to follow, would find it slip-sliding away because faith, she learned, was not enough.

Howard O'Brien remarried in 1957 and, with his new bride, moved the family to Richardson, Texas. For Anne, who socially and intellectually felt set apart from her peers and the world around her, the move was traumatic. To her, New Orleans was and always would be her home, an anchor to her childhood and everything she held dear—Richardson, Texas, on the other hand, was terra incognita.

In time, Anne adjusted to life and, in fact, found Richardson High to be a liberating experience after attending Redemptorist. At Richardson, in journalism class, she found herself attracted to a bright, intense young man named Stan Rice.

George Beahm

Front view of the house that Rice grew up in, at 2301 St. Charles Street

Anne Rice: The Literary Queen of the Damned

After graduation, Anne attended the nearby Texas Woman's University and, later, North Texas State, which Stan Rice attended. At a chance meeting downtown, Anne saw Stan and, as Ramsland wrote in *Prism of the Night*, "hope was rekindled. They spoke briefly, but Stan showed no inclination to follow up. . . . It seemed to her that things were pretty much finished with Stan."

As it turned out, Stan, like her, was in the process of discovering himself, a process that, among other things, uncovered his bliss: poetry—and, as he admitted to himself, Anne.

After a letter and a visit to San Francisco, Stan returned home and soon proposed. She left San Francisco and headed back to Texas, where they were married on October 14, 1961. It was, it seemed, a marriage made in heaven.

Stan never finished college at North Texas State. Leaving Texas permanently behind, they moved to San Francisco and began new lives, this time together.

California Dreaming

Working full time and attending night courses at the University of San Francisco, the Rices later transferred to San Francisco State University, where Stan earned a degree in creative writing and Anne earned a degree in political science. Stan, not Anne, looked to be the writer in the family. It was Stan who published poetry, gave readings, and became part of the literary community. Anne, in contrast, played the role of the supportive wife and mother—in 1966, her daughter Michele was born. The joy of being parents, as it turned out, was short-lived: Four years later Michele was diagnosed with leukemia and finally succumbed in 1972.

Just as her mother's death marked a turning point in her life, causing her to evaluate the belief systems that were supposed to insulate her and give meaning to life, so now the death of her daughter reinforced the notion that there was no God—how could He be so cruel, so unfeeling?—and that life was existential, meaningless.

Both Stan and Anne found refuge, but not in themselves (unable to save their daughter), and not in religion (unable to provide answers or solace), but in alcohol.

At this low point of her life, Anne worked full time but found the work meaningless. Eventually quitting at the behest of Stan, Anne turned to fiction and wrote her way through her private grief. A short story, "An Interview with the Vampire," would be the vehicle that would carry her outside her world filled with pain—a vehicle that would allow Michele to be reborn in the fictional guise of Claudia, a child vampire who would live . . . *forever*.

Interview with the Vampire

Written in one sustained piece in five weeks, *Interview with the Vampire* pulled together Anne Rice's trademark writing skills: the textured history, the sublimated eroticism, the philosophical questions. Going for baroque, Rice's horrific tale transmuted her personal pain into a tale laden with symbolic overtones.

When Stan read the manuscript, it reaffirmed what he had known for years—his wife was the writer; he was the poet. He knew, then, that their lives would change forever—eventually, since he knew the publication process was daunting and, at best, chimerical.

In 1974 Anne Rice attended a writer's conference with *Interview with the Vampire* in hand. There she met Phyllis Seidel, who in turn sold it to Knopf, a prestigious New York publisher. Two years later *Interview* was published, and the novel immediately won her a legion of fans, but not among book critics, who were put off by the subject matter. It would also be the beginning of her growing disenchantment with, and later abandonment of, book reviewers as impartial critics. As Rice later explained to an interviewer, "Book reviewing is a mess. There's no indication of what the book is attempting or accomplishing. It's not like opera reviewing. The opera guy has to know something about opera. He can't just go in and say, 'Why are they screaming in Italian?' But a book reviewer can do that. 'Why are all these people *vampires*?'"

The novel's movie option was picked up by Paramount for $150,000, and the paperback sale garnered $700,000.

Rice did not write the second book in what became the Vampire Chronicles until 1985. In the interim, she explored her interests in historical fiction, sexuality, and erotica with books that confused and fragmented her audience wanting more supernatural fare.

In 1978 the Rices had a second child—a son, Christopher.

In 1979, she published *The Feast of All* Saints, followed in 1982 by *Cry to Heaven*, another historical novel. She then wrote three erotic novels under her pen name A. N. Roquelaure (*The Claiming of Sleeping Beauty*, 1983; *Beauty's Punishment*, 1984; *Beauty's Release*, 1985), and a contemporary erotic novel, *Exit to Eden* (1985), under another pen name, Anne Rampling, which secured a $35,000 advance—a far cry from the big money that had marked her first novel published nearly a decade earlier.

Predictably, when she returned to the Vampire Chronicles with *The Vampire Lestat*, publisher and public interest spiked up sharply. Knopf paid $100,000 for hardback rights, and her fans propelled it onto the bestseller list.

Anne Rice, though aware of the market forces that shaped her acceptance in the marketplace, was more concerned with writing what appealed to her at the time; and if it meant changing fictional voices—from historical fiction to erotica to the supernatural—so be it. Her fans would have to trust her as she explored the facets of her fictional world.

In 1986 she published another erotica novel, *Belinda*, then began writing the third vampire novel, *The Queen of the Damned* (1988).

Haunted City, Haunted Past

In retrospect it seemed inevitable that Rice would eventually return to New Orleans. By her father's choice, she had moved to Texas; and by her own choice, she had moved twice to California, but the more she drew literary inspiration from the past, the more she realized that New Orleans, not San Francisco, was home—a feeling aggravated when the hometown paper published what she perceived to be irresponsible reviews of her early novels.

Stan took a leave from teaching and in 1988 they sold their California home and bought a house in New Orleans. In contrast to the frigid California literary climate, the Big Easy was easy on Anne, and she immediately felt welcomed as part of the literary community—here, it *felt* right.

After the 1988 publication of *The Queen of the Damned*, which had earned her a $500,000 advance, the Rice family made a permanent move to New Orleans in 1989. Freed from the financial need to teach for a living, Stan gave up academic life to pursue painting, an early interest. Anne Rice's financial success almost meant that they could afford their dream house, which they found in the Historic Garden District: a stately manse set on a quiet residential corner sheltered by large, overhanging trees.

In 1989 Anne Rice published *The Mummy, or Ramses the Damned*, a screenplay recycled as a novel. Though she has not to date written a second book about Ramses, she will undoubtedly do so when the spirit moves her.

The series that did take shape, the Lives of the Mayfair Witches, began in 1990 with the publication of *The Witching Hour*. The novel almost marked a record advance: $5 million for it and the next novel in the Vampire Chronicles.

The next year, personal tragedy struck: Anne Rice's father passed away. That reinforced her notions of the importance of family, as well as reminded her of the fragility of human life, as she gathered her three sisters together in New Orleans, encouraging them to live nearby as one extended family.

In 1992 *The Tale of the Body Thief*, the fourth Vampire Chronicles novel, was published, marking the completion of her two-book contract. In 1993 Rice signed another record-breaking contract, this time for $17 million.

Just as the two-book deal allowed her to buy the mansion on First Street, the new book deal allowed her to fulfill another childhood dream: buying and restoring St. Elizabeth's, a 47,000-square-foot structure occupying one city block, which had stood empty for years. It would, Rice said, house her growing doll collection and allow her room for her other collectibles, as well as give her the space for studios for family and guest quarters for visitors.

That year also saw the publication of *Lasher*, the second in the series Lives of the Mayfair Witches. The following year she began writing *Memnoch the Devil*, a dark and depressing writing experience.

Though several of Rice's novels had been optioned by Hollywood over the years, none had been produced until 1994. Predictably, the forgettable adaptation of *Exit to Eden* came and went like a ghost, but in November, when *Interview with a Vampire* was released, Rice fans bit hard. After months of agonizing over casting calls—notably Tom Cruise as the vampire Lestat—Rice, bewitched by her fans' overwrought concerns, recanted and embraced Cruise as Lestat. The David Geffen movie would go on to be one of the top ten moneymakers in Hollywood for the year, grossing $100.7 million.

Gushing with joy, Rice published two lengthy pieces to clarify her new perspective on the film—a full-page ad followed by an insert, both initially published in *Variety*, the film industry's trade journal.

Like King, Clancy, and Grisham, Rice saw her book sales spike upward as moviegoers, thirsting for more, haunted the bookstores, searching for *The Vampire Lestat*, *The Queen of the Damned*, and *The Tale of the Body Thief*, all conveniently available in hardback and mass-market paperback, usually in attractive displays that drew attention.

The success of her movie also boosted the sales of her new novel, *Taltos*, the third book in her Lives of the Mayfair Witches series.

In 1995, amid much fanfare, Knopf released what Rice had prematurely

Anne Rice: The Literary Queen of the Damned

Robert Beamer

Rice signs *Memnoch the Devil* at the Rizzoli bookstore in Casa Mesa, California, on September 9, 1995.

said would be the last Vampire Chronicle, *Memnoch the Devil*. Boasting a monstrous first printing of 759,000 copies, *Memnoch the Devil* was also the theme of a ball held over Halloween at her newly restored house/museum, St. Elizabeth's. The ball, which drew several thousand ardent readers, officially marked the end of her national tour which began on August 12 when her mock jazz funeral made its way through the steamy streets of New Orleans.

Now fifty-four, Anne Rice has indisputably become the literary queen of the damned, whose tales of the supernatural—to her surprise—grew beyond her cult audience and into a mainstream audience with a ravenous appetite for more.

A doll from the Rice collection

Kat Frazier

Anne Rice: The Literary Queen of the Damned

Her fans are legion and they are the ones whom she trusts, not the book critics and not the academicians who, in recent years, have begun to take her seriously. Her fans, she discovered, love her . . . and she loves them back. She willingly sits for marathon signing sessions on national book tours that would make most writers blanch; she records her thoughts on tape and fans call her telephone number to hear them and leave messages; she publishes her own zine, *Commotion Strange*, supplemented by contributions to the newsletter for the Vampire Lestat Fan Club.

The horrors of success have meant that Anne Rice has seen all vestiges of privacy disappear. Because her home's location is well known and has become a favorite tourist stop, she has reluctantly installed security to keep the fans at bay—feel free to look, she says, but come no closer.

Success has also meant that she's seen her words twisted and taken out of context by the media, always looking for another bit of gossip or bit of sensationalism to hawk a few more papers or magazines, or to ensnare a few more viewers.

With fame, wealth, and the freedom to write whatever she damned well pleases, Rice knows only one fear: "My own talent vanishing away from me," as she told TV talk host Charlie Rose on an August 1995 show.

Her fans, however, need not fear a Rice literary drought because she has completed *The Servant of the Bones*, to be published in 1996.

Beyond her wildest dreams, the little girl who grew up as an outsider would, finally, as an adult see her work and herself accepted on her own terms, by the people in the city she loves, as well as millions of fans worldwide.

Coming out of the shadows, Anne Rice now feels the sunlight on her skin, and, as she might tell you, it feels fine, just fine.

The House at 1239 First Street

by Martha Ann Brett Samuel and Ray Samuel

In The Great Days of the Garden District and the Old City of Lafayette, *Martha Ann Brett Samuel and Ray Samuel profile some of the more famous and distinctive homes, to "satisfy the continuous requests made by the hundreds of visitors who take the [Parents' League of McGehee]-sponsored Garden District home tours."*

What follows is their entry for the house at 1239 First Street —the Rice home, formerly known as the John A. Mmahat House, as listed in the Samuels' book.

◆

Roses, their beauty captured in iron, embellish the grillwork of this palatial Garden District mansion. The interesting facade with double galleries is distinguished by the use of "columns in antae," Corinthian and Ionic columns between the square pilasters at the corners.

The contract for construction of the building was signed on January 3, 1857. For $13,000, so modest by present day standards, the owner, Albert Hamilton Brevard, erected a mansion of many spacious rooms, ornamented in the best classic fashion, with all the carved wood in the house of solid mahogany.

The architect of this splendid, typically New Orleans interpretation of the Greek Revival was James Calrow. Charles Pride was the builder. Originally, the lot comprised half a square extending all the way to Camp Street, boundaries which are still defined by identical fencing along the block. This decorative fence was a patented design and as such was a forerunner of the unaesthetic chain link fences of today. A century ago it was unthinkable that beauty and utility not go hand in hand.

Two years after the completion of the house, Brevard died and his daughter inherited the property. In 1869 she sold it to Emory Clapp for his bride. In preparation for the newlyweds, special mirrors were ordered from France for the double parlor, where they hang today. Made of rosewood, these four mirrors are ornamented with the monogram of the bride and groom. A pair of the mirrors hangs over the marble mantels; the other pair, hung at opposite

The House at 1239 First Street

Front view of the Rice residence on First Street

Scott Stewart

ends of the huge parlor, reflects the handsome crystal chandelier *ad infinitum*, a source of delight to visitors.

On the south side of the house are double galleries of the same delicate ironwork. The hexagonal library with bedroom above and the accompanying grillwork gallery were added by the Clapps. For over 65 years Mrs. Clapp made her home here, taking a loving interest in both house and grounds. Upon her death in 1934 the house was purchased by Mrs. Frank Brostom. Next owners were Federal Judge and Mrs. John Minor Wisdom, who occupied the house from 1947 until 1972. The next owners, Mr. and Mrs. John A. Mmahat, tastefully preserved the various outstanding features of the house.

Both inside and outside walls are of brick. The recessed entrance provides space to fold back the tremendous storm doors. Door and window frames in the house follow several patterns but for the most part are topped with egg and dart molding and a Roman classic design of great charm. Especially elaborate treatment of the woodwork was used in the dining room. Among the many beautiful plaster ceiling centerpieces, the medallion in the library is considered the finest.

THE HAUNTING HOUSE ON FIRST STREET

Sitting on a half acre of land, flanked by large trees that obscure the house from the front, the house on First Street haunted Anne Rice. It was, as she explained to Janet Plume of the New Orleans *Times-Picayune*, "always my dream to own a Greek revival in the Garden District."

As Rice told Plume, a few days after they saw the house, she "was in the Trinity Church listening to a cellist playing and I thought, 'That music is that house.' That house is that beautiful, rich, slightly dark but lustrous sound, and it was calling to me to buy it."

Fulfilling her dream, Rice bought the 11,000-square-foot house, which gave her the room necessary for her growing book and doll collections.

A favorite tourist spot, the Rice house draws the faithful fans and the curious alike to its quiet residential street a few blocks from the house in which she grew up on St. Charles Avenue.

The House at 1239 First Street

From the entrance hall the stairway, which has rails and spindles of mahogany, extends in an unbroken flight to the floor above. The typical double parlor is divided by a large arch, necessary to support the ceiling. The arch of carved mahogany terminates in a decorative corbel at either end. Two fireplaces warmed the area in winter and many windows, all with handmade glass, provided the necessary summer ventilation. The marble mantels are unusual in that they are an unidentical pair. One depicts spring; the other, autumn. Throughout the house are rare antiques, paintings, and *objets d'art*.

The front portion of the beautiful garden has a formal arrangement focusing on a classical statue. There is also a bird bath backed with a long bed containing cherry laurels (*Prunus laurocerasus*), yews (*podicarpus*), myrtles, a seasoning bay tree (*Laurus nobilis*), a large cocculus, *Camellia japonica*, and azaleas, edged with boxwood. A huge purple bougainvillea climbs the iron lacework on the front, while the back of the gallery supports a *Quisqualis indica* vine, a tropical plant sometimes called Rangoon creeper. The bed alongside the house has camellias, multifleur, and Confederate jasmine vines (*Trachelospermum jasminoides*).

An integral part of the landscape design is the limestone balustrade which encloses the garden and runs along the flagstone paving. There are formal boxwood parterres in the back garden and an inviting circular bench which surrounds an exceptionally large sweet olive tree (*Osmanthes fragrans*). The planting around the fish pond includes podicarpus, sansaquas, bottlebrush (*Callistemon lanceolatus*), shrimp plant (*Beloperone guttata*), loquat, viburnums, and barberries. White azaleas in profusion lend springtime beauty.

Novel End for Landmark: Rices Purchase St. Elizabeth's for New Home

by Ronette King
(from New Orleans *Times-Picayune*, May 29, 1993)

Until now, it has been home to girls without families or those who couldn't make it on their own.

But in its latest incarnation, St. Elizabeth's will be the compound for an extended family happy to live under one roof—albeit with 47,000 square feet of space under it.

Anne and Stan Rice, novelist and artist, respectively, have bought the complex and are turning it into their private home. When she saw it, Rice said, she knew immediately she wanted it.

"I had been in a lot of places like these before," she said. The interior brick walls and space to add large pieces to the family's art collection that they never had room for helped sealed the deal.

St. Elizabeth's was built as a school in 1865, turned into an orphanage for girls in 1871 and later became a boarding school. The Daughters of Charity closed the school in 1989 and moved the program to Marrero, where they already operated a similar program for boys.

The religious order put the Napoleon Avenue complex on the market. It could have become apartments to feed those on the prowl for upscale living. And it was almost turned into housing for seniors.

Then Rice toured it and found in it her ideal home—inspired by the Italian Palazzo with grand rooms, massive furniture, vintage fabrics and room to expand and display her collection of African and other primitive art.

There will be living quarters for the Rices and their extended family, plenty of space for guests, painting and writing studios, a grand dining hall that can double as ballroom and a "Mardi Gras Room" for viewing parades on Napoleon Avenue.

Novel End for Landmark: Rices Purchase St. Elizabeth's for New Home

The entrance to St. Elizabeth's

Front view of St. Elizabeth's

Renovation Work Begins

This collection of three connected buildings—the first constructed in 1865—offers ample room. They represent the largest cluster of Second Empire design architecture in the city and are on the National Register of Historic Places.

The Rices bought St. Elizabeth's for $1 million and have already started work to renovate and restore the structure. They're tearing out old classroom partitions and removing aged plaster from interior red brick walls. One thing that will remain is the chapel on the second floor of the Prytania Street wing. With its jewel-like stained-glass windows that soar two stories high, the chapel will be used as a recital hall. The statues, communion rail and stations of the cross will remain and several pews will be reinstalled.

Early plans call for the first floor to have drawing rooms, a large family dining room and grand dining hall which can double as a ballroom. The second floor will have six large guest bedrooms, a huge library and the chapel. The third floor will be private living quarters for the Rices and their son, Chris, said Nancy Diamond, operations manager.

Novel End for Landmark: Rices Purchase St. Elizabeth's for New Home

The four-story towers that connect the main building with two added in 1993 and 1994 will be used as a painting studio for Stan, a writing studio for Anne, apartment for Diamond (Stan's sister) and another for Anne's sister, Karen O'Brien.

Discoveries Being Made

So far they've made a few discoveries about the place: an inner stairwell in one wing that had been walled off and what appears to be the original kitchen on the first floor. The place still held remnants of St. Elizabeth's previous life, boxes of handbags and books left behind after the last yard sale, when the facility was relocated. And in the attic where older girls lived, a weathered slip of paper pinned to the door says, "Sister's Storage." There, tucked away under the eaves of the building, the Blessed Mother oversees the inner courtyard.

"Usually Americans have to go to Europe to obtain an old villa, palazzo or chateau," Rice wrote in a press release announcing the purchase. "We have found one right here in one of the most beautiful cities in America. And all our plans are in complete harmony with the lovely work of the architects who built St. Elizabeth's Home."

This is a novel ending to a historical landmark. Early reviews from Rice's new neighbors are favorable:

"We're ecstatic," said Wayne Lake, president of the Faubourg Bouligny Neighborhood Improvement Association.

"I think it's a wonderful expression of faith in an old New Orleans neighborhood," said Patty Gay, director of the Preservation Resource Center.

The Rices plan to keep their Garden District home at First and Chestnut streets. And Anne Rice is still looking for a place to establish a museum for her collection of antique dolls.

Asked if she thought St. Elizabeth's would be enough space for home, Rice replied, "Maybe."

Rice Plans Museum for Dolls at Home

by Coleman Warner
(New Orleans *Times-Picayune*, April 26, 1995)

Vampire novelist Anne Rice has always seen a dark side to dolls.

"Dolls are inherently spooky," she once said. "Some people can't stand to have them around."

But Rice loves having them around, so much so that assemblages of dolls have long greeted visitors to her Garden District home.

And now Rice and her husband, Stan, a poet and painter, have found a spooky place to display a large collection of handmade dolls from around the world: St. Elizabeth's, a 19th century, former girls' orphanage they bought last year, planning to turn it into their home.

Facing Napoleon Avenue and occupying a city block, St. Elizabeth's once inspired tales of dead nuns who returned to haunt the place, prompting even Rice to say she fears visiting after dark.

Recently the Rices asked city planners for permission to open a doll museum on the ground floor of a wing that faces Prytania Street.

Opening a museum in the historic Bouligny neighborhood requires City Council approval and perhaps a waiver of off-street parking requirements. The plan, which does not yet include many specific details, is scheduled for a City Planning Commission hearing. . . .

A description of the museum filed with the commission offered little elaboration on the collection, calling it simply an enormous collection of "contemporary doll art" as well as rare antique dolls. Attorneys and aides for the Rices said the couple is not giving interviews.

But in their proposal the Rices emphasize that the museum is unlikely to attract large numbers of visitors and that it will occupy less than one-tenth of the property.

"The entire vision is of a private collection in a private home—something gracious and beautiful and interesting—offered to the public in a remarkable but very dignified style," the proposal says.

The museum has aroused little concern among neighbors, who were relieved when the Rices bought the handsome brick complex for $1 million and began renovations and landscaping.

26

THE MEMNOCH BALL:
A MONSTROUS CREATION

Under renovation since its purchase, the orphanage was the site of the 1995 Memnoch Ball; the theme: Vampires Through the Ages. Attendees dressed in costume.

As Rice explained in *Commotion Strange #3*, "This year I am taking over (the annual ball), and the party will be throughout the building, and more or less my own monstrous creation. . . .

". . . St. Elizabeth *was* a real orphanage for over one hundred years. It was an empty, benignly haunted building when I bought it. I restored the two story chapel which is one of our major ball rooms, and restoration continues throughout. If you come you will find yourself in the midst of vampires, ghosts, mummies, waltzing nineteenth-century vampires in one ball room, and minueting eighteenth-century vampires in another—people from all over the world in an atmosphere of brick, beam, shining wood floors, velvet and silk drapes by the mile. . . . The building occupies an entire city block. . . .

"Also my entire doll collection will be on display, including the French and German dolls, and it gives me exquisite pleasure for people to see this collection, which includes original contemporary dolls from all over the world, and the French Bru that was described as Ash's doll in *Taltos*. We have a marvelous Nosferatu, full size, made for us by a doll maker in Chicago. And we have a lovely female vampire doll made specially for us by a doll artist in New Zealand. . . .

"My seven foot replica of Pumpkinhead (spongy but great) bought from the Sharper Image will be on display downstairs in the Pumpkinhead Pool Room which also has a real jukebox crammed with oldies. . . .

"It's my special pleasure to take over this year and fill the air with Strauss waltzes, Baroque music, as well as the usual rock."

There had been fear since the orphanage closed a few years ago that the building might be converted to a high-density use, such as a restaurant or medical complex.

The only neighborhood worry has been tour buses stopping at the museum, said Dr. Wayne Lake, president of the Bouligny Improvement Association. But he said attorneys for the Rices have assured residents that buses

A painting, perhaps by Stan Rice, on display at the Memnoch Ball 1995

would be confined to Napoleon Avenue and Prytania Street, which already have heavy traffic.

One neighbor, Jena Street resident Cornelius Crusel, said the Rices have saved St. Elizabeth's and he isn't about to complain about a modest doll museum.

"How many people are going to come to see a doll museum?" he asked. "Now if she had vampires, it might be different."

An Interview with Anne:
The New Orleans Experience

conducted by Ronnie Virgets
(*New Orleans Magazine*, June 1991)

NEW ORLEANS MAGAZINE (NOM): So where were you in 1966?

ANNE RICE: I was in the Haight-Ashbury district of San Francisco, right there on Clayton Street, where it was all happening that summer. I had been in Texas for a couple of years after leaving New Orleans, last year of high school, first year of college, in the Dallas area. After that I went to California and worked my way through school. Stan was just starting to teach at State and those were pretty amazing days. You know, I was telling the photographer here that I was wearing a new dress, a Laura Ashley dress, and it looks just like a granny dress from those flower child days. You can wear anything now; it's nice.

NOM: After you went away, did you come back to New Orleans?

RICE: Oh yes, I came back every chance I got, just for a couple of days at a time. I remember one time driving all the way into town at midnight and going right to the Pearl to get an oyster sandwich, and it was like heaven. Here I am, home again! There's so much here you can't get anywhere else. . . .

NOM: There are frequent comparisons between San Francisco and New Orleans; can you compare the two?

RICE: They're really nothing alike. But what makes them similar is their differences from all other American cities. It's been said that there are only three American cities that have their own look—New Orleans, Boston and San Francisco—and I think that's true, but they're nothing alike. This is the only Catholic city in America. San Francisco may have a big Catholic population, but they really have a Protestant work ethic that dominates there in a healthy way. But this city really is like a piece of the Caribbean or the Mediterranean. We don't care about the Protestant work ethic here; we care more about the po-boy or whether our rice and beans have the right consistency. We know that life's a series of feast days—Jazz Fest, Sugar Bowl, Mardi Gras—and that's a very Catholic outlook. And again, it doesn't matter if

29

you're Catholic or Protestant or Jewish; it's the milieu of the city we're talking about. Also, San Francisco and New Orleans are different from other cities architecturally. San Francisco is a trolley city, a streetcar city, too, and has that wonderful old dense architecture, too. But other than that, it's not really too much like New Orleans.

NOM: They say that much about New Orleans is illogical or absurd; do you find it so?

RICE: Absolutely. Sometimes you think you're in a different world. So much of the physical past is still here. And I think that's good. I mean, if we were caught up in the New York minute, so to speak, most of our buildings would have been bulldozed down already. I mean, every time I bump over one of the potholes on State Street, I tell myself it's great to be home. Things are allowed to mature here.

NOM: Much of your subject matter deals with the un-dead. This is a town that prides itself on its rembrances of the dead. You wrote a novel called *The Feast of All Saints* about All Saints' Day. Do you yourself have any memories of that day?

RICE: I remember going to clean up the graves and flowers being sold on the streets, though the day wasn't especially big in my immediate family. But I was certainly aware of it, as any child growing up here in the '40s and '50s would have been aware of it. We don't run from the dead, we don't try to hide. And the saints we grow up with—St. Patrick, St. Joseph, St. Jude—the saints were all very real, very alive, for us. People ask me how can you write about such things and I say how can I write about anything else? I grew up in a world where people believed in the miraculous. I mean, what about the saint who forgot to turn off the water and the angel came and turned off the water for him and the faucet turned to gold?

NOM: Did you see much superstition in your immediate family or neighbors?

RICE: No. But there was that absolutely firm belief in the Catholic Church and the miraculous. And in ghosts and what would now be called the mythology of the devil. My mother told me that the devil could take the form of loved ones and come back to see us. Of course, I was never scared of such things because we were also taught that the sign of the cross took care of everything; just make the sign of the cross and everything would be okay.

An Interview with Anne: The New Orleans Experience

NOM: This is, or was, a city of neighborhoods. What was yours like?

RICE: You know, I really didn't grow up in a neighborhood. I grew up on the corner of St. Charles and Phillip. We were on the edge of the Garden District, but not really part of it. We had family in the Irish Channel, but we were miles away from that. I went uptown to school for a while, Holy Name, but we certainly weren't part of that. So I would say that I sort of grew up at a crossroads. I remember going to the grocery on Jackson Avenue, and buying comic books next to the Pontchartrain, but I never really felt a sense of neighborhood. I mean, on St. Charles there were millionaires and boarding houses at that juncture. There was a beautiful mansion designed by Gallier across St. Charles and there was Fortier's, a very respectable boarding house for rich old ladies and their chauffeur-driven limos, and yet right around the corner was a boarding house for sailors and old men who were always sitting outside on the porch. It was almost semi-commercial. . . .

NOM: So you were a kind of frontier person?

RICE: A marginal person. People ask why do you feel so much of an outcast or loner . . . well, in a way it had nothing to do with that, but in another way, it did.

NOM: Another way people here define themselves is where they went to school—not college, but high school. Were you aware of this when you lived here?

RICE: Oh, sure. Like I said, I went to Holy Name right through the beginning of high school, then I transferred back to Redemptorist. It was a very exciting time; we had just won the city championship in football and all. But people from there did not like to be told "We knew you were from Redemptorist by the way you talk." Nowadays it's different. You celebrate being from the Irish Channel. But not back in 1956. I didn't have the accent because my parents didn't have it. But I was keenly aware that people looked down on it— and I didn't like it.

NOM: Later on you spent a year at St. Joseph's Academy . . . in boarding school.

RICE: It was a very 19th-century Gothic place. We boarded up in the attic. All the boarders slept in one room, on old iron beds that looked like they had once held mosquito netting. It was a very hard place. Writers are always glad for any experiences they have, and I have some great memories of many friends there. But the place itself was very hard. We went to bed at

8:30 PM; it would practically be light outside. You could hear the music coming from jukeboxes from the bars on Dumaine Street. I describe what living at St. Joseph's was like in *The Witching Hour*. I call it St. Rose's in the book, but it was St. Joseph's.

NOM: Describe a bit of your childhood home in New Orleans.

RICE: Well, like I said, it was the corner of Phillip and St. Charles. It's still here, all boarded up now and I have dreams of one day buying it and having it restored, but I haven't been able yet.[Ed. note: Rice did eventually buy the house.] It was a very relaxed, carefree home. My mother was a Bohemian, very ahead of her time. She believed in a creative atmosphere and all of that, so I can't really say I had a room. It was more like a communal arrangement. There were four of us and at various times, I slept in different bedrooms. Very high ceilings, airy, looked out over Phillip. A big backyard, where I dug for pirate gold. A very high tree that my sister Alice used to climb to the very top to look out for World War II enemies. We used to take brisk walks to Lee Circle to the library there and that was always lots of fun. And Smith's Drug Store loomed large in our lives. When we were kids, it was a large, swanky, air-conditioned drugstore with a great cosmetics counter under glass, a soda fountain and a wonderful comic-book selection that we'd read until they'd run us out. "This isn't the library!" But we had a lot of fun, going there at nine or ten o'clock at night and always feeling safe. . . .

NOM: Where did you go to the movies?

RICE: We went to the Grenada Theater on Baronne. It's gone—I checked it out right away when I got back and it's so sad that it's gone. Anyhow, it was on the corner of Phillip and Baronne, a wonderful old neighborhood theater, where we saw lots of black-and-white movies—which I now realize were old re-runs of the 1930s they were palming off on us—but we didn't care.

Those old Rocket-Man serials, and Superman, and—I can't remember—was there a Frog-Man? We saw lots of Abbot and Costello there, and Errol Flynn—everything he did. On Sundays were the Technicolor movies, on Friday nights, the horror movies and I think Tuesday nights were the adult movie nights. Dreadful adult movies. I do remember seeing *On the Waterfront* there, and I remember thinking I'd better pay attention because my father was taking this movie seriously, so maybe something was going on. . . . We went other places, too. The Tivoli, over there where Louisiana and Washington sort of run into one another and the Prytania, which was a nice neighborhood show then. And, of course, the big shows downtown, the Loew's and the Saenger.

We always went on Christmas Day—I remember going to see *Quo Vadis*. I think I went to see *The Ten Commandments* with the entire Redemptorist high school in my sophomore year. We all laughed when we saw Yul Brynner with that single braid running down the side of his head.

NOM: Were you musical?

RICE: I tried to play the violin. It was the most crushing defeat of my life. I really didn't have an ear. My teacher promised me if I practiced real hard, I could make the school orchestra. But I didn't want to be in an orchestra; I wanted to be the star. So if I couldn't be a Heifetz, I didn't want to play. When you're a writer, you can be a virtuoso. You're in control.

NOM: Any special memories of Mardi Gras?

RICE: Oh, yeah. Well, we lived right on the parade route. In those days, the parades started on Felicity and St. Charles, came past our house going uptown, turned back on Washington, and came past our house again. We'd just run right across the neutral ground. And those were the only parades there were then. I don't think there were any parades in the suburbs then. Yes, many happy memories of Mardi Gras. Because we were on the route, everyone came to our house. My mother would put a big ham on the table with a lot of crackers. Very simple, but very good.

In a way, the whole Mardi Gras scene was sort of like our belief in the saints. The idea that someone would spend a year building a giant grasshopper to go on the side of a float didn't seem strange. You believed in the power of magic, the great and gilded figures of the imagination. That people would build a papier-mâché bed of roses to run on for one day—that's legitimate. That's what you get when you live here: a belief in the spiritual. To me, that's a spiritual thing. Mowing your grass is very seldom a spiritual thing, but dressing up in a Mardi Gras costume is a venting of the Dionysian side of ourselves.

NOM: Do you see New Orleans as a tolerant sort of place?

RICE: Very much so. Still is. You live in a town like Dallas, you see what real bigotry is. Even San Francisco. San Francisco has the reputation of being a very liberal, enlightened city, and maybe it is in some of its political aspects. But you don't see black people there in the wide variety of jobs you see them in here. There are all kinds of black craftsmen here. In my time in California, I never saw a black carpenter, a black mason, a black house-painter. Those jobs are all dominated by whites. I don't mean we're a perfect city, and Lord knows there are prejudiced people. But I also think there's been real integration here in a way there hasn't been in other places.

We're decadent. We are chaotic. We are inefficient. But we are tolerant. I don't think homosexuality's ever been really persecuted here. There's always been a charming spirit, a friendly spirit, in the French Quarter anyhow, where people from all walks of life can come and live in peace. There's a large gay community in San Francisco. Okay. But there's been violence, too. People come into the gay community and murder people.

NOM: Your vampire characters possess a certain androgyny.

RICE: Well, I like to write about characters who transcend gender and whose love transcends gender. It's a part of the way I see the world, and I have a large gay audience. I think they like the way I write about characters and relationships that aren't heterosexual or homosexual, that do transcend gender.

NOM: Some people have noticed a certain androgyny about New Orleans . . .

RICE: I think that's true. Southern men are more relaxed, more able to enjoy all aspects of life. They don't feel like they have to put on three-piece suits all the time to prove their masculinity. They don't mind telling you their own recipe for crawfish boil or their own way of cooking fish. Or dressing up for Mardi Gras. They let all of those different dimensions of themselves come out, the artistic dimensions. And they have the ability to enjoy celebrations and that kind of thing, which a lot of American men completely suppress—they can only focus on work. And our men are much more talkative than men in many other parts of the country. . . .

NOM: When did you come back to New Orleans?
RICE: In 1988.

NOM: And was the reason complex?
RICE: I always wanted to come back. We were just waiting for the right moment to come back . . . when my husband was able to take early retirement.

NOM: What changes did you notice?
RICE: I tell you the truth, I was so happy with the number of things that hadn't changed, that I hardly focused on the changes at all. I guess the biggest changes that I noticed were that a lot of the old houses were being saved and restored, whereas twenty years ago they would have been torn down. And the French Quarter has been cleaned up some and restored some. I know

some people are critical of what has happened here, but I'm very happy with it. New Orleans had a renewed consciousness of its architecture and was making the necessary sacrifices to save it.

NOM: Did you look up any old school acquaintances?

RICE: Well, I really had lost contact with most of my old school friends. But I have a very large extended family here—30 cousins and now their children and even their children's children. So it's been fun getting back close to them. I love all my big extended family.

NOM: There's quite a difference of opinion about whether New Orleans is a good place to do creative work. How is it for you?

RICE: It's always been good for me. For instance, I wrote passages for *The Witching Hour* here that I never would have been able to write in California.

NOM: It's also a town that reportedly does not honor its own prophets . . .

RICE: All I can say is that I haven't seen it. My reception here has been great and everyone's been very, very nice. I found there are a lot of young men and women who are writing here and I really feel like New Orleans is undergoing a revival of the arts. My husband has been painting since he's been here and he's painted over 30 canvases, some of which are being shown at Simonne Stern's. I really think a creative renaissance is going on here. You know, years ago, we were taught mostly about local colorists, Lyle Saxon, and that was about it. But now, people are talking about all types of writing. . . .

NOM: Are any of your characters based on real New Orleans people?

RICE: Not really. All of my characters are really compilations of people I've known. But *The Witching Hour* is my most New Orleans–type book. . . .

NOM: In one of your books, you have a character say, in effect, that humanity has never learned to deal with evil, assign it to its proper place in the human infrastructure. Do New Orleanians have a different vision of evil?

RICE: No. They have a different vision of good. We don't think that eating and drinking and celebrating are evil, that Dionysian side of ourselves. We have that Catholic tradition that after fasting comes a feast and that concept is good. . . .

NOM: One standard literary-interview question: Who were and are your literary influences?

RICE: Especially early on, it was more English and European than American. At Redemptorist, the Brontë sisters. Certainly not the modern American.

Not the novel of middle-class manners, of adultery in Connecticut. They don't have enough scope. They're having their hour on the stage, but it won't last. The only new guys I read are the Chinese-Americans. . . . Yet certainly always Tennessee Williams, Eudora Welty and Faulkner's *The Sound and the Fury*. Storytelling comes naturally to me, but I turn to the Southern writers for their language. I love that wild side of Southern writing. . . .

A gravesite at the Lafayette cemetery

PART TWO

◆

The Unreal World of Anne Rice

When a writer makes the transition from unknown to known, from unpublished to published, from little known to well known, the work assumes a life of its own. Taken seriously by readers, fans, booksellers, and the critics, the work is the nucleus, the center that holds the writer's world together.

This section takes a look at the unreal world of Anne Rice—the fans, of course, but also the world of book publishing, and the world of literary criticism as seen from within the fantasy field, as well as herself in a *Playboy* interview.

Playboy Interview

conducted by Digby Diehl
(March 1993)

*When it comes to interviewing writers of the fantastique, most mainstream inter-
views are sadly lacking. Part of it is that the interviewer has, at most, a few hours
to conduct the interview; and by the time a rapport is established, the interviewer
has moved on, in search of the next profile. Also, most interviewers don't have the
luxury of boning up on the subject at hand—ideally, to interview Rice, it requires not
only a knowledge of fantasy literature, Christian theology (especially Catholicism),
New Orleans history, and philosophy (especially existentialism), but also a working
knowledge of the kinkier aspects of sexuality, notably bondage and discipline,
which are integral to several of her novels, penned under other names.*

To its credit, Playboy *takes great care in selecting the interviewer—almost as
much, it seems, as it does the interviewee. The ground rules, laid out by the magazine, require that the subject be interviewed thoroughly, which means no short
cuts. And, afterward, the hours of tape are carefully edited to provide a thought-
provoking piece of reading, prefaced by an illuminating introduction properly
orienting the reader.*

*Published in its March 1993 issue, this interview with Rice is her best to date, a
look at the writer from the perspective that informs the most: the writer's view-
point.*

◆

From the Introduction to the *Playboy* Interview:

To learn more about Anne Rice and her world of ghosts and vampires, we
dispatched *Playboy's* book columnist, Digby Diehl, to New Orleans, where
by day he visited with Rice in her home and by night searched for Lestat on
Bourbon Street. Diehl's report:

"When I spoke with Anne on the telephone prior to our meetings, she was
terse and businesslike. There were no restrictions on what we would talk
about. But she made clear that she would only be available for four hours each
afternoon for four consecutive days. No lunch, no cocktails, no socializing.

As she promised, our talks were interrupted only for periodic refillings of diet Coke and the afternoon arrivals of her son from school.

"What surprised me a bit more each day was not only Anne's energy but her subtle chameleon ability to shift intonation and delivery as the conversation changed. Anecdotes about her youth were told with a charming sparkle. Ghost tales were offered in a spooky, slightly lowered voice, and denunciations of censorship came booming out angrily.

"In the end, I realized that her initial formality was a way of protecting herself from her own warm nature. There is an openness, a generosity of spirit about her that would make it easy for a visitor to impose upon. It is better she should set limits and save the time to spend at her word processor."

PLAYBOY: You are a feminist and yet you have written explicit sexual fantasies. How do you reconcile those two things?

RICE: I believe absolutely in the right of women to fantasize what they want to fantasize, to read what they want to read. I would go to the Supreme Court to fight for the right of a little woman in a trailer park to read pornography— or write it, if she wants to. I think one of the worst turns feminism took was its puritanical turn, where it tried to tell women what was politically correct sexually. I mean, we had that for thousands of years. I got that from the nuns at school: what you were supposed to feel as a temple of the Holy Ghost, what you were supposed to allow. And to hear the feminists then telling me that having masochistic fantasies or rape fantasies just isn't politically correct, I just thought, oh, bullshit. You're not going to come in and politicize my imagination.

PLAYBOY: Not all feminists agree with you. The Los Angeles chapter of the National Organization for Women called for a boycott of most Random House books because it published Bret Easton Ellis's *American Psycho*, which featured the murder and mutilation of men and women.

RICE: I was outraged by the boycott. If Random House doesn't have the right to publish a disgusting book, then young editors all over New York will never get radical books through their publishing houses. Those women are treating Random House as if it were a great, big, monolithic publishing house. It's not. Publishing has always been made up of courageous individual editors fighting for individual books. I was furious. I hate censorship. I hate it in any form. Can't those people see that if they could win that battle and force the book not to be published, other interest groups could then force all kinds of other books not to be published? I was just horrified. I would have defended Random House with a wooden sword in front of the building.

Part Two: The Unreal World of Anne Rice

PLAYBOY: Have you had problems with censorship of your own books?

RICE: Not really very much. Knopf didn't want to publish my pornography, but that was the individual decision of my editor, Vicky Wilson. She read the first book and said, "I can't publish this." But she recommended Bill White-head at Dutton, who published it. So I stayed at Knopf as Anne Rice and went off to Dutton and wrote the A. N. Roquelaure books. Vicky really is a dedicated editor, but she can't publish something she doesn't understand. She really just didn't get it. It is pornography. She said, "If I were to publish this, all the sex slaves would have to fight to be free and to escape." I just said, "Oh, Vicky, I don't want to do that. This is a sex fantasy about *being* a slave. They don't want to get away."

PLAYBOY: Why did you decide to write explicit erotic fiction?

RICE: First of all, I think the masochistic fantasies explored in my pornography, and rape fantasies in general, are fascinating things. They have to do with our deep psyche and they transcend gender. Both men and women have these fantasies. And to pretend that they don't exist is ridiculous. I don't believe the old argument that people read pornography and go out and commit crimes. The vast majority of crimes are committed by people who aren't reading anything. They don't need *Beauty's Punishment* to go attack some old woman in Oakland, steal her welfare check and rape her. It doesn't work like that. I'm fascinated by sadomasochism. I'm fascinated by the way that the fantasies recur all over, in all kinds of people from all kinds of lives. I'm not particularly interested in the people who act them out. I have nothing against them, and I've found them interesting when I've run into them. They come to my book signings sometimes and say, "Do you want to come to our demonstration of how to tie all the knots?"

PLAYBOY: They invite you to bondage demonstrations?

RICE: Yes. There are groups in Northern California that believe in healthy, safe-sex S&M. They'll give a lecture on how to tie up your lover but make the knots so that you can get them undone quickly. Or if you're going to use locks and chains on your lover, to be sure that all the locks use the same key, so that you can unlock them quickly. An organization up there invited me to their demonstrations. One night they had a dungeon tour: They were going to visit this one's torture chamber and that one's room. The organization was mainly made up, as I recall, of people who just liked to practice S&M. There were married couples in it, there were a lot of lesbians in it and there were a lot of professional women. The women did this professionally, largely for male customers. They were very hygienic.

PLAYBOY: What do you mean by "professionally"?

RICE: They charge money. Dominatrixes. What fascinated me about them was that there were no males who did it to women for money. If you wanted to go to San Francisco and say, "I would like to be dominated by a pirate for sixty minutes in a completely safe atmosphere, where he'll just take over but never get really rough," you can't do it. But men do it all the time. They go in and get dominated for an hour in a safe context. It's amazing to me. So my books are for the women who can't get that.

PLAYBOY: Did you go on the dungeon tour?

RICE: No, I didn't go. I'm shy. I did go to the house of one of the people, and I did see all of the whips and the chains that she had. The little phalluses and everything. She was dedicated. This was a gay activist who wrote all the time for gay publications. She's very much an S&M dyke, I believe she would call herself. She showed me all of these beautiful leather handcuffs and stuff that she had made, this entire lovely armoire filled with them. And a drawer filled with all these little dildos and things. I was fascinated, but that was enough. I mean, I really am a retiring person. I don't show up dressed in black leather as Madame Roquelaure. I'm not a dominatrix. I have almost no interest in acting it out. That was never what mattered to me. It was the fantasy, and I have discovered how many of us share that fantasy. Over the years, because of those books, I've run into thousands of people. Now those books are in the suburbs. They're everywhere, and women come up with babies in strollers and say, "We love your dirty books. Are you going to write some more Roquelaure?" They put it right in the stroller with the kid, at the bookstore. I think that's great.

PLAYBOY: What is the answer to their question? Will you write any more explicitly erotic books?

RICE: No, I don't think I will. I wanted to write some top-notch pornography in the genre, material that was just pornography. Where every page was a kick. I think I did it, and it would just be repetitious to write more. Also, I have to confess, since I've grown older and I've lost more friends from AIDS, and just experienced more of life, my vision has darkened a bit. I'm not sure I could put myself in the happy-go-lucky frame of mind I was in when I wrote the *Beauty* books. But I'm glad I wrote them. I'm proud.

PLAYBOY: You're clearly not in sympathy with Catherine MacKinnon or Andrea Dworkin, who have proposed recent antipornography legislation.

RICE: I think they're absolute fools. If two Baptist ministers from Oklahoma came up with their arguments, they would have been immediately laughed out of the public arena. They got away with their nonsensical arguments because they were feminists, and because they confused well-meaning liberals everywhere. But the idea that you can blame a piece of writing or a picture or a film or a magazine for inciting you to rape a woman is absolutely absurd. If you give the woman the right to sue and say that a magazine was the cause of the rape, there's only one step from that for the man to say, "Yes, it was the magazine that made me do it, and it was also the way she was dressed." Why can't he sue her?

PLAYBOY: And her dress designer.

RICE: Good point. Her dress designer and the guy who ran the bar. That MacKinnon and Dworkin don't see this drives me crazy. I think that is the most evil piece of legislation I have ever heard of. We've spent all this time trying to get men to take responsibility for rape. When I was a kid in the Fifties, we knew that half of the time the police blamed the victim. Women didn't want to report it. OK, we've reached a time when we're urging women to report the crime. The man is responsible if he does it. He can't blame it on the woman, he can't say she asked for it, he can't say she shouldn't have been in that bar, or that she shouldn't have gone to his apartment. And those two, MacKinnon and Dworkin, in their madness, want to take that responsibility off the man again and put it on *Playboy*, or whatever he was reading. That's bullshit! It's not true. We know statistically that pornography does not incite people to commit crimes.

PLAYBOY: Don't women need special protection in some cases?

RICE: Two things have gone side by side throughout the feminist movement: a protectionist idea that women are victims and have to be protected, and the belief that women are equal and have to have equal rights and equal access to everything. The two really clash on this issue. I don't believe women are victims who have to be protected from everything. I believe when someone is a victim of a crime, that person is entitled to protection of the law and the courts. But I don't think that women per se are so gullible or foolish that they have to be protected by legislation like that. These people think that if a woman can be made to have sex with a donkey, like for an erotic film, she can be made to sign a contract. The fact that she signed a contract doesn't necessarily mean that she wasn't a victim. That's absurd. If they can't be trusted to sign a valid contract because they're women, then women shouldn't drive, they shouldn't vote, they shouldn't hold jobs.

PLAYBOY: Rape is another issue, isn't it?

RICE: I think this is a crisis time with regard to rape. I don't think there's ever been a time when women have been so vulnerable to rape and there's been such an outcry against it. As a student of Western civilization and law, I'm fascinated by what's going to happen with the notion that when she says no—no matter when it is—it's over. I think it's important to women's freedom, and important to our dignity and our rights as human beings, that rape be a crime, that nobody has a right to force himself on you, whatever you are.

PLAYBOY: Have you been following some of the public rape trials?

RICE: I didn't think there was sufficient proof in the William Kennedy Smith case to bring an indictment. I thought a real injustice was done to that woman when she was taken that far by the legal system.

PLAYBOY: What is your reaction to the Mike Tyson rape case?

RICE: Again, you have to extend the protection of the law even to a girl who's stupid enough to go to Mike Tyson's bedroom at two o'clock in the morning. She has the full protection of the law. She may be an idiot, and she may be doing something that none of us would have done when we were her age—we would have had more brains! If Mike Tyson had said to me, "Come up to my hotel room," I would have said no.

PLAYBOY: Do you think you would have known what to expect?

RICE: From what I could tell, what happened in that case was that she did expect something to happen, but she expected it to be romantic and she expected it to be nice. And what she got was unpleasant and nasty. And she was entitled to the protection of the law against that. You cannot invite someone to your house for a party and then beat them up and say, "Well, you accepted my invitation, and that was the nature of the party: It was a beating-up party." That's what I suspect happened, but I really don't know. I think she was prepared for sex and consummation, but wasn't prepared to be mauled or bullied or hurt. I think she felt outraged afterward, and she had the courage to say that shouldn't happen to someone. That is really what rape is.

Part Two: The Unreal World of Anne Rice

PLAYBOY: Are we always stuck with the he-said-she-said problem?

RICE: I think we have to fight each one out. We have to guarantee women this protection. You cannot tell women that the price of equality is that they might get raped. I think that as a culture we're desensitized to how awful rape is. We see it played with so much, and we see it on television in so many forms all the time, that it is hard for us to imagine what an outrage it is when someone has to force himself on a person that way. I think the movie that brought it home to me most honestly was *Thelma & Louise*. I would have shot the guy immediately. If he had done that to my friend, I would have blown his head off. That was so outrageous a violation of that woman's privacy and dignity that I didn't see why Louise waited. I praise that movie because I think it's hard to show it without its being sexy because it is sexy. And rape fantasies are part of our brain. They're part of our genetic heritage, and that's not going to go away if you ban pornography. It's an archetypal fantasy.

PLAYBOY: What about the argument that sexual images in movies and TV affect public consciousness?

RICE: When you're talking about the content of programs, I'm leery of anybody trying to turn the media into propaganda. I feel that we need a creative jungle out there, that we have to put up with some people who use the First Amendment and use free speech in a way we find repulsive. And it's worth it for the price of free speech. Also, I feel that there are certain people whose function it is to outrage us. Madonna, to me, is wonderful. She would be the one person to whom I would sell video or film rights to the *Beauty* books. Or course, she has not knocked on my door asking for them, but I would not consider anyone else. I think what she's done in those videos is so courageous, the way she's played with those fantasies and those images. The idea that somebody tried to censor her or keep one of those things off MTV is outrageous. We ought to know that those people are going to stretch the limits and are going to say outrageous things.

PLAYBOY: How do you feel about the extreme case of child pornography?

RICE: I think the crime there is the making of the pornography, the using of a child to commit a crime. And if what you're watching is a record of the crime, an act that's involved with the commission of that crime, I can see laws against that. A child has certain protections until he or she is eighteen. But you prosecute people for exploiting children. You don't prosecute on the content of the film. I am really pro-freedom. Freedom means that somebody is going to abuse it or use it in a way you don't like. It's not freedom if they don't do that.

PLAYBOY: Do you think pornography has any effect?

RICE: It's almost a superstitious reaction to think that people are going to act out pornography. We know, for example, that thousands of people read Agatha Christie mysteries. They don't try to become Miss Marple. They read Mickey Spillane and they don't shoot one another. The readers of Louis L'Amour do not carry six-guns and tobacco pouches everywhere they go. So to think that for some reason the readers of erotic fiction are going to be different, that they're going to jump right up and act out everything in the book, is absurd. It doesn't work that way. They're taking a mental trip with that book, just like the readers of Agatha Christie. And good pornography does what good mystery fiction does or good Western fiction or good science fiction: It takes you to another place. It allows you to enjoy that place for a little while, and then you come back. If it's really good, you know something you didn't know before you went.

PLAYBOY: On what kind of mental trip are you taking the readers of the Vampire Chronicles?

RICE: What interests me about vampires is their mythic qualities. They're characters in our literature, and they're great. But I have never met anyone who was a real vampire. I do believe in a lot of the rest of the occult. I think that there probably are ghosts. There's an abundant amount of proof that there are some sorts of apparitions and spirits and things like that. But a vampire, I think, is strictly a mythic character, almost out of ancient religion. It's like writing about angels or devils. There's a great deal of meaning there. Whether you believe people have ever really seen an angel or a devil isn't the point. What I have done is to take a B-movie image and say that it is as significant as a magical character in the Renaissance and treat it that way. Because the book is a special world—with language, thoughts, ideas, concepts and characters you are drawn into—you forgive the fact that it's basically absurd.

PLAYBOY: Speaking of the B-movie image, will we ever see the Vampire Chronicles on the screen?

RICE: *Interview* was sold to Paramount in 1976. Richard Sylbert, who was the head of the studio at the time, really wanted to make it. Before the contract was even signed, he left Paramount. Michael Eisner and Barry Diller came in. Then John Travolta came in and made some sort of deal with Paramount. His managers were interested in his doing *Interview with the Vampire*. They took it as part of a package with Paramount, and they took control of that property for a long time. The truth was, Travolta didn't want to do it, so it never got made. Years passed, and more and more was charged to the picture—scripts and so forth—until finally, I think, it had a debt against it of six or seven hundred thousand dollars. They dumped it on the television division about 1984. A television producer then began to develop a script for it. In the meantime, I'd written *The Vampire Lestat*. Because of the sequel rights in my original contract, I had the right to sell the movie rights to *Lestat* if Paramount didn't want them. They didn't. So other people became very interested in developing *The Vampire Lestat*. Julia Phillips, the producer, was particularly interested.

PLAYBOY: Thus you came to play a role in her book, *You'll Never Eat Lunch in This Town Again*.

RICE: Isn't that wild? Julia and I are very different. I wish she had not hurt so many people's feelings. But I do think she's a talented writer. Anyway, she did come into my life being interested in *The Vampire Lestat* because she couldn't get *Interview* away from Paramount. She pitched it to the studios and really started it off on a life of its own. Meanwhile, *Interview* reverted back to me. Julia and I tried to get the properties united with one company. For a while, Julia had a brilliant idea to develop *The Vampire Lestat* as a movie while she did *Interview* on Broadway as an opera or a musical. At that point she began to talk to David Geffen about it. David was kind enough to give me a shot at writing the script, and I submitted a revised version to him. But who knows? Right now, *Interview* is still in development.

PLAYBOY: So *The Witching Hour* will probably be the first of your books to make it to the screen?

RICE: It's supposed to start shooting soon. But *The Witching Hour* is easy compared to the Vampire Chronicles. It's mostly humans.

PLAYBOY: And they're going to shoot it in New Orleans?

RICE: They have told the mayor's office that they want to shoot some of the movie in New Orleans. It's exciting. It's never been this close before, it's always been just at the script stage.

PLAYBOY: Do you like dealing with Hollywood?

RICE: I went there a lot at Julia Phillips' behest. Julia dragged me down there enough times that I lost my fear of those people. I sat at so many dinners at

Morton's with Julia, meeting Adrian Lyne and Mel Gibson and blah-blah-blah that she really defused that world for me. I realize that these were, in fact, often limited people who had jobs only for short periods of time.

PLAYBOY: What insight did you gain about how to deal with Hollywood?
RICE: My primary insight is don't eat lunch in that town, except with David Geffen. He can make your project a reality. Just don't eat your heart out for somebody who comes back and whines, "I couldn't get them to read it."

PLAYBOY: In your life as a novelist—
RICE: My real life!

PLAYBOY: You've written a breakthrough book. In *The Tale of the Body Thief,* the vampire Lestat finally has the opportunity to be human again.
RICE: A good opportunity. A good shot at it.

PLAYBOY: But he chooses to remain a vampire.
RICE: I always thought that's exactly what would happen, but I was ready to let the book go in whichever direction it wanted to go. I felt he had to confront the fact that he really loved being what he was. The fourth vampire volume in the Vampire Chronicles is really about the ruthlessness, the evil, in us all. You and I are sitting here, and we know right now people are dying horribly in Iraq or in Ethiopia. But we choose to sit here. We've made that choice. We're not going to spend our lives trying to save one village in India. That's what the book is about. Lestat chooses to remain a powerful, immortal being. And I think most people would make that choice.

PLAYBOY: The minute Lestat gets out of his vampire self and into a human body in *The Tale of the Body Thief,* he has exclusively heterosexual encounters—and unhappy ones at that. Some readers identify vampires with gay sexuality. Isn't this going to fuel that stereotype?
RICE: Well, probably. I really see the vampire as transcending gender. If you make them absolutely straight or gay, you limit the material. They can be either one. They have a polymorphous sexuality. They see everything as beautiful. To them, it no longer matters whether the victim is a woman or a man. And I do see Lestat as a real 18th-century bisexual. Either the village girls or the village boys, depending on who's around. It was really a middle-class idea that came in with the revolution that homosexuality was a perversion.

Part Two: The Unreal World of Anne Rice

PLAYBOY: How do women readers react to the Vampire Chronicles' androgyny?

RICE: I would say that there is certainly a kind of woman who finds two men together very attractive, and I have a lot of those readers. But, by and large, most of the women I've known are afraid of homosexual men. We have deep-rooted fears when we see people of the same sex kissing and embracing, no matter how sophisticated we are. There can be a genetic rush of fear. The species is threatened. I have to remind myself of what that's about, because I don't feel it. I've always rather romanticized gay people as outsiders bravely fighting for sexual freedom and being willing to take the slings and arrows from the middle class. Certainly Lestat is an outsider, an immortal who is offered the choice and chooses to remain a vampire.

PLAYBOY: Critics have pointed out that *The Body Thief* is a real departure from the other vampire books.

RICE: To me, *The Body Thief* was the first modern Vampire Chronicle in that the exploration was inner, psychological. All the other Chronicles were really devoted to going back and finding the answers in the past—reading history, finding secrets, crashing into sanctums and discovering truths, and encountering over and over again the statement: "History doesn't really help." You always wind up back where you started. I like it very much, going in this other way, the psychological way. If I hadn't been pleased with this book, I would have thrown it away.

PLAYBOY: Have you thrown away books before?

RICE: Just before taking up *The Body Thief*, I wanted to do this book, *In the Frankenstein Tradition*, about an artificial man. For some reason, that has just not come together. I don't know why. I went back and read Mary Shelley's *Frankenstein,* and I was terribly excited about it. What an incredible book. What a brain she had at nineteen! I just loved it. I really wanted to do something with those concepts, and I began to see that I couldn't do what I wanted to do.

PLAYBOY: Like Mary Shelley, you've absorbed a lot of things that are out there—ideas, things that people are thinking about and feeling. They're not necessarily expressed in a direct way, but they're addressed by your characters and their concerns.

RICE: I always felt that any book that's going to be really good is about everything you know or everything that's on your mind. At least for me that's the way it always works. In the beginning, when I first started having books published, one of the distressing things was to watch critics view them as historical novels and not see that they had to do with the present moment. But American fiction is so influenced by the idea that to be profound a book has to be about the middle class and about some specific domestic problem of the middle class, that it's hard to make your own path. You're really working against that. Unless you're a South American surrealist, you have a hard time.

PLAYBOY: Why do you write serious books about such strange stuff?

RICE: I came of age in the Sixties in California, and the prejudice was that a really profound book dealt with one's own recent experience hitchhiking in Big Sur. Somebody writing books like I wrote was writing trash, basically, according to the conventional wisdom. I sort of had to fight against that because I didn't know any other way to write. I recently have been reading books about what art was like before the Reformation. And what became very clear to me was that the novel today—John Updike, Anne Tyler, Alice Adams—is really the triumph of Protestantism. It's a Protestant novel. It's about real people. People who work, usually, and who have small problems. It's about their interior changes and their moments of illumination. And that is the essence of what Protestantism came to be in America. Out with the stained-glass windows, out with the saints, out with the chants and the Latin and the incense. Out with Faust and the Devil. It's you, your Bible, and God. Those novels are personal. They affirm the Protestant vision that everything is sort of an interior decision to make—as you make a good living and as you fit into the community in which you live.

PLAYBOY: Were you aware of feeling separate from the cultural mainstream early in your career?

RICE: Having grown up in New Orleans—the only Catholic city in America—amid all this decadence, I grew up with a completely different feeling. I was nourished on those stories of the saints and miracles and so forth. I really thought it was fine to write a book in which everybody was a vampire and they all talked about good and evil. The industrial revolution and Protestantism came together in America in a way it didn't in any other country in the world, with such force and power. To see our literature finally dominated by things that used to be *Saturday Evening Post* short stories is really the final triumph of the Protestant vision in art. It's basically a vision that says if it's about God and the Devil, it has to be junk. It's science fiction; it's dismissible.

PLAYBOY: Do you mean all fantasy is Catholic?

RICE: If you think back to before Martin Luther about what literature was, the spiritual exercises of Saint Ignatius encouraged you to use your imagination. You'd sit there and close your eyes and think about what Christ felt like as they drove the nails through his hands. See, I grew up on that. We *did* those exercises. That was an approach to imagination that was entirely natural to me. All that came to an end with Protestantism. Protestantism put its faith in the less magical, more practical, more down-to-earth and—in this country, ultimately—the more sterile. But I see that now. I love living here, and this really is a Catholic city in the sense that it doesn't fix its potholes.

PLAYBOY: Are potholes Catholic, too?

RICE: They're Catholic because people don't really care that much about progress or cleaning up. Think about it. Go to Venice or to Mexico. Think of the countries that are Catholic. Think of the people who came to America who have been gangsters. They've almost all been Catholics—Italians, Irish. You don't hear a lot about German gangsters or Swiss gangsters—except for Dutch Schultz. Catholics still live in a world that's filled with dash and flair and color and drama and terrible injustice. There's a sort of acceptance of things. This city moves at its own pace. People here are natural storytellers. They really are spiritual, in a Catholic sense. They really do care more about a good cup of coffee than mowing the grass. In a city like Dallas it's much more important to mow your grass. The cup of coffee comes next. In San Francisco it's more important to go to work, get a job, sweep the pavement. And that's wonderful. I'm glad we live in a Protestant country. I'm talking about this strictly in terms of cultural movements.

PLAYBOY: Do people in New Orleans have a different vision of reality?

RICE: I have met countless people in New Orleans who have told me their personal experiences of seeing ghosts. I never met these people in California. Not in thirty years have I ever met anyone in New York or California who claimed to have seen a ghost. And since I've been here, people look me right in the eye and describe the ghost's clothes and what it did as it came up the stairs. They tell me absolutely I should come to their house and see this ghost, that it really is there. I'm amazed.

PLAYBOY: When did you break away from the church?

RICE: I didn't know anything about the modern world when I lived in New Orleans. I never read a line of Hemingway until I was twenty. I didn't even know such people existed. I grew up in such a closed, Catholic environment that when I moved to Texas and went to college and discovered things like existentialism, it was like emerging into the modern world. I thought, I have to know what's out there. I have to read Walter Kaufmann's books on existentialism. I have to see who Jean-Paul Sartre is. But I wasn't supposed to read all this. It was a mortal sin if I read it. That's when I broke with the church. It was astonishing. I'm thinking about this a lot lately. I guess now that I've come home, thirty years later, I see a lot of it in perspective I didn't before. I was sort of battling these voices and demons and different things, trying to figure out things. Why did everything work for me when I introduced a character who is a vampire? Why did I suddenly start to be able to write about everything I felt when, for other people, the opposite was true? I don't know, but I see it now, and I do think it's this battle of the Protestant and the Catholic.

PLAYBOY: Where would a writer such as Stephen King fit into your cultural division of Catholic and Protestant visions?

RICE: I read all of Stephen King's early books. I have not caught up with his output because I'm a slow reader. But I think Stephen King is a very fine writer, and I learned a lot from *'Salem's Lot* and from *Firestarter*. He's the master of talking about ordinary people in ordinary situations and then confronting them with the supernatural or the horrible. That's American and Protestant to take horror and put it in that context. He did a kind of genius thing. He created a proletarian horror genre. He departed from the European tradition of spooky houses and doomed aristocrats, and he created this wonderful world of horror in middle-class America. It's brilliant!

PLAYBOY: We've never heard anyone describe Stephen King quite that way.

RICE: He is absolutely a brilliant, Protestant, middle-class American writer. He's really great at that. But there was one point when I was reading the reissue of *The Stand*—I was into it and I loved the writing—and I thought, No one has survived this flu who is really an interesting person. They're all these wonderful Stephen King people, but I would really like some truly heroic person. Heroism to me is real. People can be heroic. And what interests me in fiction is creating these exceptional people—Lestat, Ramses—people, as I've said, who are bigger than the book. King doesn't do that.

Part Two: The Unreal World of Anne Rice

PLAYBOY: In Stephen King's books and in your own books there is a lot of violence. How do you feel about that?

RICE: I love it. It's obvious, isn't it?

PLAYBOY: Many people would find your reaction troubling.

RICE: I don't think we can have great art in our society without violence. Everything is how you do it: the context. Prime-time TV really hurts kids because again and again it presents mindless, senseless, motivationless, sadistic people hurting one another. It's horrible. Crimes committed by sneering, tough-job, nasty, snarling criminals. We don't know where they came from or why they're the way they are. Prime time presents them all in these cops shows as the reality of the streets. I think that's been terrible for our morale. But I think when you take a movie like *Scarface*, written by Oliver Stone and directed by Brian De Palma, you have a symphony of violence that's a real masterpiece. It has a beginning, an end, a middle and a moral: the rise and fall of Tony Montana, the cocaine dealer. I love that movie and I watch it over and over again. I wanted to dedicate *The Body Thief* to Tony Montana, but I didn't have the guts. And, by the way, I once had an opportunity to meet Oliver Stone, and I said just what I said to you, that I love violence, and he said, "So do I." We laughed. I think he was being honest.

PLAYBOY: Are the people who oppose violence less than honest?

RICE: We Americans are such hypocrites about violence. Maybe there are a few Americans out there who really never watch anything with violence in it. But ask them if they've watched *Gone with the Wind*. Everything depends on context. To me, the context has to be really strong. The moral tone of a work is important, the depth of the psychology is important, the lessons, the feeling afterward of moral exhilaration as well as of having been entertained. All that is very important about a work of art. But I would be lying if I said I didn't enjoy violence in a strong context, because the best of our art contains violence. *Moby Dick* is violent, don't you think? If we cleanse all the violence out of our work, we will really have the *Saturday Evening Post* short story triumphant. That will be our art. We've gone through phases where we've nearly done that, and it's pretty dismal stuff.

But I do love violence, I absolutely love it. I loved *The Godfather*. I remember people coming home and saying it was too violent, the horse's head, oh my God. I thought it was great. I thought it was a masterful use of violence. That's my field and I love it.

Playboy Interview

PLAYBOY: You're also a big boxing fan, aren't you?

RICE: Yeah. We had a writer friend, Floyd Salas, who introduced Stan and me to boxing. We got into it and would go with him to the Golden Gloves in San Francisco every year. But the amateur matches in Oakland and Richmond with kids sponsored by the police were really a trip. I'll never forget how sensuous the Oakland Auditorium was. The auditorium is vast, much larger than the crowd. We would get in that audience surrounding the ring, down in the middle of the auditorium. Those two beautiful spotlights would hit it, and out would come these gorgeous bodies and they would start hitting each other. I thought it was terrific. I really developed a love for boxing then that I've never lost.

PLAYBOY: Didn't Salas get you to put on the gloves once?

RICE: Floyd was always helping the boxing team at Cal, and one time I got in the ring with him. I found it a bit too rough. I mean, one blow to the head, even with that mask, is enough. It was a bit too rough, but it was fun. I don't have—well, I do have a killer instinct, I guess. No, I really don't. I think that it was great fun to pretend, until somebody—me—got hurt for a second.

PLAYBOY: Fighters get hurt all the time.

RICE: I remember one awful moment at the Golden Gloves. The place was packed and I was just coming back into the auditorium with a hot dog or something. Two guys were in the ring, one of whom was a medical student. Just as I entered the auditorium, the medical student had been almost knocked out, and he had dropped to his knees. He was clearly dazed—he didn't know what he was doing. At that moment, the whole crowd stood and began to roar. There was something horrible about that moment of seeing that kid. There he was, obviously badly hurt, and that whole crowd was roaring because this is exactly what they had come to see. I realized that we were screaming as much to see these guys go down as to go up. I hadn't quite thought about it that way. I had though of it as screaming more for the guy who scored a punch, for his triumph over something. Yet here's this med student who really should be protecting his brain, and he's on his knees, dazed, in front of all these people who are screaming as if they were in a Roman arena.

PLAYBOY: Now that you have moved back to New Orleans, do you see yourself more as a Southern writer?

RICE: I was always a Southern writer. It was good to come home and acknowledge that. Books that I have cherished and loved are books like Faulkner's *The Sound and the Fury*. Reading over and over again the language in that book and loving it. Eudora Welty's short stories, I just pick them up and read words. I don't even have to know what the plot of the story is—if she happens to have one. Sometimes she doesn't. She has a great story about two people who meet in New Orleans and drive south along the river, down the road. I believe that's all that happens in the story. They drive and become almost narcotized by the landscape. Then they go back to New Orleans and they part. I love that story. I feel like my writing has always been very much influenced by these lush Southern writers.

PLAYBOY: There is something about a lot of your material—dealing with the supernatural and time travel—that's fundamentally anti-intellectual. But you're an intellectual. Isn't that a contradiction?

RICE: Well, it's that Protestant-Catholic thing again. I'm a serious intellectual, and I certainly was a serious spiritual person who wanted to be a great writer. I had Carson McCullers and Hemingway and Dickens and Stendahl stacked on my desk, but I couldn't find my way in contemporary literature until I hit the supernatural and its advantages. And then I took everything I had to give and put it there. That's always been the contradiction of my work.

PLAYBOY: What did you read as a child?

RICE: *The Lives of the Saints*, that's what I read as a kid. Soap operas, yes, they made a big difference. And radio made a big difference. I'm increasingly realizing how much radio was an influence—*Lux Radio Theater, Suspense,* Lamont Cranston. I had forgotten. But playing tapes of old radio shows, I'm really beginning to realize how much my work sounds like a radio show. It really does, to a large extent.

PLAYBOY: How did you come up with the idea of doing *Interview with the Vampire*?

RICE: It was haphazard. I was sitting at the typewriter and I thought, What would it be like to interview a vampire? And I started typing. I was very much a think-at-the-typewriter writer then, more so than now. I would start with a blank page and have no idea what I was going to write for several hours. And I just started the idea of this boy having a vampire in the room, and the vampire wanting to tell the truth about what it was all about. The vampire explained all about drinking blood and absorbing the life of the victim, that it was sort of a sacramental thing. He talked about being immortal and so forth and so on. I took that story out several times over the years and rewrote it. It was at one of those points when I was rewriting it, to include in some short stories that I hoped to enter into a contest at Iowa, that it took off and became the novel. And, of course, I had encouragment from friends. Friends had said, "I think you really have something with that story; that story is so unusual." I really began to let it go, and something like five weeks later, the novel was finished. I had forgotten the contest. I never finished the short stories. They all went back in the drawer.

PLAYBOY: You really wrote most of that novel in five weeks?

RICE: Yes, but that was the period when my daughter had just died, and I wasn't doing anything except drinking and writing—often all night long.

PLAYBOY: That must have been a terrible time.

RICE: I was just a drunk, hysterical person with no job, no identity, no nothing. There was a two-year period after her death when I just drank a lot and wrote a lot, like crazy. Then I sort of came out of it and wrote *Interview with the Vampire.* My husband had told me, "I really believe in your writing." He was working at San Francisco State University. He wasn't chairman yet, but he was a creative writing professor with tenure there. He was the bread-winner. I went out and got a job for a while and was miserable. He said, "Quit the job. I believe in you and I believe in your writing. We have my pay, so just write." I've always felt that that was one of the greatest things he ever did for me, other than being his wonderful self.

PLAYBOY: Do you think in some ways the shock of your daughter's death shaped your literary vision?

RICE: No doubt about it. It had a devastating effect. There's a period after a death like that when you don't think the lights will ever go back on. I mean, you don't like doing anything—vacuuming the floor or cooking a meal or walking out of the house. I remember even in the immediate weeks after her death it was hard for me to swallow food. I felt a disgust for every-thing physical. I kept thinking of her in the cemetery. And even though I don't believe she's in that body, I couldn't get it off my mind. That went on for a long time, as a matter of fact. Particularly late at night. Until very re-cently, I've had thoughts about the fear of death and thoughts of her. In fact, only on the return to New Orleans would I say I let go of that. I felt that I could perhaps have her in another way. It doesn't have to be such a painful thing every night. I think we cling to these things because we don't want to lose the person. It's a form of fidelity to keep grieving like that.

PLAYBOY: Was the writing of *Interview with the Vampire* a conscious effort to sublimate your grief?

RICE: An interesting thing to me about *Interview*, in retrospect, is that I never really connected her with it. I remember the night I told Stan the whole story of *Interview*. We went over to the Cheshire Cat in Berkeley and we were having some beer. I had been writing the book and I said there was this little girl vampire in it and she's four years old, and Stan said, "Oh, no, no, no, no, not a four-year-old vampire. You can't have a vampire that young." I said, "All right, all right, a *six*-year-old vampire?" But neither of us said, "Michele?" If I had done that I would have been blocked. The character, Claudia, was a little fiend. When I look back on it I think, How in the world could I have been so detached? But I really didn't think of that as being about my life. I just thought, I'm writing this thing, and for some reason when I work with these comic-book vampire characters, these fantasy characters, I can see reality. I can touch reality. This is a context. My books before that had been uneasy mixtures of contemporary California and the French Quarter and Garden District in New Orleans. People thought I was making up all this stuff about the South. They thought I was getting it out of Dickens or something. Miss Havisham and her big house. So it never worked. But anyway, that is what strikes me as so strange, in retrospect, that I didn't completely connect it. It's like I had a dream. The novel was a dream of everything that had gone on, but I didn't make the connection.

PLAYBOY: And it really was connected with the deeper reality.

RICE: Yeah, I think it's a novel all about grief and about the loss of faith and about being shattered—yet wanting to live, being sensual and wanting to live. And the sensuality of drinking is certainly in there. I don't like to talk about it because I think it's a trivial aspect of the book, but it's about alcoholism. It's about being drunk. The whole experience of the dark gift is like a drunken swoon. It's almost a drug experience. It's like the golden moment of drinking, when everything makes sense. It was a lot of talking about the craving for booze, the need to drink. That wonderful feeling of transcending and everything meaning something when you are drunk, and yet it was crumbling away.

PLAYBOY: You say that it came from your own drinking experiences, but there are people who connected it with drugs.

RICE: Marijuana. I had powerful experiences on marijuana that were so intense that I quit smoking. And I never touched it again. But I had what other people might refer to as psychedelic experiences just smoking grass and drinking beer. I was describing that in *Interview*. I was describing that entire knowledge, you might say, of listening to Bach when very stoned, so that the music is just lapping and lapping. I had absolutely ghastly experiences of perceiving that we were going to die and that there was no explanation, that we might die without ever knowing what this was all about. And I never recovered. I described it in *The Vampire Lestat*. He saw death in the golden moment, and that has exactly happened to me.

PLAYBOY: Is the issue of immortality what the Vampire Chronicles are essentially about?

RICE: The Chronicles are about how all of us feel about being outsiders. How we feel that we're really outsiders in a world where everybody else understands something that we don't. It's about our horror of death. It's about how most of us would probably take that blood and be immortal, even if we had to kill. It's about being trapped in the flesh when you have a mind that can soar. It's the human dilemma. What does Yeats say in the poem? "Consume my heart away; sick with desire / And fasten to a dying animal." That's what I feel it's really true to. People are shaken by those things.

PLAYBOY: For your fans, I understand that there's a lighter side to the vampire fantasy, too.

RICE: Yeah. I have some readers who go to the dentist and they get these little fangs made that fit on their teeth. They get them fitted by the dentist and made the same color as the rest of their teeth. In fact, I heard that I have a whole gang of fans in Los Angeles who do that. They put on their teeth and go out at night and sit in cafes, show their fangs. They've come to my door, the people with the fangs. They come to the coven party. They call me on the telephone. Let me emphasize again: All of these people know this is fiction. We're talking about people in their thirties and forties. This is fun to them. This is almost a hobby to be part of the fan club, to dress up like a vampire and to love vampire movies. They're vampire groupies. It represents the romance in their lives. They're wonderful people. I have never met a single one who's been a sinister Satan-worshipping person or anything like that. They just exude goodwill and cheerfulness and laughter. Lots of laughter. It's all fun. Even when they won't step out of their vampire persona, they're just pretending to be vampires and they won't answer questions as anything but a vampire, they're laughing. It's all a gag.

PLAYBOY: You said people call. How do they get your number?
RICE: It's listed, with the address, in the phone book.

PLAYBOY: You're sure you want to say that in print?
RICE: Yes, that's fine. It is listed, but only a certain type of person takes the trouble to find your number and call you, so it tends to be very similar people who call. They're usually young, they're usually college students and high school students. They're enthusiastic about the books and they're nice. They just want to talk for a minute. They just want to say how they enjoyed the books, or they just want to know if there's another one coming out.

PLAYBOY: What books can we expect after *The Body Thief*?
RICE: I've completed a sequel to *The Witching Hour* entitled *Lasher*, which plunges again into the Mayfair family. I've kind of resigned myself to the fact that it's a hybrid science-haunting novel, because Lasher is here with us on this side. I'm fascinated by genetics and science and DNA and evolution, so I get into questions of a mutilation. And then I want to get back to Lestat. Then there are all kinds of other books I want to do. Also, I still don't believe I've really done a great haunting novel. That was my goal with *The Witching Hour*, but it became a witchcraft novel. I'd like to do one really about just pure haunting, like *The Turn of the Screw*. Just have ghosts. I'd love to do that, and I'd love to go back to Egypt. So I have all these stories in my head. I just have to find enough time to spend at the keyboard to write them.

◆ FANS ◆

Unlike her bestselling contemporaries like Stephen King, Tom Clancy, and John Grisham, Anne Rice is very accessible to her fans. Although her publisher will forward mail, the easiest way to get a letter to Anne Rice is to write to her directly or phone her. Since she makes no secret of her home address or one of her home phone numbers, she gets, as you'd expect, a lot of mail and phone calls.

In her personal zine, Commotion Strange, *she wrote: "Our addresses are well known, including that of St. Elizabeth's Orphanage. But do remember, please; the family lives in our houses; they are private residences. And though we love you, we cannot come to the door, or meet with people personally. We thank you for your understanding. We do have a great deal of security; men on patrol; dogs, all of that. But in general, we have found that our readers are the kindest, gentlest people in the world, and we are honored that some times you want to stop on the corner of First and Chestnut, or of Napoleon and Prytania. We love to look at New Orleans houses too, and always have."*

You obviously won't get through the locked gates, but you can always call her number. She usually has an answering machine on, and offers a long update on her new projects, and asks you leave a message if you wish. According to her Lestat fan club newsletter: "She welcomes comments about the movie [Interview with the Vampire], *her books,* Red Heaven [a band that played at the last Coven party] *or whatever. Sometimes she answers in person!"*

For those who want to meet Rice in person, the best bet is to attend a book signing. Unlike some authors who will sign for two hours maximum, Rice enthusiastically signs for hours. On the Memnoch *book tour, she signed for nine hours at a signing at St. Petersburg, Florida. Afterward, in a recorded phone message on her hotline, she said that she'd try to set a new record with a ten to eleven hour signing. No question: If you've got the stamina to stand in line for hours, you'll get a personal moment with Rice as well as a signed book. (Signing tip: If you are the first or last person in line, Rice will, in addition to signing, render an original drawing in your book.)*

Anne Rice's
Vampire Lestat Fan Club

Officially sanctioned by Anne Rice, the Vampire Lestat Fan Club is always looking for new blood. The brainchild of Sue Quiroz, the idea came to her when she and several of her friends stood in line at de Ville Books and Prints for an autograph party for Anne Rice in 1988. "Look at all these people. Wouldn't it be great if we could form a fan club?" Quiroz asked.

As Teresa Simmons, one of its founding members, explained in an article for *The Vampire Companion*, they immediately began canvassing other fans in line, collecting names for a mailing.

Rice subsequently gave her approval and assistance, which gave the fan club a cachet that most lack. This also meant that the club was privy to insider information, which made the club indispensable for the hard-core fans who preferred to get their news from the source.

Since its inception, the fan club's rolls have swollen to over three thousand members worldwide, each paying $13 for a one-year membership ($18 overseas). For their money, members get a membership card; a bumper sticker, perfect for your car; a postcard of Anne Rice; and one year's worth of newsletters.

Unlike other, similar publications—such as Stephen King's late *Castle Rock*—the Rice newsletter is published sporadically. "Let us explain: newsletter frequency depends on the availability of information, the workload and the amount of help we have. We apologize for the long delay but have faith! We exist and intend to network information as soon as we can."

The newsletter also features ads (free, available on a space-available basis). You can order privately published chapbooks of poetry about vampires, get on the mailing lists of book dealers that specialize in dark tomes, subscribe to magazines and journals, buy limited editions of Rice's books, and buy memorabilia from the fan club itself—bumper stickers, Anne Rice photo T-shirts, and the official Lestat fan club T-shirt.

The real bonus, however, is keeping abreast of the biggest event of the year, insofar as Rice is concerned: news of the annual Coven party, which grows larger each year. Dressing in costumes, attendees pay a modest fee for admission and, depending on the year, may get an opportunity to see the bewitching novelist herself.

Anne Rice's Vampire Lestat Fan Club

Even if Rice isn't present, thousands of diehard Rice fans attend and party late into the night, listening to bands like Red Heaven, Trio Nocturna, and Ex-Voto fill the place with unearthly and appropriately macabre music. The fan club, operated by volunteers, can be reached at: Anne Rice's Vampire Lestat Fan Club, P.O. Box 58277, New Orleans, LA 70158-8211. (And tell them George sent you. . . .)

HOW TO GET A TICKET TO THE ANNUAL BALL

Though 1994 tickets to the annual ball were not available by mail, they were sold through retail stores in New Orleans. For the 1995 ball, the procedure changed: Tickets were initially offered through the mail on a senority basis to members of the fan club. (The week of the ball, the remainder of the unsold tickets were available through Trice's bookstore, the Garden District Book Shop.)

An estimated four thousand people attended the 1995 ball, most of them fan club members and their guests, so your best bet is to join the fan club to receive advance notification, order tickets immediately, book your flight and hotel reservations as soon as you get the word, and plan on heading down to New Orleans for a hell of a good time. (If you don't get a ticket through the fan club, contact Trice's bookstore to see if they have been given any tickets at the eleventh hour.)

Anne Rice's Vampire Lestat Fan Club

requests your honored presence in costumed-attire to revel in the festivities of the

Annual Gathering of the Coven

Revel is defined by Funk & Wagnall's as "to take delight in: to engage in boisterous festivities: merry-making: carousing." A perfect description of the activities of the more than 1,400 attendees who came from as far away as Connecticut, Pennsylvania, and Australia to partake in this year's Gathering. A more splendid evening could not have been found elsewhere.

The scheduled entertainment consisted of four acts spanning the musical spectrum. TRIO NOCTURNA, from Atlanta, played their haunting melodies. A chilling set of Gothic songs was performed by EX-VOTO, who count among their members A.R.V.L.F.C. staffer Linda Rainwater. Longtime fan club friends JOHNNA WHITE, from New Jersey, and L.A.'s RED HEAVEN (who were celebrating the release of their debut CD) closed the show. Also, a last minute surprise rounded out the already-packed bill. In town for their own show across town, HOLE arrived and asked if they could play a short set to open our party. Partiers were treated to a free thirty minutes of COURTNEY LOVE and crew pounding out tracks from their newest CD: *Live Through This.*

The high-point of the evening for most was

Anne Rice who addressed the crowd on two separate occasions. First, from the balcony, Mrs. Rice assured the multitude that the motion picture *INTERVIEW WITH THE VAMPIRE* was "fantastic." "I give you my word of honor: Tom Cruise actually becomes Lestat. He takes over that role without taking it away from me. So I feel like Tom Cruise wins the Balls Award for 1994!" A tumultuous cheer rose from the crowd. "I think you're going to love the movie," Rice continued, "and if you don't, call me." She said that her home phone number was newly relisted and available from Information for this purpose. Later, as she and her family were departing, Mrs. Rice took the stage to say farewell and give her blessings to the party-goers.

More than twenty amazing door prizes — everything from signed books to T-shirts to vampfire hot sauce—were awarded to delighted winners. In addition, a raffle was conducted for a copy of the limited edition of *Taltos.* Published as a 500-copy edition, this book was made extra special by an inscription from Anne Rice commemorating the Coven party. The lucky winner was Jason Krause of Baton Rouge. No one left empty handed, however, since fan club staffers handed out 1500 plastic rats signed by Mrs. Rice as well as loads of continued on page .. 11

George Beahm

First page to the Club newsletter, January 20, 1995, issue

A Hell of a Good Time: The Memnoch Ball 1995

by Sascha Mabus-Vosper

We met on America Online as Geo Beahm and Rowan24601. When Rowan24601—excuse me, Sascha Mabus-Vosper—told me she had attended the 1994 Gathering of the Coven Ball at Tipatina's in New Orleans, I asked her to write a firsthand report for this book, which she did.

Since then, she attended the 1995 Gathering of the Coven, the Memnoch Ball. It seemed more appropriate to use an updated version, especially since Anne Rice was hosting the ball at her new home, the former St. Elizabeth's orphanage, with the theme "Vampires through the Ages."

A Rice reader since the age of sixteen, Sascha is very much a fan in the best sense of the word—enthusiastic, upbeat, and eager to spread the gospel according to Rice.

In the piece that follows, Sascha, in the company of her boyfriend, Greg, takes us inside the new Rice residence, in what had to be the biggest housewarming in New Orleans, with four thousand guests . . . dressed to kill.

◆

Having a Ball

When we arrived at St. Elizabeth's, the limo driver let us out a little way from the entrance because the block had been closed off by police barricades. We stepped out and walked to the entrance, following hundreds of vampire-clad fans.

When we reached the first barricade on the Prytania Street entrance, the security guards checked to see if we had tickets, then motioned us inside to the second barricade, where we were handed programs for the night's events.

We went to the ticket table, where our tickets were ripped and our hands were stamped in red ink with a design of the devil. The volunteer bade us a good time, and we were off to enjoy the evening.

The first of several outdoor pavilions was packed with people. As the sounds of the Bedrocks filled the New Orleans night with rock 'n' roll music, we stopped to take pictures and to have our pictures taken, and to talk with the other guests.

Fan from the Memnoch Ball 1995

George Beahm

A Hell of a Good Time: The Memnoch Ball 1995

Be Our Guest

Clearly, Rice had the guests' comfort in mind. The main walkway was lined with chairs and refreshment tables. After popping open my can of beer, custom brewed by Abita Brewing Company, I looked closely at the label, designed by Anne. Victim (the beer's name) bore the legend: "Memnoch Ball 1995, Compliments of Anne Rice. . . . 'Lestat,' he said . . . 'you want to taste it, don't you?'" (This was an allusion to *Interview with the Vampire*.)

As did others, we took a few bottles home for keepsakes.

Beers in hand, we headed inside St. Elizabeth's.

Because the stairwell was packed, the line moved slowly. Once inside, we walked down the first of many hallways, this one flanked with Stan Rice's oil paintings. As we were viewing them, Jamie Ferguson, dressed as a rose peddler, passed out a red carnation to each woman. (Later that evening, she and Sarah Namer passed out dozens of old-style church fans: on one side, the words "Coven Party '95/ St. Elizabeth's/ New Orleans, Louisiana," with a wash drawing by Patricia Hardin, bearing Anne's signature in red ink; on the other, printed in reverse type, a poem by Stan Rice, "Living in New Orleans," with his signature below.)

The hall emptied into a large line of people leading to a stairwell. We were told that the Chapel Ballroom and the doll collection were upstairs on the second floor. According to the printed program, the scheduled entertainment in the Chapel Ballroom was to be The Mardi Gras Salon Orchestra and the Vampire Dancers. Both were to perform until midnight. Discouraged that the line was not moving, we decided to wait until it thinned out a bit.

The second floor contained two other rooms with performances. In "Chris's Cabaret Room," under the direction of Chris Rice, Broadway tunes were to be played. The second attraction was "Miss Havisham's Room" containing a replica of Miss Havisham's famous wedding cake from Dickens's *Great Expectations*. The wedding cake was cut and served early in the evening; unfortunately, when we finally reached the second floor, only crumbs remained. Judging from the size of the plate, the cake must have been immense.

With beers and flowers in hand, we wandered around the first floor. One room contained an elegant table filled with finger sandwiches and tasty treats. Adjacent to the food room was a guest lounge where you could watch television or play pool. In the corner of the lounge stood a monstrous doll in the image of Pumpkinhead, from the movie of the same name. For a brief moment, I actually thought the doll was a real person in costume because it looked so lifelike.

It was only nine P.M., so we made our way to the Chapel, on the third floor. Security guards kept vigil on the stairwells and kept guests from ascending to the private quarters. One stairwell was blocked by a life-size skeleton woman dressed in a wedding gown. The message at her feet said "End thy upward climb."

We decided to explore the five rooms on the third floor.

The first room was called the "Theatre of Art," appropriately named because it housed a slide show of Stan Rice's paintings. The second room was occupied by Epic Winds, a woodwind trio that played a delightful mix of classical and contemporary selections while dressed in eccentric costumes. The third room contained all of the fan club merchandise for sale and party mementos. Because we had no money with us to buy fan club T-shirts or posters, we secured some free medallions. A fourth room was called the Band Promotional Room, which contained recordings for sale of Trio Nocturna and the other bands at the ball.

The fifth—and oddest—room was called the "Chamber of Les Innocents and the Bat Cave." The hallway leading into the Chamber was decorated with plastic bats hanging from the ceiling and eerie ultraviolet lighting. The Chamber itself was a museum of the macabre, strewn with coffins, vats with floating eyeballs, spider webs, sadomasochistic mannequins, dismembered hands, and general peculiarities.

Because it was nearly ten P.M., we made our way to the Green Velvet Ballroom, which was packed with people awaiting the appearance of Anne Rice. As the musical group Peabody left the stage, fan club staff member Ritchie Champagne took the stage and told everyone that there would be a big surprise soon, but we had to move back so the security guards could set up barriers in front of the stage. Slowly, the crowd moved back, hampered by the fact that nobody wanted to lose his or her place.

Finally, Anne Rice appeared. Incongruously dressed in an elegant black ball gown and wearing a baseball cap, Anne Rice was accompanied by son Chris, husband Stan, and the teaser "surprise"—dressed in an elegant blue gown, child actress Kirsten Dunst ascended the stage to the cheers of the crowd.

Fan Club President Susie Miller, representing the collective Anne Rice fans, pleaded with Anne to continue the Vampire Chronicles—a concern raised by her public pronouncements that Lestat had left her and there would

The program book cover for the Memnoch Ball 1995

be no more tales about him. Susie said that there was no way we would let Lestat's or Armand's adventures end in such an open-ended manner.

She was followed by Chris Rice, who commented that Anne was the best mother in the world.

When Anne took the microphone, she thanked everyone for coming to the ball and for supporting her. She also thanked fan club creator Susie Miller and gave her a dozen roses. She then introduced Kirsten Dunst and presented her with two gifts: an antique watch and a mirror to "watch herself and her brilliant career grow."

The group stood for pictures, then made their way out of the Green Velvet Room to a podium situated outside of the main entrance of St. Elizabeth's. The procession was followed by a percussion band.

At the podium, Anne posed for pictures, signed a few books, and talked to her entourage and guests, as Kirsten Dunst signed autographs for her fans.

TRAVEL TIPS FOR OUT-OF-TOWNERS

1. Get an information packet about the city of New Orleans from the Visitor's Bureau and take in the other Anne Rice sites of interest.

2. Because New Orleans is a popular convention site, be sure to book reservations for lodging early. (Be sure to specify to your travel agent that you want lodging in the Garden District.)

3. When coming in from the airport, rent a car. You'll need it to get around, especially if you want to see all the Rice sites: the French Quarter, the Historic District, and the cemeteries.

4. Bring plenty of color print film; you'll want to take pictures.

5. Book through a local travel agency in New Orleans. Rice fans are advised to deal with Tours by Andrea (2838 Touro Street, New Orleans, LA 70122 ◆ 1-800-535-2732 ◆ fax 1-504-942-5737). The owner, a member of the Vampire Lestat Fan Club, can handle all your travel needs and, unlike other in-town agencies, can tailor your trip to your Rice-specific destinations. (Tours by Andrea was the agency that the Vampire Lestat Fan Club worked with in providing packages for out-of-towners for the 1995 Memnoch Ball.)

6. Cautionary note: Because some of the cemeteries are not in secure areas of the city, it's best to stick to organized tour groups—there's safety in numbers.

A Hell of a Good Time: The Memnoch Ball 1995

In what was to me the most touching moment of the evening, an elderly man was escorted and helped onto the podium. Anne affectionately hugged the gentleman and spoke to him privately. It brought some of us close to tears.

The evening winding down, we took the opportunity to view what I considered to be the most beautiful displays and rooms in the building—the Chapel and the doll rooms.

The Chapel room is the most magnificent room I have ever seen. When I first stepped inside, past the statues and pictures of saints, Christ, and the Virgin Mary, I was nearly breathless.

The Chapel was approximately the size of a small nave, lacking pews. Hundreds of guests mingled, awaiting the next musical set. On the far end of the chapel was a balcony on the second floor. At the head of the room stood the altar, sectioned off by an ornate rail, separating the Mardi Gras Salon Orchestra from the guests.

The Witching Hour

As the witching hour—midnight, marking the formal end of the ball—approached, we headed to the rooms with Rice's doll collection.

Earl G. Perry, Jr.

Two vampire dolls

I noticed a small wooden rocking horse. When I bent down to look at it, I noticed that the horse was made by Howard O'Brien, Anne's father.

The dolls were positioned along the perimeter of the room behind a rope barrier. We moved along, attempting to view the hundreds of dolls in this room alone. Grouped by artist, arranged in small scenes, the dolls' clothing and lifelike faces were testaments to their artistry.

The room overflowed with lace, fur coats, flowers, curls, and ribbons representing all periods of fashion and time. In addition, fantasy-themed dolls of mermaids and vampires decorated the room.

Also on exhibit, two eye-catching pieces: a life-size doll of Nosferatu and a handcrafted Victorian dollhouse, designed by Pat Newman, which was perfect in every detail. It contained six main rooms, an attic room, a bathroom, and a stairwell; the beds had tiny lace bedspreads, the dining room chairs were made of red velvet, and the stairwell was carpeted. Outside the dollhouse stood miniature dolls going about their business.

The second doll room was just as memorable as the first. The dolls were similarly arranged, positioned on couches, rocking horses, on tables, and in rocking chairs. It appeared to be a room full of children who were sitting quietly.

A beautiful chess set was the centerpiece to the room. The pieces were carved in the uniforms of soldiers at the Battle of Hastings. Greg, an avid chess player, was particularly drawn to this display. As I walked around the room and viewed the dolls, he snapped photographs of the chess board.

The tour of the second room concluded with a viewing of a shelf of miniature knickknack dolls. There were hundreds of little dolls arranged in small cubicles. In addition to child and baby dolls, Anne collected smaller, ethnic dolls as well.

It was close to midnight as we made our way to the front entrance. The crowds had thinned considerably, so moving within the building was much easier. We left her house through the Napoleon Street exit and, after Rice left in her limousine, we left for our hotel.

To this day, I am still surprised that a public figure like Anne Rice would open her home to all of those strangers. But as I thought about this, I realized that we are not strangers to her. Perhaps she doesn't know our names, but she knows what is in our hearts. Anne Rice is passionate about what she writes, and we are passionate about listening to what she has to say. Perhaps that is why she allowed us to share with her what was in retrospect an unforgettable night.

*If you're like most Rice fans, chances are good that you rely on your local inde-
pendent bookstore, chain store (like Waldenbooks, Barnes and Noble, or B. Dalton
Bookseller), or discount store (like Sam's Club or the Price Club) for forthcoming
Rice novels.*

*Did you know that several of the books in the Vampire Chronicles were adapted
as graphic novels?*

*Did you know that a bookstore within walking distance of Rice's home on First
Street offers signed copies of her books and caters to Rice readers worldwide?*

*Did you know that signed, limited editions of some of her books have been
published?*

These are worlds you've probably never dreamed of. . . .

Knopf's book design for Anne Rice's novels, stamped on the front cover, bearing her initials

An Interview with the Illustrator: Colleen Doran

Even among Anne Rice's most ardent readers, "The Master of Rampling Gate" is likely to be, if not unknown, a little-seen work. A short story that originally appeared in *Redbook*, the story was subsequently revised by Rice for its graphic album adaptation published by Innovation.

Fortunately, Innovation did not approach John Bolton—or any other male comic-book artist—to render the interior art. Recognizing, perhaps, that the work is a gothic romance, Innovation approached Colleen Doran, a young artist who has illustrated comic books for Marvel, D.C., independent publishers, and Disney. The result: an evocative graphic adaptation of a short story that, through her art, makes the leap from prose on a page to pictures in the mind, enhanced by her love of history and period pieces, her painstaking approach to watercolor illustration, her fascination for the fantastic, and her own romantic nature.

The "splash" page (the first page of the book, designed to grab your attention and set the mood) shows Rampling Gate, an imposing estate with immaculate grounds, a blue-black sky boiling with clouds, and the sun breaking through.

Unfortunately, the publication of this adaptation—like the story on which it was based—was probably unseen by most of Rice's readers, since the publisher's distribution was limited to retail comic-book stores. Out of print, *The Master of Rampling Gate* is a visual delight and worth your effort in tracking it down through secondhand book dealers that specialize in comic-book-related material.

The Master of Rampling Gate, trade paperback,
6.5 x 10 inches, 64 pages; June 1991, $6.95.

BOOK CREDITS
Adapted by James Schlosser
Painted by Colleen Doran
Lettered by Vickie Williams
Edited by David Campiti
Cover painting by John Bolton
Book design by David Campiti
Logo design by George Broderick Jr.

An Interview with the Illustrator: Colleen Doran

Original art by Colleen Doran from the splash page of *Master of Rampling Gate*

Part Two: The Unreal World of Anne Rice

◆

GEORGE BEAHM: Had you read "The Master of Rampling Gate" in short-story form before being asked to illustrate it?

COLLEEN DORAN: I didn't know it existed. I was [erroneously] told it was the only short story she had ever written; and when Innovation asked me if I'd be interested in doing this assignment, they actually offered me my choice of *The Master of Rampling Gate, Interview with the Vampire,* or *The Queen of the Damned.*

The time commitments on *Interview with the Vampire* or *The Queen of the Damned* would have taken up to three years to complete, so I chose *The Master of Rampling Gate* instead, which ultimately turned out to be a good decision because the company went under before finishing *The Queen of the Damned.*

I got to work with Anne Rice, I got to do an entire book, and then I moved on.

BEAHM: In comparison to straight text, what does the graphic novel format add to Anne Rice's work?

DORAN: It's not a question of adding; it's more like taking a step sideways. I'm always happy to see many different versions of something I enjoy; and

---

ARIA PRESS

An aria is "an elaborate melody sung solo with accompaniment, as in an opera or oratorio" (from *Random House Dictionary of the English Language,* second edition, unabridged). It is an appropriate symbol for Colleen Doran's small press, which she started as a necessary alternative to mainstream publishing. A veteran of the comic-book industry, Colleen has worked for Marvel, D.C., and numerous independent publishers, but in recent years has put a priority on her self-published ventures, including a bimonthly comic book, *A Distant Soil,* limited editions, T-shirts, and her own fan club (self-directed by necessity after a disheartening experience with a start-up fan venture).

For information on Colleen's publishing activities, include a self-addressed, stamped envelope with sufficient postage for first class, and ask for a flyer on her latest projects. Write to: Aria Press, 12638–28 Jefferson Avenue, Suite 173, Newport News, VA 23602.

An Interview with the Illustrator: Colleen Doran

Orginial art by Colleen Doran from a two-page spread in *Master of Rampling Gate*

as a very visual person, I *like* seeing representations of the characters—it's much harder to find people who not only are gorgeous as they are in her books, but are also great actors and fit your vision of exactly what *you* want for a story.

As a cartoonist, I can make the heroes and heroines look exactly the way I want, and presumably they look pretty much like what the readers wanted, too.

The advantage with *Rampling Gate* was that because so few people knew the story even existed, they didn't have any preconceptions of what the characters should look like.

BEAHM: What contact did you have with Anne Rice while working on the project?

DORAN: I spoke to her and got a couple of letters through her secretary. The one thing I do know about this book was that she was really happy about how the characters looked. Apparently, I came really close to what her versions of her characters looked like. Also, Anne likes deep, rich coloring, and she commented that she liked my coloring style as well.

BEAHM: Do you think your book would have looked different if a man had drawn it?

DORAN: Oh, yeah! [laughter] I don't think the people would have been as good-looking!

BEAHM: This is a very romantic story—

DORAN: I think all of her work is romantic, even if it is horror; it's *extremely* romantic work, and I think that people lose sight of the fact that a lot of the appeal of her stories is carried by the characters and their interpersonal relationships—that's the most important thing about her work. Almost everything else is incidental to me; the characters are what's really important, and how they deal with these bizarre situations, of course.

BEAHM: Have you gotten any feedback from people in the comic-book community regarding your adaptation?

DORAN: It was really positive.

BEAHM: And what of your own evaluation of the work?

DORAN: I don't have complaints on at least half the pages of the book, which is unusual for me because I usually complain about something on every single page I do.

Almost all the original art from the book I no longer own, though I did save about four pages that I really wanted.

BEAHM: How much research did you have to do?

DORAN: There was a *lot* of research. I spent an awful lot of time in the library. That first page of *Rampling Gate* is a combination of three different buildings and grounds. On the second page—the double page of the train station— I was actually supposed to be doing a different train station, but there was no reference to be found on *that* particular train station in that particular year, so I found an old painting by a gentleman named Firth.

I was able to find some very specific references in the library for the costumes. Of course, the big dining room scene was full of reference material— I had a whole file.

It was an awkward time to be working on the book because it was a schizophrenic period for me—I was also working on *The Beauty and the Beast* for Disney and Clive Barker's *Hellraiser*.

BEAHM: It seems to me that if a male artist had done the book, there would not have been the emphasis you put on the romantic aspect of the story.

An Interview with the Illustrator: Colleen Doran

DORAN: The story is just a gothic romance, isn't it? I think all of Rice's work is very romantic.

BEAHM: Absolutely. . . . Is there any reason why John Bolton was used as the cover artist?

DORAN: He had a contract with the company that gave him the right to do the covers to all of Rice's graphic novel adaptations, which was a great disappointment to me because his cover doesn't reflect the story or what's going on inside the book—it doesn't hold with the rest of the art: The heroine is described as a blonde [Bolton portrays a brunette], and the vampire hero is supposed to be very youthful, innocent, and romantic-looking, but he looks quite menacing in Bolton's shot. . . .

The book was actually supposed to be longer than it was. It was going to include a section on the preproduction color sketches I had done, and an interview with Anne.

BEAHM: If time were not a problem—as it always is when you're juggling so many projects for different publishers, including yourself—is there something she's written that you would have loved to illustrate?

DORAN: I would have loved doing *all* of the vampire books, frankly, but I don't see a time when I'd have a decade to paint comic-book adaptations. Of all of them, I would have liked to do *The Queen of the Damned* because it's got all the best characters in it. It spans thousands of years in time, so it'd be fun to represent all those different costumes and time periods—everybody's in that one.

Britton E. Trice:
An Interview with a Bookseller

For Rice fans who want a one-stop shop for their needful things, you can't do any better than the Garden District Book Shop, conveniently located six blocks from Anne Rice's house. Owned by Britton E. Trice, bookseller and publisher, the Garden District Book Shop has become *the* place to go for Rice's books (in print and out of print), audiotape adaptations, limited editions, and ephemeras.

For locals and tourists, it's best just to stop in; the store is open seven days a week (Monday to Saturday, 10–6; Sunday, 11–4), but Trice also does a brisk mail-order business, catering to out-of-town readers that have seen his ads in the Anne Rice newsletter.

To reach Britton in a trice:
- phone: (504) 895-2266
- fax: (504) 895-0111
- electronic mail on America Online: BETbooks

◆

GEORGE BEAHM: Tell me a little about your bookstore.

BRITTEN E. TRICE: I have no idea about the number of volumes stocked. It is mostly a new book shop, but I do have a small selection of used and rare books on New Orleans and Louisiana, including some first editions of contemporary southern and New Orleans authors—especially Anne Rice.

We also have a good selection of books about gardening and decorative arts.

BEAHM: What is the relationship between your store and Anne Rice?

TRICE: I met Anne when she and her family moved back to New Orleans in 1988. We saw each other infrequently but spoke on the phone whenever Anne had a book request or needed some information about books.

I immediately sensed Anne's intelligence by the way she zeroed in on a problem or subject matter. She would question me about certain things until she knew everything I did about the subject. It was intimidating at first, but I got used to her method of rapid-fire questions.

Britton E. Trice: An Interview with a Bookseller

George Beahm

Britton E. Trice, owner of the Garden District Book Shop, displays a copy of the limited edition of *Taltos*, published by his press.

Part Two: The Unreal World of Anne Rice

We are only six blocks from Anne's house, so it was natural that we hosted her first local autograph party. We have continued these signings and have done six to date.

BEAHM: How did you get started in publishing Rice's limited editions?

TRICE: After starting my own publishing company in 1992, I knew that I wanted to publish something of Anne's. I had in mind a short story or a piece on New Orleans with photographs by Sandra Russell Clark. I tried to set up a short meeting with Anne to discuss these projects, but she was in one of her writing periods when she does little else but write.

A few months passed and I heard about *Taltos* being finished, so I spoke with her editor, Vicky Wilson, about the possibility of doing a limited edition. Vicky told me to send her a proposal, and the rest is history. The limited edition was published in two states: twenty-six lettered copies ($350) bound in full leather, signed and slipcased, which sold out one week after my announcing its publication; and five hundred numbered copies ($150) bound in linen, signed and slipcased.

BEAHM: Which signings has Rice done at your store?

TRICE: We have had six autograph parties: *The Queen of the Damned* in 1988; *The Witching Hour* in 1990; a joint signing with Rice and Katherine Ramsland for *The Witching Hour* (paperback) and *Prism of the Night* in 1991; *The Tale of the Body Thief* in 1992; *Lasher* in 1993; and *Memnoch the Devil* in 1995.

Although Anne made no public appearances for *Taltos* in 1994, she signed over fifteen hundred copies for us to sell at the book shop and for our mail-order customers.

We advertise these autograph parties through our mailing list, the newspapers here in New Orleans, the Anne Rice Vampire Lestat Fan Club newsletter, and more recently through the Internet and other computer on-line services.

These autograph parties draw huge crowds, with people starting to queue up several hours before the start of the party. When in full swing, the line of people stretches for at least two blocks with a wait up to two-and-a-half hours.

Anne is one of the more gracious authors we have had at our shop. (In fact, she even hired a New Orleans brass band to play at the signing in 1993. She wanted her fans to be entertained while having to wait in line for an autograph.) We also provided refreshments for the crowds while they waited.

As you can imagine, these signings are quite an event, with national and local television crews on hand to cover them.

Britton E. Trice: An Interview with a Bookseller

Anne not only signs books, comic books, T-shirts, napkins, etc., she also inscribes them. All during the signing, she keeps up a steady stream of answers and comments to the people who are having their books signed.

I'm always amazed at her ability to answer all these different questions so quickly and with an incredible depth of knowledge in so many different areas, which she keeps up until the last book is signed. It's quite a performance, usually lasting about five hours.

BEAHM: As for Rice collectibles, can you give us a feel for what's really collectible—what the diehard fans really want to buy?

TRICE: It varies. As for value and collectibility, *Interview with the Vampire* and *The Vampire Lestat* seem to be the ones I get asked for the most, but the people who collect Anne's books want them all—from the Vampire Chronicles to the erotica.

Right now, the longest waiting list is for *The Feast of All Saints* and, interestingly enough, the British edition of *The Mummy*, which is very popular because there was never a hardcover edition in the U.S.

One of the hardest books to find is the first U.S. edition of *The Claiming of Sleeping Beauty*. (I'd be interested to find out the print run of that one.)

BEAHM: Is your store *the* watering hole for Rice fans in town?

TRICE: I'd have to say yes. We are constantly directing people to Anne's houses or places in New Orleans that she writes about. We get people in the shop every day from all parts of the world who have come to New Orleans *just* because of reading Anne Rice's novels.

She is the best spokesperson for New Orleans. To bring people to a city just by writing about it . . . that says something about the power of Anne's writing.

I'd venture to say that her house on First Street (the setting of *The Witching Hour*) is one of the most photographed buildings in New Orleans.

BEAHM: Which of her books sell best in your store? The vampire books, the witches books, the contemporary erotica, the historical erotica, or the historical novels?

TRICE: That's a hard one. It's close—the vampire books and the witches books—but I'd have to say the vampire books have the edge, especially now that *Interview with the Vampire* has been released.

The "Beauty" trilogy seems to outsell the Rampling books, and *Feast of All Saints* sells more than *Cry to Heaven* or *The Mummy*.

BEAHM: Is it possible to characterize the typical Anne Rice reader? Give me a feel for who reads Rice.

TRICE: It really isn't possible to pigeonhole her "typical" reader. I see *all* types reading her books, but I'd characterize them as younger—the concept of alienation in Anne's books is something her younger readers can readily identify with.

BEAHM: What's your bestselling book *about* Anne Rice?
TRICE: *Prism of the Night*, the biography by Katherine Ramsland, but her companion books (*The Vampire Companion*, and *The Witches Companion*) are not that far behind.

BEAHM: Do you carry the audiotapes of her books and, if so, how do they sell?
TRICE: I carry all of the cassettes, and although they are steady sellers they don't come close to the number of books that are sold.

I have been selling a lot of copies of a locally produced tape, *Tableaux de Lestat*, which is music written to accompany a play that was performed here in New Orleans.

BEAHM: Among Rice's works, what's your favorite book and why?
TRICE: I'd have to say *Interview with the Vampire*. Even after eighteen years, I can still remember how remarkable I thought this book was after my first reading.

The person who got me into the book business in New Orleans had to talk me into reading this book; she made several tries before I would agree to read it. Needless to say, I finished the book the same night I started it. I remember being amazed at how believable the whole thing was—not your usual horror novel where you have to suspend disbelief in order to read it. This novel was *really* believable.

BEAHM: Do you do most of your business retail, or it is mostly mail order?
TRICE: We do most of our business directly from the shop, but each year sees an increase in our mail-order business.

This year, we had a marked increase in mail orders because I got a new computer and began playing around on the Internet, which led me to discover all of the Anne Rice news groups on the online services. (We got a good number of orders for Anne's books through these groups.) Also, Anne did not do a tour in 1994, and, fortuitously, my shop was one of the few places in the country to get signed copies of Anne's new book.

Collecting Rice:
A Price Guide by George Beahm
with Britton E. Trice

For signed, first editions in hardback, the following prices are a reliable barometer of what you can expect to pay for *signed* books, according to Anne Rice expert Britton E. Trice.

Obviously, as Anne Rice's readers increase in number, the demand for each new book grows correspondingly, as it does for first printings. *Memnoch the Devil* had a first printing of 750,000 copies—contrast this to the estimated 25,000 copies of *Interview with the Vampire*.

◆

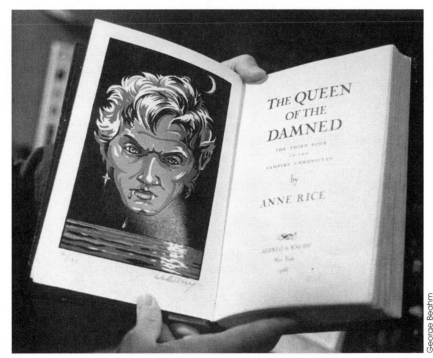

Britton E. Trice displays a copy of the Ultramarine Press edition of *The Queen of the Damned*.

MOST COLLECTIBLE AUTHOR

Barry Levin, of Barry Levin Science Fiction & Fantasy Literature, presents an annual award to the author his discriminating clientele agrees is the most collectible. For 1994, Anne Rice was the recipient of this award and received a beautiful Lucite sculpture with a sphere mounted on top.

Beauty's Punishment, $200 (U.S. edition); $165 for the British edition

Beauty's Release, $200 (U.S. edition only; no British edition was published)

Belinda, $95 to $125

The Claiming of Sleeping Beauty, $350 to $400 (U.S. edition); $165 for the British edition

Cry to Heaven, $125

Exit to Eden, $100 to $125

The Feast of All Saints, $150 to $175

Interview with the Vampire, $600 to $700, though copies have sold for as much as $1,000

Lasher, $35

Memnoch the Devil, $35

The Mummy, or Ramses the Damned, $175 to $200. (Note: This is for the British edition; there was no U.S. hardback edition)

The Queen of the Damned, $100

The Tale of the Body Thief, $35

Taltos, $35

The Vampire Lestat, $250 to $300

The Witching Hour, $60 to $100

George Beahm

Anne Rice's signature on a limited edition of *Interview with the Vampire*

The Limited Editions

As for collectibility, first editions are always in demand, but in recent years Rice has seen several of her books published as limited editions, with prices to match, listed chronologically:

Ultramarine Press

The Queen of the Damned was published in 1988 in two states: a lettered state of 26 copies bound in leather, published at $325 (current value, $900, according to its publisher), and a numbered state of 150 copies, bound in cloth, published at $150 (current value, $350, according to its publisher). Rebound with folded and gathered sheets from the Knopf edition, this edition also had a signed and numbered lithograph in color by Ron Worlowski. (This was the only Rice book Ultramarine Press co-published with Knopf; there are no plans to publish any other Rice books.)

Alfred A. Knopf

At the 1992 American Booksellers Association convention, Knopf gave out limited editions of *Interview with the Vampire;* the limitation sheet stated: "The first one thousand copies / of the reissue of / *Interview with the Vampire* / HAVE BEEN SPECIALLY PREPARED AND NUMBERED / FOR PRESENTATION AT THE / AMERICAN BOOKSELLERS ASSOCIATION CONVENTION, / MAY 1992 / NO. ———— [hand-numbered in ink, 1–1,000] / [Anne Rice's signature in black ink].

This edition also sported a "belly band" in red, with white lettering: "Coming from Knopf / October 31, 1992 / THE TALE OF THE BODY THIEF / The Vampire Chronicles continue . . ."

The belly band wrapped around the yellow-gold dust jacket.

At the convention Anne Rice passed out these free copies and spoke briefly with each bookseller. No copies were inscribed; all copies had been presigned.

In November 1990 Knopf published a boxed, three-volume set of signed Rice books under the title "The Vampire Chronicles." The paper box was decorated with a photograph by David Finn, a detailed shot of Antonio Canova's *The Farewell of Venus and Adonis* (1789). The ribbon frame was created by Brian Sharkey. The design was by Virginia Tan.

Part Two: The Unreal World of Anne Rice

The set of three books originally retailed for $100. The books did not have dust jackets. Bound in black cloth, all three books were signed on the flyleaf by Rice in black ink; on the legal page is the notation, "Reset, boxed edition, November 14, 1990."

B. E. Trice Publishing

To date, this company has co-published two limited editions with Knopf. The first was *Taltos*, in September 1994, in two states: twenty-six lettered copies, slipcased, bound in full leather, at $350 (out of print); and 500 copies, slipcased, bound in linen, at $150 (in print).

The second was *Memnoch the Devil*, in August 1995, in three states: 26 lettered copies, bound in full leather, $375 (out of print); 50 copies in quarter leather, $250 (out of print); and 425 copies in cloth, $150 (in print).

Like the Ultramarine Press edition of *The Queen of the Damned*, these copies use the folded and gathered sheets from the trade edition; the sheets were then rebound.

Row of masoleums at Lafayette Cemetery

George Beahm

Sponsoring an Anne Rice Event

One of the advantages of being a bestselling author is that book signings are not exercises in embarrassment. Unlike less popular or unknown authors, bestselling writers draw hundreds of devoted readers who will patiently line up for hours before the scheduled signing to insure they get an autographed book.

Most bestselling authors would prefer to stay at home, avoiding the dreaded book tour in which interviews, book signings, and in-store appearances become the orders of the day—a way of life for one or two hectic weeks.

Rice is an exception to this rule. Flourishing under conditions that make other authors wilt, Rice seemingly thrives on the publicity, the interviewing, and especially the book signings, where she will patiently sit for hours and sign books with a preternatural stamina.

To promote *Memnoch the Devil*, Rice went to dozens of bookstores from coast to coast, to the delight of her publishers and her fans. Predictably, the number of signings scheduled was dwarfed by the number of requests, as Knopf pointed out in a five-page form letter sent to the stores that were selected to host a Rice event.

"At last count," Knopf's letter said, "426 of your colleagues—bookstores from all over America—had called, faxed, written letters, sent proposals, composed poems, delivered paintings, coffins and dolls to the Alfred A. Knopf offices in an effort to lure Anne Rice to their bookstore for *Memnoch the Devil* booksigning. You made the cut. Now here's a few things we can do together to make your Anne Rice event one to remember."

I've summarized the five-page letter in the bulleted list below:

- The bookseller must put up around town 100 posters promoting the signing. (Knopf wants three photos of the posters on display.)
- The bookseller must put up a window display or an in-store display. (Anne Rice will judge displays and the winning store will receive two tickets to Rice's Memnoch Ball; three runners-up will receive the limited edition of *Memnoch the Devil*.)
- The bookseller must advertise the signing.
- Knopf will provide *Memnoch the Devil* T-shirts for store employees to wear during the signing.

+ Knopf expects to see in-store promotional efforts used to maximum effect: newsletter mailings, calendar listings in local papers, and bag stuffers.

+ For security purposes, the store must hire "one local, off-duty police officer" and confirm details with Knopf.

+ The bookseller must provide live entertainment. (Though the book signing itself will be approximately five hours, fans start queuing up early, and need to be entertained during the interim. "Stores that call asking 'What do you mean by live entertainment' run the risk of being ridiculed by Knopf Director of Promotion Paul Bogaards.")

+ Anne Rice will do a fifteen-minute radio or print interview prior to the signing to promote it, in addition to an in-store fifteen-minute press conference (all media must be cleared by Knopf).

+ Anne Rice will get a half-hour break at the midpoint, so she "can retreat to a backroom, relax and snack."

+ Because of the large number of persons that may show up, stores should cap attendance at 2,000. Tickets are recommended.

+ The bookstore must have in place a mechanism for determining the number of people in the line at all times. ("Anne's publicist . . . will need to know how many people are in line, have passed through the line, or are left in line at a moment's notice.")

+ A sturdy table should be provided, with a comfortable, sturdy chair also provided—preferably, someone of Rice's height (5 feet, 4 inches) should try out the set-up for comfort. A small pillow should be provided as well.

+ The line must feed from Rice's left side; her publicist will sit to her left and pass books to sign; on the right, a store employee will make sure the line is flowing smoothly.

+ Store employees "with *neat handwriting*" are responsible for lettering cards that will be inserted in each book to be signed. "The employees should use a black Sharpie pen, fill out the customer's first name in *large block letters*, and insert the finished cards in said customer's copy. . . ."

+ The store employee on Rice's righthand side will pass on the signed books to the customers.

+ Provisions to have on hand: "Anne signs with black medium-point Sharpies. Have plenty of pens. Have at least one 'metallic' pen for the one or two customers who will want their leather jackets autographed. Anne drinks Tab but will drink Diet Coke in a pinch. Have one or the other (cold, in cans). She also drinks bottled water (flat, noncarbonated). She likes Hall's cough drops and Puff's tissues. . . ."

♦ Rice will sign the customer's *first name only* in copies of *Memnoch*. "No limit on quantity."

♦ Rice will sign *her name only* in any other Rice book bought from the store. "No limit on quantity *time permitting*."

♦ Fans cannot bring items to the signing; only Rice books bought in-store will be signed.

♦ A staffer from the store will be designated as "store photographer" and "will take the camera from the individual wishing to have their [sic] photo taken with Anne and snap the picture while Anne is signing their [sic] book."

♦ No video cameras allowed.

♦ On the expectation that fans will bring gifts for Rice, the bookstore should have a carton on hand for UPS shipment to Rice's personal residence in New Orleans. ("Pack the carton with care. . . .")

♦ Advance phone orders and store staff copies will be signed prior to the book signing at Rice's hotel room. "All phone orders will be *signature and date only*. Staff copies will be personalized."

Row of masoleums at Lafayette Cemetery

Scott Stewart

Mel Graziano's *Tableaux de Lestat*

Tableaux de Lestat by Graziano. Recorded on chrome cassette with Dolby, from Mel Man Productions, 3917 Ferran Drive, Metairie, LA 70002. Side one: 5 selections; side two, 6 selections. $10.

When Britton E. Trice, proprietor of the Garden District Book Shop, recommended this recording to me, I wondered why it wasn't available nationally, but when I found a copy at Trice's bookstore, I knew the reason why: It's a local effort, thoroughly professional, and hellishly delightful listening—it's the music of the night.

Obviously, the liner notes, printed separately, are a prerequisite to understanding why and how the music was composed, so in the event you don't get a copy when you get a copy of the recording, the following notes should help you understand and appreciate a masterful, original work that richly deserves a wider audience.

◆

Buried in the Garden District: So named because that's how the novel opens up—Lestat has buried himself under his home in the Garden District in uptown New Orleans. Here we hear what Lestat hears: the sounds of streetcars, amplified radio music, electric guitars, the emergence of Jazz/Dixieland, and an uncontrollable urge to rise and become a part of this new world. The melismatic organ portion that follows symbolizes his rising and his "tooling around" on his newly purchased Harley motorcycle. Next, the contrapuntal section, a variation on the secondary melody previously expressed, is his feeding on his victims. In the recapitulation of the melismatic texture, his ideas for his new life take form in his mind. The final section is his ideas being organized and put into action.

Magnus: Because Magnus was an ancient vampire, I used a lot of very old melodies. The familiar chime that opens the piece is actually based on an old Gregorian Chant. Then the three bells for three o'clock, the time when Magnus first abducts the young mortal Lestat. We hear Magnus say, "Wolfkiller." The main melody is plainchant—The Kyrie from Mass XI ("Orbis factor"), which I variate and add accompaniment to. An ostinato line and more bells are Lestat becoming a vampire. Finally, he succumbs to his fate and starts out on his quest. Here I use rhythmic augmentation and diminution of the original theme.

Mel Graziano's *Tableaux de Lestat*

Gabrielle Made: This is when Lestat makes his mother a vampire. Anne Rice treats this scene with love and compassion, so I also do the same; slow-moving and beautiful, with ritards symbolizing her being "bit."

The Coven's Trial: "A curse on the outlaws . . ." is the opening sound. Lestat senses danger but also views the whole proceeding as a farce and contradictory in nature. The music is a pleading of the "case," melodies take on a conversational feel, with repeats to symbolize the coven membership swaying from one opinion to another. The use of "Blasphemy" and "Dark Gift" are the prosecution's base for their case. Lestat is victorious in his arguments and we hear the old queen vampire, in giving her pardon, say "Ride the devil's road."

Théâtre des Vampyres: Lestat tries to help his fledgling Nicki to overcome his insanity by making him return to his one love—music! A violin is the chosen instrument. Nicki is timid at first, tuning the violin and playing a little melody. Soon, his new vampire powers give an unequaled virtuosity to his playing ability and a feverish atmosphere is reached. The music form used is one that would have been common at that time for a solo artist—a type of Bach partita that, at the tempo given, would be hard for a mortal to cleanly achieve. Soon we find strange triple and quadruple stop glissandos adorn the musical madness until the end.

The Release of Marius: So named because Marius was about to be captured and thrown into a fire by an ancient coven. Though the fire meant certain death, it could also be seen as a release of sorts from the earthly bonds and torments. I took Latin text from the Catholic Requiem Mass because it fit the mold of the unfolding scene. First, there is the banging on the door, and then the cries, "Devils who paint angels." Marius is taken prisoner and destroyed, leaving his fledgling Armand to be interrogated and persuaded to join the coven. "Where are those who must be kept," "Join the children of darkness," and "Serve Satan" set up that part of the scene. The end comes with a descent into the earth by all those involved; music scale motion also goes down.

Armand's Admonitions: A solemn treatment is offered here to represent the scene in which Armand teaches Lestat that vampires cannot stay in each other's company too long and that eventually Gabrielle will leave to go on her way. The music sets the mood as Lestat sees Armand's predictions come true as she departs and Lestat is consumed by overwhelming loneliness.

Rescue from the Cairo Sands: Lestat has buried himself deep in the sands of Cairo to revitalize and escape for a while. Too weak to rise from his grave, he is rescued by the ancient vampire Marius, whose counsel Lestat has sought for many years. Marius' heartbeat and cannon booms are heard as he draws near. An eastern-sounding motif is used and the music lightens up as Lestat is lifted out of the ground and takes his first breath of air. A familiar ostinato pattern is heard as Lestat drinks from Marius. The piece concludes with a recapitulation of the original motif. And when Lestat realizes who has saved him, he asks, "Marius!" To which he is answered, "Yes!"

Steps to the Sanctum: Rice's description of the stairway leading to where Those Who Must Be Kept was so vivid I had to touch on it. Water sounds—drips, rushing seas, trickles—give us a feel for our surroundings. An ostinato accompaniment, made to sound like walking down a flight of stairs, lies underneath a very slippery solo line (dampness and mold). The ending notes tell us Lestat and Marius have reached the bottom and the doorway to the chamber of Those Who Must Be Kept.

The Concert: The opening night in San Francisco for the band, the Vampire Lestat. Crowds shout and chant "Lestat." Because of time constraints, I tried to touch a little bit on all the major songs described in the novel. The Vampire Lestat: "I am the Vampire Lestat," "You can't resist the lords of the night." The Children of Darkness: "Children of darkness meet the children of light." Age of Innocence: "This is the age of innocence," "Understand what you see when you see me!" The music here may not have all the heavy-sounding guitar that the book calls for, but I had to weigh continuity of the recording very high on my list of priorities. When the song called for a fast tempo, I did it; likewise for the opposite. Concluding this section is the melee between the opposing vampire factions, with unearthly screams and explosions. Lestat and company are successful in their escape, helped by some unknown, unseen force, and we hear police sirens in the background as everyone flees the scene.

Finale: Everyone conjectures as to who had helped them survive such an onslaught, but for now it is time to retire before the sun comes up. As Lestat settles into his crypt for the day, he feels a stone-cold hand touch his hand. It is Akasha! She was the one who had vanquished his enemies. "'Oh, please, my darling, my beautiful one, please!' I wanted to say. But my eyes were closing! My lips wouldn't move. I was losing consciousness. The sun had risen above." At this point it seemed only appropriate to reuse the main theme of the whole piece. I variate its texture and recapitulate some of the motifs and sounds used earlier for other pieces.

PART THREE

◆

On Anne Rice

Typically, in the fantasy and science fiction fields, literary criticism is published by a small or academic press that specializes in the field, like Borgo Press or Starmont House (now defunct).

Ironically, Anne Rice has not been the subject of book-length criticism in the field, but instead has had several books published by mainstream houses, mostly written by one person: Katherine Ramsland.

In this section, we meet Anne Rice's chronicler, look at her books on Rice, and hear from Rice herself, from her self-published, informally distributed zine, *Commotion Strange*, as well as in an interview conducted by Dale Rice.

◆

Why I Wrote a Biography of Anne Rice

by Katherine Ramsland

A well-written life is almost as rare as a well-spent one.

Thomas Carlyle

◆

First, I'd like to say that I was rather naive when I decided to approach Anne about writing her biography. I figured that someone ought to write it, so why not me? I'd already written one book and had credentials in psychology and literary interpretation. Only after I had committed myself to writing it within a year did I find out that most biographers spend five to ten years working on their books. So the question really was, how hard can it be to squeeze five years of work into one? The answer should be obvious.

Nevertheless, I'd do it again.

I first approached Anne after reading her third Vampire Chronicle, *The Queen of the Damned*. I was impressed by how she had addressed philosophical themes in a way that echoed Camus, Conrad, and Sartre. I wondered what her background was, and whether she had consciously constructed her fiction around literary writers or had developed the themes in her own way in synchronicity with them. I knew it would enhance my own reading pleasure to find out.

◆

RICE ON *PRISM OF THE NIGHT*

Because you ask, there is Katherine Ramsland's *Prism of the Night*, a full scale biography with which I cooperated, but which I never sought to control. It's out there in paperback and is fairly up to date. I have not read all of it. I mean it's my life, for God's sakes! But my father did read the first edition and approved of it before he died. Good enough for me.

from *Commotion Strange #3*

94

Why I Wrote a Biography of Anne Rice

I also noticed that everywhere I went with the novel, people approached and expressed interest not only in how far I'd read or who my favorite character was, but also in Anne, herself. I thought that was unusual. Oftentimes, people read a novel and can't even recall the author's name. The interest in Anne was clear. So I decided to give her a call.

She was friendly and flattered, but reserved. I told her I'd write a proposal for her to see. Just as I finished it, she called to say that people had advised her not to cooperate, that her time was valuable and no one had ever heard of me. I said, "Okay, but I do have the proposal written. How about just taking a look at it?" She agreed, and the result was my book about her life and work, *Prism of the Night*.

As I had suspected, the more I found out about Anne, the more eager I was to go back to her fiction again and again to see how the metaphors blossomed. Her inner life was a rich panorama of experiences and images that infused her novels with psychological and literary depth. I began teaching the Vampire Chronicles in my philosophy courses and watched students grow more and more enthused about the ideas and the style of Anne's writing. At no time did I ever doubt my vision for this biography. In fact, the finished product went well beyond the original proposal, thanks to the complementary vision of my editor at NAL, John Silbersack.

There were people who predicted to Anne that I'd never write it. Fortunately, she decided to take a wait-and-see attitude, and was willing to answer questions and write a general letter of introduction to her friends.

There were people who told me she was too young or not famous enough. Some editors even said she had to be dead before they'd be interested in a biography (which became a joke in Anne's family). I ignored all but those who encouraged me. And now I have an elegantly packaged hardcover book that has been critically received and is selling very well. Even better, I have a friend, Anne Rice. She is thrilled with what I've done, and has called several times to tell me.

So the moral is, if you have a vision, go for it.

A Look at Ramsland's Books
on Anne Rice

As any biographer will tell you, it's difficult enough to write a biography on a deceased figure—a task that usually consumes several years of research, even before the writing can begin—but writing a biography on a living person is, in ways, even more difficult. To write an unauthorized book means, typically, no access or assistance from official sources, families, and friends; and to write an authorized book means, typically, needing the diplomatic skills of a foreign service agent, since the writer must walk the tightrope of telling the unvarnished truth and ensuring that the subject is not offended.

Katherine Ramsland, Anne Rice's Boswell, took on the unenviable task of writing a biography that, even with the consent and active cooperation of Rice herself, was no easy task. Compressing several years of activity in one year in order to write *Prism of the Night*, Ramsland found herself appending a chapter with each new edition.

Rice is well served by Ramsland. An academician by training and inclination, Ramsland is the expert on Anne Rice's life and fiction.

Her books on Rice, chronologically listed, are:

- *Prism of the Night: A Biography of Anne Rice* (1991)
- *The Vampire Companion: The Official Guide to Anne Rice's "The Vampire Chronicles"* (1993; revised and expanded, 1995)
- *The Witches' Companion: The Official Guide to Anne Rice's "Lives of the Mayfair Witches"* (1994)
- *The Anne Rice Trivia Book* (1995)
- *The Roquelaure Reader* (1996)
- *The Anne Rice Reader* (tentative publication date: fall 1996)

Prism of the Night: A Biography of Anne Rice

Edition in print: trade paperback from Plume/Penguin, 414 pages, $12.95. Indexed, with a 16-page photo insert.

Originally published in hardback by Dutton, Ramsland's biography is now available in trade paperback. Updated with a new chapter with each new edition, the biography is required reading for Rice readers.

A Look at Ramsland's Books on Anne Rice

Because the project was authorized by Rice, the book features extensive interview material with Rice, her family, and friends, complete with private photographs from her photo albums that, otherwise, might never have seen book publication.

If the book had been nothing but a straightforward, chronological recitation of the facts of Rice's life, the book would still be fascinating reading. However, Ramsland's academic training—she has a master's degree in clinical psychology and a Ph.D. in philosophy—makes her ideally suited to discuss the Rice canon as a literary mosaic. The end result: a penetrating, insightful, and authoritative book that sheds light on Anne Rice as writer and individual.

Eschewing sensationalism, Ramsland is quick to point out that this is "a serious book, not an exposé. I had no agenda other than to discover and articulate the sources of Anne's multi-faceted creativity," as she wrote in "Biographical Reflections: A Look at *Prism of the Night*," published in Innovation's *The Vampire Companion #3*.

The Vampire Companion: The Official Guide to Anne Rice's "The Vampire Chronicles"

Preferred edition: trade paperback, 640 pages, $17.95 (includes the full text of the short story "Interview with the Vampire").

Organized from A to Z with over one thousand encyclopedic entries, this book provides a wealth of detail about the Vampire Chronicles, with the help of the Vampire Chronicler herself, Anne Rice. As Ramsland explains in the introduction to the book:

> Shortly after the biography was published, Rice asked me if I'd like to work on an interpretive guide to *The Vampire Chronicles*; she had been approached to do it herself but preferred to concentrate on writing novels. . . . What could be more wonderful than to go back to those themes and interpretations I'd left behind? . . . the *Companion* also includes a chronology of events that begin with the vampire origins; maps of significant locations; cross-references; and over one hundred drawings and photographs. I organized the entries in encyclopedic fashion and added background material, expanding the significance of key events and ideas. I categorized the contents of Rice's novels according to characters, places, themes, literary allusions and devices, symbols, famous quotes, and vampire-related terminology.

What makes this book special is that, unlike similar books, this one provides "more than a plot summary, so Rice agreed to provide deleted material from early drafts of her novels and to talk about background influences. . . ."

The end result: a fascinating, in-depth, single-volume reference book that ties together the first five books of the Vampire Chronicles: *Interview with the Vampire*, *The Vampire Lestat*, *The Queen of the Damned*, *The Tale of the Body Thief*, and *Memnoch the Devil*. (There are also references to *The Witching Hour*.)

In a letter to me, Ramsland wrote: "I'd appreciate it if you'd make it clear that the vision for [the companion guides] was created by Anne and myself together. I've heard fans complain that there's too much detail, but that's the way Anne wanted it. She wanted something that would be rich and literary and philosophical, with lots of illustrations, not just a quickie concordance. We talked about it at length and went over many of the entries."

The Witches' Companion: The Official Guide to Anne Rice's "Lives of the Mayfair Witches"

Edition in print: trade hardback from Ballantine Books, 528 pages, $29.95. Extensively illustrated with photos and art. (A trade paperback reprint is tentatively scheduled for fall 1996.)

Like *The Vampire Companion*, this book is organized from A to Z in encyclopedic fashion, covering in detail *The Witching Hour*, *Lasher*, and *Taltos*. And, like *The Vampire Companion*, Anne Rice assisted Ramsland to ensure that this reference work would reflect their unified vision.

As Ramsland wrote in the introduction, this book "is intended as a supplement to, not a substitute for, the novels. . . . The following pages contain an alphabetical list of characters, places, literary and historical references, symbols, terminology, plot summaries, page references, cross-references, drawings, and photographs. Also included are maps of significant locations, a chronology of events, and a genealogical Mayfair family tree."

The Anne Rice Trivia Book

Edition in print: paperback from Ballantine Books, 242 pages, $5.99.

Organized thematically instead of by book, this trivia quiz collection—cunningly crafted as only a college professor could—uses questions, multiple choice, matching, and fill-in-the-blank to pose puzzlers on the entire Rice canon, with the exception of the three erotic novels Rice published as A. N. Roquelaure.

A Look at Ramsland's Books on Anne Rice

The first part, "The Dark Universe"; the second part, "Anne Rice: Life and Writings"; the third part, "Super Bonus Questions"; and the fourth part, "Answers."

No matter how much you *think* you know about Rice's work, this book—as the back cover points out—will help you discover "how much you really know about the realm of Rice. . . . Ramsland has conjured up more than 1,000 queries covering 12 novels, more than 150 characters, and enough fascinating lore to give even the most devoted Rice fans a chance to test their knowledge of their favorite books."

The Roquelaure Reader

Edition in print: trade paperback from Plume, $12.95.

Focusing on Rice's erotic material, this reference book is a marked departure from Ramsland's two previous companion books. Approximately three hundred pages with no photos or drawings, the book has three parts, according to Ramsland: "a concordance, a long biographical essay with lots of quotes from Anne on her erotic imagination (e.g., more detail than I could put in a mainstream biography), and a trivia section. Also, it contains excerpts cut from *Exit to Eden*. Rice is a participant in this as she was in the companion guides to the supernatural works and to the *Anne Rice Trivia Book*."

The Anne Rice Reader

Scheduled publication date: spring 1997.

Organized in four parts, this book is a reader *about*, not *by*, Anne Rice: Part I, Anne Rice's novels (fourteen articles by various writers); Part II, *Interview with the Vampire* movie, including interviews with David Geffen and Tom Cruise, a Jungian analysis by John Beebe, and from *Variety*, Rice's letter to her readers; Part III, two Rice short stories ("October 9, 1948" and "Nicholas and Jean"); Part IV, an interview with Rice, an article by Kathleen Mackay, and comments on the future.

Prism of the Night:
A Biography of Anne Rice

a review from *Publishers Weekly*
(September 13, 1991)

The life of novelist Anne Rice is almost as unusual as her fiction. Her birthname was Howard Allen O'Brien, and she changed her first name to Anne before marrying Stan Rice. Born in 1941, she grew up in a New Orleans full of Southern gothic ambience; her father enjoyed taking her through cemeteries. The death of her alcoholic, highly religious mother, and the later loss of her own daughter to leukemia, plunged her into grief, obsessive-compulsive behavior and nearly fragmented her. Through her supernatural tales and erotica written under a number of pseudonyms, she explored her own masochistic impulses, "sought to unite the male and female within herself" and expressed her desire for humanity's "enlightenment free of religious tyranny," according to Ramsland, who teaches philosophy at Rutgers. In a revelatory, intimate biography that fans will relish, Ramsland interprets Rice's vampires as metaphors of seduction and submission to a higher mystery and power.

Of Vampires and Their Ilk: Traditions, Transformations, and the UnDead

by Dr. Michael R. Collings

Dr. Collings, who teaches at Pepperdine University, is an advocate of fantastic fiction, which sets him apart from most of his peers. A prolific writer, critic, and poet, Dr. Collings is a member of the UnDead Poets Society and author of A Vapor of Vampires. *In this piece, written especially for this book, Collings sheds light on the vampire in literature and film.*

◆

The vampire as we know (and sometimes seem to love) it today is actually a relatively new creature.

Unlike ghosts and ghouls and other denizens of the dark that have inhabited our collective nightmares for millennia, and like its compeer, the Frankenstein-monster, the literary (and usually at least marginally symbolic) vampire really dates back only about two centuries. To be sure, highly sexual, feminine vampire-like creatures appeared in classical mythology under the name *Lamia*, later subsumed under the more generic term *Succubus*, but the version of the monster that we readily recognize today as the *Vampire* really began with a number of stories and, almost immediately, highly successful stage presentations in the early and middle nineteenth century, including one purportedly told first by Lord Byron at the same story-fest that resulted in Mary Shelley's *Frankenstein*.

It remained, however, for Bram Stoker to crystallize the contemporary vampire into a single figure, embedding in our imaginations the suave Count Dracula as the archetype of his kind. It seems appropriate that Stoker's compendium of all things vampiric appeared almost a century ago, in 1897, during the closing decade of the Victorian period, that era of complacency and of increasing faith in the powers of science to unravel all of the remaining mysteries of the universe. (The story goes that about the same time, there was a subtle undercurrent of panic in the Patent Office in London, where it was

101

feared that the office would have to close before the year 1900 rolled around, since almost everything that could be invented had obviously already been invented.)

In a sense, that period closely approximated the closing decade of the eighteenth century—western culture's nominal Age of Reason, when the final vestiges of superstition had been thrown off and suddenly it seemed possible that we would finally unravel all of the remaining mysteries of the universe. And, just as that Age of Reason closed with a period of frighteningly intense irrationality in literature, generally classified as the "Gothic" period and characterized by such extreme (and extremely sensational) novels as Matthew G. "Monk" Lewis's truly horrific *The Monk* (1796) and Charles Maturin's *Melmoth the Wanderer* (1820), so the final decade of the nineteenth century seems to have triggered a resurgence in Gothic irrationality that continues to this day. At the same time that science was identifying and defeating age-old killers, including the cholera that periodically devastated Victorian London, Stoker and others like him were creating the mythos of the walking UnDead, of nocturnal creatures outside of science and understanding and human society. Almost by virtue of the circumstances surrounding its literary birth, the twentieth-century vampire seemed destined to be an antirational, antiscientific, antilogical extension of fundamental human fears.

Now, after almost a century has passed since *Dracula* appeared, and almost two centuries since Lewis's *The Monk*, the vampire is a staple in horror literature, film, and art. Over the past two decades, the figure has seen a resurgence, particularly since the appearance of Stephen King's now-classic version of the vampire in *'Salem's Lot* (1975). After a period memorable primarily for re-visions of Stoker as interpreted by the director Tod Browning and the actor Christopher Lee, King's novel revitalized a genre that was threatening to slip into parody—either unconsciously, as in the never-ending flood of exploitative "B"-rated (and often lower) vampire films and stories; or self-consciously, as in Stan Dragoti's 1979 film, *Love at First Bite*. By the end of the 1970s, however, the vampire was again a central figure in American literary and visual art, triggering a number of modifications in the mythos.

Many writers chose to remain true to Stoker's initial vision of evil incarnate, of a supernatural *and* unnatural creature feeding on the living blood of humans, occasionally transforming one of its hapless victims into a monster like itself. Admittedly, to do so would require that the writer work in the shadow of both Stoker and King, but it would also provide a ready-made resource file of themes and images, archetypes and actions. Often, the more traditional, sexually oriented vampire stories infuse the fundamental horror with sociological themes: examinations of the breakdown of contemporary communities, of instability within the family, of the demise of religion as source of values and of strength. Rick Dees' *Blood Lust* (1990) is a typical example of how all of these elements might be compressed into a single narrative that still retains its initial thrust—to retell the vampire story, virtually unaltered from Stoker and King. Rarely, however, do these strictly traditional vampires rise to the level of their progenitors; in most instances, they remain conventional, stereotypic, and predictable. When they do attempt more than re-creation, they generally do so by putting a spin on the central character, as in S. P. Somtow's *Vampire Junction* (1984). The novel's rock-star vampire capitalizes on the inherent symbolic connections between literary vampirism and the kind of psychic-vampirism implicit in the rock phenomenon—a motif that writers such as Anne Rice and Nancy A. Collins would use extensively. The result was what Edward Bryant characterized as "the first ambitious attempt at post-King dark fantasy."

Once the vampires made their way into the limelight, it was not a far reach for Robert McCammon to take them all the way to Hollywood. In *They Thirst* (1988), McCammon moves away from the small, almost claustrophobic sense of King's *'Salem's Lot*, or even of Stoker's Transylvania and late Victorian London suburbs, to imagine the vampire loose in Los Angeles. Taking advantage of the sociological and narrative implications of Los Angeles' sheer physical size, and the impact that such a large expanse of landscape would have on community, McCammon gives us a colony of vampires that are literally unstoppable through any human intervention; in good California fashion, it takes "The Big One," the cataclysmic earthquake that is part of California's own mythos, to destroy the monsters. McCammon consciously builds on recognizable conventions (as he does so well in his other horror novels). His own comment is that he "wanted a vampire novel with a huge cast"; in this he succeeded, but the traditional outlines of his monsters are apparent from the beginning.

Other writers, however, have chosen to diverge from the conventions. In the past twenty years, readers have been inundated with attempts not merely to revitalize but to reimagine wholesale the vampire tradition. While acknowledging the mastery of a Stoker or a King, they have attempted to wrest the vampire from traditional niches and transform the UnDead into something new, something uniquely contemporary. One of the best examples of this trend is F. Paul Wilson's masterpiece of indirection, *The Keep* (1981). Initially, Wilson presents us with meticulously re-created evidences of a conventional vampire embedded in a story set in World War II. Setting, characters, the milieu he painstakingly evokes—all convince the reader that the story, while unusually well told, is 'just another vampire story' until, with a suddenness that surprises, he adroitly reverses the direction of the novel and immerses us in something akin to Lovecraftian Cosmic Horror. The vampire lore is revealed as a false trail that we have willingly and complacently followed, never guessing until it is too late that the meanings assigned to the clues we have been given will ultimately be reversed.

Even more intriguing, however, is the twist on conventions explored by Whitley Strieber in *The Hunger* (1981). Again, the story begins conventionally enough; then Strieber reveals that his vampires are neither supernatural nor unnatural. Strieber's lamia-vampires are, like his Wolfen (his other memorable contribution to horror literature), products of an alternate evolution, uniquely understandable in twentieth-century terms although they have co-existed on this planet with unknowing humans for eons. They prey on humans, are ultimately dependent upon humans, and are related to humans in scientifically verifiable ways—but they are not human. Rather than inviting sociological metaphor, Strieber's story seems as much (if not more) concerned with humanity's place in a planetary ecology as with the more conventional themes and images of vampire tales.

In a further transformation of expectation, Dan Simmons' ambitious and remarkable *Carrion Comfort* (1989) elevates the traditional bloodsuckers of folklore to etiolated psychic vampires, linked to the horrors of Nazism and living off excesses of violence in contemporary American society. Outside of and indifferent to the mores of human society, they feed on the energy of their victims; for them, warfare is merely one more form of violence to be encouraged and tended, regardless of the suffering it entails. Simmons' creations are in some senses the apotheosis of the twentieth-century vampire, released from the physical need to consume something so gross and elemental as blood, and freed to devour the energy—the psyches—that makes humans human.

Effecting the transformation from supernatural monster to true alien, along the lines explored almost three decades ago by Colin Wilson in *The Mind Parasites* (1967) and *The Space Vampires* (1976), Brian Lumley's continuing Necroscope series combines the new with the old. The vampires' setting is no longer Transylvania, a dark and Lovecraftian New England, or even faceless and remorseless Los Angeles; it is a new world, a science-fictional world, an epic fantasy planet with all of the ramifications of its geographical features carefully worked out. And its vampires are, like Strieber's, not so much the

Of Vampires and Their Ilk: Traditions, Transformations, and the UnDead

George Beahm

A plastic rat, signed by Rice, inscribed to Britton E. Trice, on the occasion of the Gathering of the Coven Ball in 1994

Walking UnDead as a parallel life form, in this case the Wamphyri Lords, putative masters of their world. While many of the conventions are present, they are recombined to create the effect of a lushness and an exotic eroticism at times merely suggested, at other times explicit. Much of the mystery of the vampire as monster is defused, and the vampire as alien becomes paramount.

Of all the writers mentioned, arguably the most popular and successful as "vampirist" is Anne Rice. King, Strieber, McCammon, Simmons have all used the vampire motif occasionally; Rice has turned it, in a sense, into her own private stalking ground, with a series of novels that systematically distance the vampire as character from many of the expectations readers might bring to her novels. *Interview with the Vampire* (1976), *The Vampire Lestat* (1985), *The Queen of the Damned* (1988), *The Tale of the Body Thief* (1992), and *Memnoch the Devil* (1995)—each carries the reader further and further into the luxuriant sensuality of the vampire. If the literary vampire functions as a symbol, it generally does so against the backdrop of human society. King's Barlow, for example, is horrifying primarily because he is juxtaposed against images of normality. Simmons's soul-devouring vampires can exist only as the antithesis of human feeling and compassion.

Part Three: On Anne Rice

Rice, on the other hand, focuses on the monster, on the vampire. Humans are fodder or, at best, potential vampires. But by and large, she eliminates the critical background of humanity and tells the unending tales of monsters obsessed with love but incapable of more than lust. Although her version of the mythos explicitly denies the possibility of sexuality, her narratives insist upon images of vampires—male and female, male and male, adult and child—locked in physical embrace in their coffins by day. Although her version of the mythos equally explicitly denies the possibility of love, her vampires debate and discuss it incessantly.

The result is an approach to a traditional literary figure that systematically transmutes it into something different and not altogether satisfying. Within the tradition, the King-Vampire may eventually be killed, and humankind saved; in Rice's novels, vampires do not easily die. They return again and again, each time telling the stories of the interim years, decades, centuries. And since the vampires form a closely knit underground, she is free to pick up the stories of character after character, interweaving them, at times embedding one narrative within another within another. Time ceases to have any real meaning; distances can be surmounted with ease; and most critically, any true contact-points between vampire-kind and human-kind become so tenuous that they seem to disappear.

Rice's vampires may be sensual and alluring, exotic and erotic (particularly in light of the recent film version of *Interview with the Vampire*) . . . but they also threaten to become tedious and repetitious. They move at random through time, space, and narrative, entering and disappearing at will. As a result, they diminish the vitality of the vampire. Where Stoker inspired fear and loathing with his Dracula, Rice seems to invite empathy and identification—a dangerous process when the subject of that empathy is, indeed, monstrous.

Rice and the Gothic Tradition

by Bette B. Roberts

To present a critical study of Anne Rice's work just twenty years ago would have required a major justification; Ian Watt's influential 1957 *The Rise of the Novel*, with its emphasis on realism, virtually dominated critical assessment of the novel. Analyzing the supernatural was acceptable so long as the research was confined to Romantic poetry, such as Keats's "Lamia" figure, Coleridge's mysterious "Christabel," or Poe's "Ligeia." When these fantasy figures and the medieval ruins they inhabited moved over into the novel, the novels themselves were relegated to the realm of popular fiction and deemed unworthy of critical attention because they failed to conform to the standards of realism. Before the mid-1970s few doctoral candidates wrote dissertations on the novels of the Romantic period, and courses in the British Romantics seldom included writers like Ann Radcliffe or Mary Shelley. Early critical studies of the Gothic are sparse indeed. Nearly every scholar of the Gothic today mentions the pioneering Edith Birkhead, Montague Summers, and Devendra Varma, whose critical tasks in the 1920s through the 1950s, included the identification of Gothic texts as well as an explanation of the genre itself.

Between this early criticism and what might be called an explosion of critical interest in the Gothic beginning in the late 1970s were several important contributors whose approaches suggested avenues of significant study: J. M. S. Tompkins's *The Popular Novel in England: 1770–1800* in 1932, a cultural exploration of the relationships between popular readers' fantasies and the Gothic, among other genres; Leslie Fiedler's psychosocial commentary on the Gothic and American literature in his 1960 *Love and Death in the American Novel*; Paul Frankl's comprehensive historical study *The Gothic: Literary Sources and Interpretations Through Eight Centuries*, also in 1960; and Irving Malin's 1962 *New American Gothic*, a discussion of symbolic functions of Gothic devices in contemporary American literature not usually regarded as Gothic. Maurice Levy wrote the first major effort to update the historical survey provided by the earliest critics in *Le roman gothique anglais, 1764–1824*, where he makes interesting distinctions between the Gothic novels of male writers, beginning with Matthew Lewis, and of female writers, starting with Ann Radcliffe.

Once Robert D. Hume's article reevaluating the Gothic novel appeared in 1969 and Robert Kiely's fine exploration of *The Romantic Novel in England* in 1972, the study of the Gothic was no longer constrained by the standards of realism.

In fact, a history of critical approaches to the Gothic reveals just how much an appreciation of the genre has benefited from the recent variety of literary theories and approaches to textual analysis. In the 1970s and 1980s there appeared extremely useful genre studies, such as Elizabeth MacAndrew's *The Gothic Tradition in Fiction* and David Punter's psychological-cultural *The Literature of Terror: A History of Gothic Fictions from 1765 to the Present Day* (1980), as well as studies using feminist, psychoanalytical, reader-response, and cultural approaches to literary analysis. These last are especially enlightening in coming to terms with a genre that relies on, as Punter explains, the fictional truth of the imagination rather than the truth of real experience. Shortly after Coral Ann Howells, for instance, analyzes sensibility and the Gothic heroine in *Love, Mystery, and Misery: Feeling in Gothic Fiction* (1978), Stephen King writes his own informal psychosocial study of the genre in *Danse Macabre* in 1979. While William Patrick Day traces the Gothic as a subversion of the Romantic in his book *In the Circles of Fear and Desire* in 1985, Kate Ferguson Ellis sees the Gothic as a fantasized protest against values of the hearth in *The Contested Castle: Gothic Novels and the Subversion of Domestic Ideology* in 1989. In the same year, Joseph Grixti explores the relationship between Gothic fiction and popular audience in *Terrors of Uncertainties: The Cultural Contexts of Horror Fiction*. These and many other Gothic studies provide researchers of the Gothic today with many resources. Bibliographers of the Gothic have also produced at least two comprehensive bibliographies of primary and secondary materials: Frederick Frank's *Gothic Fiction: A Master List of Twentieth-Century Criticism and Research* and Benjamin Fisher's *The Gothic's Gothic: Study Aids to the Tradition of the Tale of Terror*.

Although elements of the Gothic occurred in all genres of literature long before the eighteenth century, coverage of novels that are predominantly Gothic begins with Horace Walpole's *The Castle of Otranto* in 1765, which was clearly a reaction against the dominant vogue of fictional realism. Stating that the reader's fancy had been "dammed up" in the novel, Walpole planned to move away from the "strict adherence to common life" to arouse the reader's imagination. The means he chose—the supernatural, the dreary castle, the prevailing atmosphere of fear—inspired many other eighteenth-century novelists, such as Clara Reeve, and influenced the two best-known eighteenth-century Gothic novelists, Ann Radcliffe and Matthew Lewis.

Ann Radcliffe and Matthew Lewis are the Samuel Richardson and Henry Fielding of the Gothic. Just as Richardson and Fielding originated two major traditions in the history of realistic novel writing—the psychological, interior focus (Richardson's *Pamela*) and the more exterior, panoramic scope (Fielding's *Tom Jones*)—Radcliffe and Lewis established two different mainstreams of Gothic fiction with identifiable characteristics still labeled as female and male. Despite the obvious variations and mixtures of these characteristics over the history of the genre, Gothic novels have been typed by gender categories.

Women writers following the Radcliffean tradition have focused on the prolonged pursuit of the pure and passive heroine by the aggressive male villain in a dark, labyrinthine setting that intensifies the anxiety and fear throughout the novel. Usually, all ends well as the threats of the villain, whose powers appear to be supernatural, are never actually realized, and the virtuous heroine, like Emily St. Aubert in Radcliffe's *The Mysteries of Udolpho*, emerges triumphant over her oppressor. This restoration of moral order is accompanied by a return to the rational as well, since the seemingly supernatural elements are reduced to the natural by an elaborate, contrived explanation at the end of the action.

This moral rationalism is not the case with Gothic novels written by men, in the tradition established by Matthew Lewis in *The Monk* and continued most powerfully in Charles Robert Maturin's *Melmoth the Wanderer*. Though the persecution of the virtuous heroine still drives the plot, the male writer shifts the focus of interest from the heroine threatened by male villainy to the villain-hero, whose evil nature may indeed be aggrandized by his supernatural nature, such as vampirism. The innocent young woman does not stand a chance against this power; unlike her Radcliffean counterparts, she may actually be murdered, or worse, seduced or raped. Lengthy atmospheric descriptions conventional in the women novelists' works are discarded in favor of erotic and violent sensationalism, as the villain indulges appetites only imagined in the women's Gothics: hence the distinction between the atmosphere of psychological terror in the female Gothic novels and that of physical horror in those written by men. The reader is asked to suspend disbelief in the actual and experience the reality of supernatural evil before the blackguard is destroyed at the end.

The varying treatments of evil suggest the traditional preference by women writers for Radcliffean Gothicism. Since the innocence of the heroine is never violated, she upholds and perpetuates the idealized virtues assigned to women in a patriarchal social structure—delicacy, fortitude, and chastity—by means of passive resistance. At the same time, she reveals the anxieties of women in a subordinate social position, particularly those who must endure persecution and imprisonment by men. As many recent feminist critics have pointed out, the nature of evil is equated with male tyranny, with the villain remaining an unsympathetic character whose powers are finally constrained by morality, reason, and social propriety. The tremendous popularity of this genre with women writers and readers in late eighteenth-century England shows that it addressed particularly female concerns. Women dominated by men related to fantasies of victory and freedom that did not require over-stepping the ideal codes of behavior. Commenting on the impact of women writers on the late eighteenth-century novel, Tompkins writes that "In their hands the novel was not so much a reflection of life as a counterpoise to it, within the covers of which they looked for compensation, for ideal pleasures and ideal revenge." The extent to which these early Gothics responded to a widespread need among female readers accounts for the popularity of this relatively new genre.

In the Gothic novels written by men, the focus on the villain-hero allows the reader to identify psychologically with the source of evil, as the torment, rebellion, and power of this larger-than-life figure call up all forbidden desires—the beast within, the id, the subconscious. Well argued by psychoanalytic critics of the Gothic as a major—if not the major—source of appeal of the eroticism and sensationalism of the genre, the escapades of the Gothic villain provide a vicarious experience normally taboo in actual life, where these desires are repressed. As Stephen King puts it, the horror scene is "an invitation to indulge in deviant, antisocial behavior by proxy—to commit gratuitous acts of violence, indulge our puerile dreams of power, to give in to our most craven fears."

This subversion of conservative, middle-class values of restraint and re-spectability was simply too great a leap for women writers to make; their more genteel Gothicism, while revealing discomfort with the status quo, certainly did not appear to be openly rebellious. As a result, the villains of the early Gothic novels written by men have exhibited a power and an evil comparable with the rebels of Romantic fiction and the Promethean figures of Romantic poetry. Early women's Gothics have been more divisive, however, with evil playing a secondary role to the portrayal of exemplary virtue and extensive didacticism justifying the sensational action. Both traditions have depended on well-defined roles of male aggression and female passivity (the moral equivalent of virtue).

Surveying the scene of Gothic fiction today to see what remains of these early characteristics is similar to tracing the influences of Richardson and Fielding in the mainstream of the novel; novelists' technical experiments have blended all kinds of conventions and devices so that the original distinctions are blurred and less meaningful. Clearly identifiable traits of the Gothic— ghosts, monsters, hauntings, and other supernatural threats to humans— have also merged with elements of other genres to form Gothic science fiction, Gothic detective fiction, Gothic erotica, and other hybrids. Vestiges of the gender distinctions are evident in the contemporary pulp extremes of both types: the purely violent Gothics that wallow in grisly gore and the equally shallow Radcliffean Gothic romances now sold widely in retail stores. With few exceptions, Radcliffean Gothicism still dominates the popular Gothic novels written by female writers for female readers. As Janice Radway explains, "Romance reading and writing might be seen therefore as a collectively elaborated female ritual through which women explore the consequences of their common social condition as the appendages of men and attempt to imagine a more perfect state where all the needs they so intensely feel and accept as given would be adequately addressed." Despite modernizations of the female protagonists, the Radcliffean model continues in that the plot hinges on the prolonged terror caused by the male who oppresses the female with threats of imprisonment.

Why this plot device continues to attract today's more liberated women readers is the source of some critical debate. Helen Hazen argues that in contemporary women's Gothics, "the tension of the story is that the heroine might be defiled, and the struggle is, without exception, sexual." The interest lies in "how to prevent the occurrence, and also in the temptation to imagine calamity when normal life seems not lively enough from day to day." Disagreeing with some feminist critics, who argue that the portrayal of actual rape prevalent in less romantic fictions and more erotic Gothics is effective in revealing female readers' real fears of male villainy, Hazen states that women do not want to read about the actual event; their fantasies do not entail explicit sexual violence. Accounting for the dominance of the romantic model, she goes further to distinguish between romantic and feminist Gothics, arguing that "Romantic gothics end happily; feminist gothics do not"; that is, sexual threats remain unrealized in the more popular romantic fiction.

Part Three: On Anne Rice

In discussing the persistence of the Radcliffean model and its contemporary variations, Cynthia Griffin Wolff states that "the specific details are different in modern Gothics, but the pattern is the same: the author assigns interesting talents and a measure of intelligence to her heroine at the beginning of the novel, and these then vanish as soon as the young woman is swept into danger." While Wolff sees female fictional identity in modern Gothics as still dependent on relationships with men, she does note a major difference between eighteenth-century and modern Gothics: today the woman "marries the demon lover" whom she would have been obliged to reject in earlier novels. Wolff sees this difference as appropriate for earlier readers, whose heroines were virtually sexless, and the sexually liberated contemporary audience, where a fictional female's choice "leads not to a rejection of feminine sexuality, but to an embracing of it: what seemed at first menacing is revealed as both tolerable and desirable." In today's more liberated female Gothics, writers may describe actual sexual violence, and acceptable choices of lovers may be expanded to include rakish Lovelace types capable of reformation. Still, the predominant Gothic novel sold over hundreds of bookstore counters to women readers remains more conservative, nonerotic, and Radcliffean.

In stark contrast to these novels, Anne Rice's non-Radcliffean Gothics explore a new vein, just as Mary Shelley's *Frankenstein* transcended the boundaries of female Gothic writers in 1818 and broke down distinctions between the two traditions established by Radcliffe and Lewis. Replacing the images of male tyranny so prevalent in contemporary female Gothics with those more commonly favored by male writers, Rice vividly depicts the horrors of physical violence enacted by supernatural villain-heroes reminiscent of Lewis's Ambrosio, Poe's Montresor, and Stevenson's Dr. Jekyll. In the postmodern world of Anne Rice, the physically horrifying and the morally depraved Gothic villain-heroes are transformed into sympathetic creatures who, like their human counterparts, must confront the existential realities of the late twentieth century. "They are lonely, prisoners of circumstance, compulsive sinners, full of self-loathing and doubt. They are, in short, Everyman Eternal." Like their great Byronic ancestors, they travel toward destruction, suffering, and renewal. The imprisonment from which they are delivered is not the stifling tyranny of men over women but that resulting from the Blakean mind-forged manacles, their own dependence on self-delusions concerning social institutions and religious myths.

Rice burdens her characters with inescapable physical conditions (vampirism, race, castration) that exaggerate their alienation from humanity and

BETTE B. ROBERTS'S *ANNE RICE*

Anne Rice, a critical study by Bette B. Roberts, was published as part of the Twayne's United States Authors Series, a series that has included book-length studies of Agatha Christie, Stephen King (two books), Ursula K. LeGuin, and J. R. R. Tolkien.

Roberts, chair of the English department at Westfield State College in Massachusetts, is also the author of *The Gothic Romance: Its Appeal to Female Writers and Readers in Late-Eighteenth-Century England*, which makes her uniquely qualified to write about Rice from a historical-literary perspective.

From the dust jacket:

"In this critical appraisal of the novels created by the contemporary queen of the Gothic, Bette B. Roberts argues that Anne Rice is more than a 'popular' writer. Reinventing the vampire figure to reflect on the human condition, Rice is both philosopher and social commentator. Her vampires are a far cry from the leering, black-caped caricature on a lonely quest for blood. Unique in the history of vampire lore, they are a feeling community of creatures, each driven by the very human needs for power, recognition, a sense of purpose, and love.

"Roberts traces the history of Gothic fiction and places Rice in the rich tradition of those writers who have used the genre to undertake what one scholar calls 'a searching analysis of human concerns.' Like Mary Shelley in *Frankenstein* and Bram Stoker in *Dracula*, Rice uses the supernatural to explore the realms of human experience that disturb or confuse. For many writers of Gothic fiction—including Rice—this has meant examining the nature of evil, of sexuality, of death, of the unconscious. Rice adds to her inquiry the existential, modernist quest for meaning in a complex, impassive world."

emphasize their need to establish their significance. In the Vampire Chronicles, humanizing the vampires' conflicts, their relationships with each other, and their often genderless natures opens up the possibilities of a genre increasingly narrowed by stereotypical conventions over the years. This expansive spirit is apparent in the wide open space and global travel of Rice's Gothics—as compared with the claustrophobic interiors of many female Gothics—and in their persistent eroticism, now a part of the liberating psychological process instead of a forbidden pleasure inherent in the male-female pursuit plot of more conventional Gothics. Since the protagonists achieve their own personal codes of moral choice in a godless universe, the restoration of order typical of female Gothics is pointless. In Rice's contemporary fictional reality, the focus shifts away from the traditional external conflicts depicting moral victories of women over men or human beings over the vampire and toward the psychological struggles of the vampires themselves seeking ways of surviving the conditions of their eternal existence.

Analyzing the cultural appeal of the Gothic, Joseph Grixti argues that the genre is a "type of narrative which deals in messages about fear and experiences associated with fear." He goes on to list some of these fears: "the discomfort we occasionally feel about our own psyche and about what may lurk in its dark depths; our worries and qualms about our own creations and about the technological advances which might be turning us into helpless robots in a ruthless world; our anxieties about the ways in which our bodies can let us down, about pain, death, and the dead, and about all forms of hostile forces which may at any moment (or so we are told) intrude into our uncertainly patched-up social and personal worlds."

While some fears are universal, others may be more intensely felt and shared by a particular group of readers at a given time. It is no accident, for instance, that during the beginnings of outerspace explorations in the 1950s, Gothic films portraying invasions of extraterrestrial monsters were extremely popular, such as *Earth vs. Flying Saucers* and *Invasion of the Body Snatchers*, while in the 1970s, films like *Demon Seed* and *The Andromeda Strain* appealed to the audience's "vision of technology as an octopus—perhaps sentient— burying us alive in red tape and information-retrieval systems." Since the most successful Gothic writers touch the reader's deepest anxieties, analyzing the threat imagined in the Gothic becomes "a process of cultural self-analysis, and the images which it throws up become the dream-figures of a troubled social group." Unforgettable film images that come to mind are the robotic women in *The Stepford Wives*, the bags of human compost in *Soylent Green*, the schizophrenic Norman Bates in *Psycho*, and the suspended human bodies kept alive in a repository as resources for organ donations in *Coma*.

Other than the Frankenstein myth, whereby the unlawful creation un- leashed on us can assume many different shapes depending on the current technology that we fear, perhaps no other Gothic image is as persistent and powerful and therefore appropriate for "cultural self-analysis" as that of the vampire. As Grixti points out, "the figure of the vampire is one whose history is interestingly intertwined with the public and private concerns of the epochs which popularized and endorsed it as an objectification of uncertainly understood and disturbing phenomena." Since the actual supernaturalism of the vampire's existence and the repeated eroticism of its attacks were considered as improper subject matter for women writers operating within codes of social propriety and moral probability, the vampire has been the province of the male Gothic fantasy perpetuated by male writers. Beginning in the early nineteenth century, John Polidori's classic forerunner *The Vampyre* was followed by James Malcolm Rymer's popular penny dreadful *Varney the Vampyre, or The Feast of Blood*, then Sheridan Le Fanu's disturbing *Carmilla*, and finally Bram Stoker's great prototype, *Dracula*.

Though there are too many variations of the vampire myth today to discuss here, Stephen King's *'Salem's Lot* and Whitley Strieber's *The Hunger* are notable, since both represent extremely successful combinations of traditional aspects of vampirism and original adaptations appealing to contemporary readers. King's frighteningly credible Mr. Barlow poses with the British Straker as a reputable antique dealer and turns a small town in southern Maine into a community of horrors. Though Ben Mears and Mark Petrie seem finally to destroy Barlow in the traditional way, with a stake through his heart, and watch his dissolution, when they return to inspect the damage, Barlow's teeth are still alive. Also, Barlow's progeny, made up of familiar townspeople, live on, as is evident from the numbers of bizarre deaths reported in the local newspaper. As Ben and Mark leave the town permanently, they realize that the fire they set will dislodge but not destroy all of the vampires. Whitley Strieber's Miriam is a highly intelligent female vampire who allows herself to be examined by her major adversary, Sarah, a doctor researching potential links between genetics and aging. In this confrontation with feminist overtones (men are clearly the weaker characters in *The Hunger*), the best human resources prove to be ineffective, as it is Sarah and not Miriam who is destroyed. Sarah ends up locked inside one of Miriam's trunks in total darkness, listening to the "little rustlings and sighs" that "filled the air around her, coming from other chests" that had lain there in the attic for centuries. Both King's and Strieber's vampires are ruthless and indestructible; as in many contemporary Gothics reflecting a loss of belief in the powers of establishment forces to overpower evil, their threat persists. They also demonstrate Leonard Wolf's description of the power of Stoker's Count Dracula: "The vampire of greatest interest is, of course, the man or woman of overwhelming ego and energy whose will for an evil life is so great that he will not die or who, when surprised by death, has reacted with a burst of rage against the inevitable and refuses to lie still."

Part Three: On Anne Rice

With few other exceptions, the contemporary popularization of the vampire myth has effected a reduction of stature that is similar to the impact of Jane Austen's *Northanger Abbey* on the overdone conventions of Gothics that became clichés between 1780 and 1830 in England. Now a friendly, familiar subject of cartoons, cereal names, and comic films, the late twentieth-century vampire has been defanged into a harmless caricature of his former self that hardly fits Wolf's description of Stoker's Dracula. As Brian Frost observes, "These days, with undead counts and countesses now considered passé the traditional image of human bloodsuckers—as vicious, self-seeking predators—has undergone a dramatic change. In contemporary horror novels the prevailing trend is to portray vampires as highly intellectual beings living a separate but not entirely incompatible existence alongside the human race, with the pursuance of knowledge (rather than nubile maidens) as their main recreation."

Though this recent demystification of the myth has made it difficult for a serious writer to employ the vampire as metaphor successfully and to overcome critical prejudice, the potential of the myth testifies to the need for careful distinctions. Sylvia Plath managed to demonstrate its power and flexibility to convey serious literary intent in her poem "Daddy" (1963), in which she attempts to free herself from male tyranny and assert her independence. After developing images of Nazi torture, the persona compares the sapping of her vitality by men to the vampire's drinking blood and her throwing off this domination to the villagers' staking the vampire in the heart. Reviewers need not assume, as some do, that any incorporation of the vampire into literature automatically debases the work's merit.

For Rice, the prejudice against Gothic conventions has larger implications. In a 1993 *Playboy* interview, she argued that critics' tendencies to believe that "to be profound a book has to be about the middle class and about some specific domestic problem of the middle class" reflect the triumph of a Protestant vision over the Catholic. Portrayals of the real, interior lives of people working out small problems and achieving moments of awareness is "the essence of what Protestantism came to be in America," a faith in "the less magical, more practical, more down-to-earth," and, for Rice, "the more sterile." She sees her own choice of the unreal and marvelous, the grand lives of supernatural characters, as the result of her being "nourished on" the miraculous stories of Catholic saints, vivid memories she brings to her vampires. The richness and power of the myth have also been well established by critical explorations of Stoker's *Dracula*, where the villain-hero becomes an ambivalent

Romantic rebel that Victorians both fear and envy. Having commented on the sources of popularity of Stoker's novel with a Victorian audience coping with repression, loss of religious faith, empiric decline, and fear of evolution, David Punter sees the "continuous oscillation between reassurance and threat" as the "central dialectic of Gothic fiction." In Stoker's version of the vampire story, the evil represented by Dracula is finally destroyed and the Victorian values of hard work, duty, and technology reaffirmed. The reader of Stoker's novel and earlier Gothics could take comfort that in the end, the menace would be defeated; virtue would indeed triumph over evil.

Rice's sympathetic and indestructible vampires are more like images of the world-weary Tithonus, who, in Tennyson's poem of that name, caught in the meaninglessness of an eternal existence, sees himself as a "grey shadow, once a man." Instead of creatures to be destroyed, her weary vampires also complain of being consumed by "cruel immortality" and run the risk of their own self-destruction. As such, they exaggerate the senselessness of existence and serve as metaphors for human beings searching for truths to live by.

Joseph Grixti, who takes up the issue of how we evaluate contemporary horror fiction, states: "A number of representatives of the genre reflect considerable artistic, imaginative, and intellectual merit in their application of the conventions of the genre to a searching analysis of human concerns, and in their employment of standard images of horror to convey insights which can form the basis of constructive action. At the same time, the genre of horror fiction can also be said to harbor an increasing amount of popular material which thrives on cliché and which projects images and interpretations of experience which are as hollow and self-enclosed as they are pretentious." As will become evident in the discussions that follow, the fictional images Rice uses in the five novels that form the Vampire Chronicles do hold up a "searching analysis of human concerns," and her technical devices and original handling of Gothic conventions represent a fascinating variation and broadening of the genre's traditions.

A serious analysis of her books in the Vampire Chronicles is warranted for both of these reasons. Most unconventional in the Vampire Chronicles is Rice's establishment of a vampire community in the first novel of the series, *Interview with the Vampire*, and her consequent development of interrelationships among vampires rather than conflicts between vampires and humans. This shift of focus causes other major departures from the tradition: vampires rather than humans tend to tell their own stories; each has individual traits that distinguish one from the other; they remember centuries of events and live in locations all over the world; they need relationships with one another and belong to small families or groups; they fear destruction from one another more than from humans; they experience loneliness and frustration. The suspense does not hinge on whether or not the humans will outlast the vampires but on whether or not the vampires will survive the aggressive actions of other vampires with power even greater than their own, and whether or not the vampires will mature enough to find ways of enduring the self-annihilating elements built into the very conditions of their undead existence. Vampires learn about their origins and histories, which are grounded in ancient myths that reveal the same enlightening, archetypal patterns of human experience. The need for blood that is both disgusting yet erotic in *Dracula* becomes less loathsome (yet still highly erotic) in Rice, as the descriptions of blood drinking involve the ecstasy between vampire and vampire. The blood also takes on symbolic overtones of family preservation and pagan rituals of human sacrifice. Human kills are still necessary, but understated so that the reader forgets how the vampire sustains itself.

Her two other Gothics, *The Mummy* and *The Witching Hour*, show her willingness to explore other occult phenomena and supernatural figures, though they do not provide quite the same opportunities for demonstrating

Louisiana cemetery

originality within a larger literary tradition. Its film-script origin, abundant eroticism, and lack of seriousness turn *The Mummy* into a near spoof of the mummy Gothics. *The Witching Hour*, however, is Rice's most ambitious book. In this novel, perhaps because of the interplay between human and supernatural characters, she conveys the ambivalences of high Gothic and integrates most effectively philosophical issues of free will, predestination, the nature of good and evil, and the relativity of reality. As in her other novels, the use of allusions to familiar literary classics and religious rituals develops layers of meaning and enriches the texts, a device that provides the fine metaphorical structure of her most literary book, *The Tale of the Body Thief*.

Since its origins with Horace Walpole's *The Castle of Otranto* in 1765, Gothic fiction has been associated with the spirit of liberation; in Walpole's case from what he saw as the damming up of fantasy in the novel, to female writers' expressions of male tyranny against women in a patriarchal society, to other novelists' revelations of anxieties and rebellions against repression. Unlike realistic novels, which depict conflicts in the contexts of probability to convey the truths of reality, Gothic novels rely on elements of fantasy and horror to address the truths of imagination. In other words, the universal significance of such mythic figures as Frankenstein's monster and Count Dracula must be explored like other Romantic images on a symbolic, psychological level. Because of her highly original adaptations of the vampire myths, Rice's vampires have this kind of power and complexity. Louis's counterpart is surely the Romantics' cast-out Cain and Lestat the modern Prometheus. With her own villain-heroes, Rice not only recaptures the richness and dignity of the tradition but perpetuates its spirit of liberation in freeing the genre from its present insignificance and opening up new realms for the vampire.

Dark Dreamer: An Interview
with Anne Rice

conducted by Stanley S. Wiater

Let's face it: Most interviews with bestselling authors are depressingly similar, focused on the writer as a personality instead of the writing that made the writer popular and famous.

The following interview, conducted by Stanley Wiater, is a noteworthy exception. A long-time horror reader (and writer), and a prominent interviewer in the field, Stan knows the field and the writer, and so you aren't going to see any asinine questions like "Where do you get your ideas?" and "How much money did you make on your latest book deal?"

◆

STANLEY WIATER: To begin at the beginning, how did *Interview with the Vampire* originate?

ANNE RICE: It was very spontaneous. There was no plan at all. I was sitting at the typewriter and just thought I wanted to try it. I wrote very spontaneously in those days—with no plan as to even what word was going to come next. At first, *Interview* was a short story. I put it away, then took it out, rewrote it, put it away, took it out, rewrote it. Again and again. It was during one of those rewrites that I got ferociously involved with it, and it grew into this very weird novel. There were a number of false turns—at one point I threw out half of it and started over. But in general it was a great deal of experimenting and throwing stuff into the pot as if you were making soup.

WIATER: How did you come to make all of the main characters vampires?

RICE: You know, I was not a person who was obsessed with vampires, or who had pictures of them around the house. I hadn't seen any vampire movies in recent years, so it didn't grow out of any active obsession with them. It just happened that when I started to write through that image, everything came together for me. I was suddenly able to talk about reality by using fantasy. So, it opened a door. In some ways, that's what it all is for me—just the opening of one door after another.

Dark Dreamer: An Interview with Anne Rice

WIATER: So you've never claimed to be an expert on vampire movies or literature?

RICE: I wrote the vampire novel I wanted to read. That's what I did—I wrote the book that I had never been able to find. That really told me what the vampire did in his "off-hours." What he really felt. That's all I was doing. But obviously, if I wanted that, somebody else is going to want to be drawn into his living room at four o'clock in the morning and learn what he has to say in argument to his fellow vampires. And that's what the reader got, that kind of intimacy. And with all due modesty, the reader also got somebody who could write [laughs].

So they got descriptions and philosophical observations that were literate. I think that even people who don't like the books and criticize them would have to admit it's a tempting notion. Whether you think it succeeds or not, the attempt was sincere. I wanted to transcend the genre—but I also wanted to write the best damn vampire novel within the genre that has ever been written.

WIATER: So literary aspirations aside, you obviously were aware of the conventions of the classic vampire novel?

RICE: And I loved the conventions! It wasn't a matter of being faithful to them, I loved them! That was the whole idea, to take the clichés: the man in the cloak, the pale face, the flickering gaslights, the struggling victims. To take all the clichés and weave them into something completely different. That's really the key to all my work: to take those clichés and conventions—which I call classic—and then attempt to find a new depth.

WIATER: Considering the immense popularity of *Interview with the Vampire*, why did it take so long for a sequel?

RICE: Well, the main reason is I wrote other books! I just really deal with whatever obsesses me at the moment. As a writer, I feel like I'm about five different people, and only one of them writes the vampire novels. Also, frankly, in the beginning I was afraid of being typecast as a horror writer.

WIATER: Yet ten years ago was also the same time that such mainstream successes as King and Straub were beginning to appear.

RICE: I'm not in the least bit afraid now. That was before I understood that it didn't really matter; that the horror fans were easily the most intelligent and perceptive fans the books could have. I mean, you can do anything in that genre. You can write a great, great, great novel in the horror genre. There's nothing in it that forces you to write less well, or to create shallow characters. I'd be very happy now if I were to write nothing but occult novels under the name Anne Rice.

Before I wrote *The Vampire Lestat*, one of the things that made me return to the genre was reading Stephen King and Peter Straub and seeing what they were able to do. I wanted to get back in there and "outdo" them [laughs]! It's a wonderful desire! I also read a lot of the great English horror writers, like M. R. James, J. Sheridan Le Fanu, and Algernon Blackwood. Blackwood is a very erotic and wonderful horror writer.

WIATER: One of the strongest qualities of your novels is the degree of perverse eroticism, isn't it?

RICE: Oh, I feel horror fiction is very erotic. People have written really brilliant essays on that subject. It's absolutely inherent in vampire material: the drinking of the blood, the taking of the victim; all of that is highly erotic. It's an echo of the sex act itself. Since the Middle Ages, people have referred to the orgasm as the "little death." So the connections are there. But when I'm writing these novels, it's not thinking consciously about that: I'm just imagining I'm a vampire.

Anne Rice at the Memnoch Ball 1995

Kat Frazier

Dark Dreamer: An Interview with Anne Rice

WIATER: You make it all sound so simple. Yet what do you say to those who would aspire to reach your phenomenal success?

RICE: What can I say? The only thing that's ever worked for me was to go where the passion is, to go where the pleasure is, to go where the pain is; to be very intense. Write like mad. Produce. Get the stuff out. I would be lying if I said I wasn't conscious of wanting to write a good story. I'm very conscious of wanting to write an exciting story, a gripping story. And I'm very aware of the fact that that is a commercial element.

WIATER: A strong story comes first, even before the characters?

RICE: With me, the storytelling has always come fairly naturally. Even my earliest work has this terrific narrative drive to it. It's always been a "and then this happened and then that happened" kind of thing. That gives a work a commercial edge. If I was giving advice, I would say don't ignore that. Remember what Aristotle said about drama: You have to have plot, character, meaning, and spectacle. So remember that spectacle is important. You had that audience gathered into the arena and you had to show them something that was entertaining. There had to be an element of color, of pageantry, of sensuality. That's how I've always interpreted the term. And in my work, I love to elaborate and amplify the sensuous and dramatic elements. I try to make a very entertaining and spellbinding texture, if I can.

Even Shakespeare would not have written a play unless it was exciting and full of surprises. So don't think that the commercial and intellectual are at odds with one another. They're not. You can write a great novel and have it be really suspenseful and have a lot of spectacle to it. Yet it can still have all the philosophy and deep meaning that your soul needs to make your writing worthwhile.

WIATER: Although your first novel had its origins as a short story, what you've published to date has been solely novels. Do you recommend that someone try publishing short stories before taking on a novel-length work?

RICE: There are no rules; they should do absolutely what they feel like doing. But I would never advise a person to write short stories if they want to write a novel. There's just no point. *Interview with the Vampire* was a short story first, but I just didn't pursue short stories; they don't interest me now. The long form is what interests me. And frankly, I think you should go where the passion is. Many, many people start with novels. There is also a very practical concern: It's easier to sell a novel than it is a short story. There's almost no market for short stories in America; they don't reach the public or have the impact that a novel makes. And in terms of career, anyone who writes novels is going to have it easier than a short story writer.

But that shouldn't be the main concern either. The main concern is that you should do what you feel comfortable doing. I feel comfortable stretching it out. Going at it from all angles. I don't want to compress it into a short story. I really don't. Almost any idea that really grips me is worth a novel.

WIATER: I'm curious to know then just how the idea of *The Queen of the Damned* originated. It does continue from where *The Vampire Lestat* ended, but deals with the "lives" of other vampire characters rather than just Lestat himself.

RICE: I was on a plane, and watching the second of the *Star Wars* movies, I believe, and suddenly the whole plot for the *The Queen of the Damned* just came into my mind. It was inspired, I guess, by little things I kept seeing in the movie that I didn't really like all that much. I remember thinking what I wanted to do, as opposed to what I was seeing on the screen. And the whole plot just flashed into my brain. It happens all the time: You read or see something, and suddenly you realize what you want to do. So I decided to break off from working on my witchcraft novel, now that I saw the whole philosophical sweep and philosophical conclusion of *The Queen of the Damned*.

A lot of this came into my head before I even wrote one word. Finally the time came when I couldn't afford to put it off any longer, and I sat down and wrote one word [laughs]. I became very determined to render exactly the book of my dreams. In other words, not to compromise in any way.

For me, it was the first book in which I really used the computer as the pure poetic tool it is capable of being. Because what the computer enables you to do is range back and forth across your work, and bring it up to your standards very easily. So even my smallest dissatisfactions, things I might have put up with if it had been typewritten, I was quickly able to boot up on the computer and change. So that's what I mean by pure and poetic: The computer really enables you to get exactly what you want to get. There's really no physical barrier anymore between you and your vision. If you can get it into words, you can really create what you see. On the typewriter, I don't think that's true. You reach a point where you have this big, ponderous draft, and even to make minor changes in early chapters would mean making a mess, losing control of pages, having to retype. . . . You're dealing with the Industrial Revolution; you're dealing with a mechanism, with labor . . . and all of that's swept away by the computer—there's very little between your

Dark Dreamer: An Interview with Anne Rice

mind and what you're putting down there. There's really no excuse for not writing the perfect book. You're no longer making the mechanical compromises that move it away from poetry. I see poetry as meaning language at its very finest, and its most intense and most compressed. And you're able to get that essence with a computer.

WIATER: When you say *The Queen of the Damned* was the "book of your dreams," do you mean in a technical sense due to the computer or more figuratively speaking?

RICE: No, frequently in the past I had imagined enormous books with many different things happening in them, and eventually that would not be the book I would ultimately produce. It would always be too big, too difficult to execute, too long, too complicated. So there was always a gulf between the books of my dreams and the books that were finally written. Like *The Feast of All Saints*, for example. That book takes place in the space of about a year or two. Originally I'd wanted it to go all the way from the 1840s to the Civil War into the twentieth century! But at that point as a writer, I couldn't write the book of my dreams. I didn't have enough skill, I didn't have enough craft to do what I envisioned. And when it came to the *The Queen of the Damned*, I firmly resolved that I was going for the whole thing; to go for the enormous vision that had been born in my brain. I had finally reached a point where I could put all of that down; I was not going to compromise out of fear that I couldn't pull off a particular scene, character, or jump in time. That's really what I was talking about.

WIATER: As already noted, an aspect of your work which has practically become a trademark is your deft intertwining of the erotic with the horrific. But how do you actually set about creating the proper mood and tone to successfully evoke this complex set of emotions?

RICE: It is a difficult question to answer, because horror and sensuality have always been linked. Good horror writing is almost always sensuous writing because the threat posed in horror fiction is usually a veiled erotic threat. But if you go back to your earliest horror stories in English, there's always a tremendous emphasis on mood, and atmosphere, and the response of the physical body to the menace. Vampire fiction in particular is always sensuous, so there's no problem really [laughs]. I mean, horror writers are almost always dealing in atmosphere and suggestion. . . . Confusion of the senses, confusion of the mind to overwhelming physical responses. That's part and parcel of the genre.

With me, there's no method. Writing to me is sensuality. It is talking about the assault on the senses, and the effect on the individual. You either do that naturally, or you don't do it. You can't school yourself necessarily in doing that. The most you can do as a writer is stand back from your material and say, "What have I left out? What was I feeling physically? What textual details are missing?" But there can be some wonderful writing with no textual details. You just have to go with whatever way it goes. You can read just a few pages of Stephen King and can see that he's a very sensuous writer. It's the way he perceives the world, how a screen door closing sounds, or the flavor of a chocolate bar or a hamburger or whatever—it's all in there. But it's in there because that's what King notices. You may notice something else entirely from your own perspective. The main thing is to immerse yourself in the material, and reach for the intensity. Again, go where the intensity is, go where the pleasure is, go where the pain is. Go for the passion. Do that honestly, and the rest will fall into place.

WIATER: Passion is a word which comes to you so readily. What do you believe makes the pursuit of a writer's life so worthy of that passion—and the heartache?

RICE: Because it's the greatest creative profession. Anyone can do it any time. Unlike moviemaking, dancing, and classical music, painting—anything at all—writing requires a minimum of equipment, yet allows for a maximum expression of passion and creativity. You can do it at the kitchen table on paper you stole from the office with an old typewriter you got at a junk store. And you can make it from there to the bestseller lists. Somebody does that just about every year. Like Judith Guest, the housewife from Ohio who wrote *Ordinary People* and sent it in over the transom.

WIATER: But are you saying that if you just keep at it long enough, you're bound to succeed?

RICE: The important thing to remember is that it is an artistic realm—even if you're writing the most commercial fiction or nonfiction. That means there's no justice. It doesn't matter how hard you work, it doesn't matter whom you know. What ultimately matters is what you put on that page—and whether somebody wants it at the moment. That's why anyone who wants to go into this profession has to believe in himself totally, work like a demon, and ignore the rejections. When you mail out a manuscript, you are not turning in a paper for a grade. You can mail out a perfectly wonderful and publishable novel and have it rejected ten times. And the reason it's rejected is that you hit

Dark Dreamer: An Interview with Anne Rice

ten different people who for various reasons don't want to work with this idea. You have to keep going. You must never interpret rejection from New York publishers as a failing grade. They are not failing grades. They mean almost nothing.

WIATER: But your first novel wasn't accepted immediately. What kept you going until it did?

RICE: Some of the rejections I received for *Interview with the Vampire* were ludicrous. Fortunately I was confident enough to know that they were ludicrous. Somebody else might have been hurt and quit. But I kept writing, and kept mailing out. My attitude was "I'm going to become a writer." I was a writer. So my advice is to remember that you're dealing with people who make decisions on the basis of a whim, and just keep going. Keep going until you connect with a person who cares enough about what you've done to publish it. And don't be discouraged if you hit twenty people who aren't that one.

WIATER: Apparently you've had a few encounters with some less-than-kind editors over the years.

RICE: I really did get scathing rejections with *Interview*. And I paid not one whit of attention to them. So you've got to throw that switch in your head that says, "I'm going to succeed." And you've got to believe in yourself, and you've got to remember that the arts have always been tough. There's no point in whining about it. Say if you wanted to become an actor. The first people you would have met would have been sitting around in a café saying, "Go home, it's too tough, don't bother." But it's always been that way in the arts— a bunch of people sitting around, telling you that you can't make it. Then others come out of nowhere and go right to the top. What's important is what you've achieved at that moment and if somebody wants it. That's it. The arts have been basically the same for two thousand years. You just have to do your best, and make others want your work, and you have to keep looking for the people who want it. Above all, keep believing in yourself, because nobody can really tell you you're no good.

Flesh for Fantasy

by Gerri Hirshey
(*Rolling Stone*, November 20, 1986)

A leering cardboard Dracula hangs pinned to the door of Anne Rice's literary workroom; below him, a sturdy plastic gate fends off the lumbering advances of Lucky, a 175-pound bull mastiff. Plaster saints, their arms spread in benediction, look down on a pair of computers. Three crisp-spined volumes of sadomasochistic pornography hold shelf space between true-crime books and histories of the Inquisition. On one wall, the red leather thongs of a custom-made S&M whip overlap a clutch of Catholic Mass cards. The writer's confessional is a tiny, cluttered room at the top of a Victorian house in San Francisco's Castro district. Conducting a tour, she is framed by leather and printed psalms.

"Behold," says Anne Rice, "the divided self."

The self is a prolific if unholy trinity. Anne Rice made her literary good name as the author of . . . exotic, elegantly written books that reside between the respected hard covers of Alfred A. Knopf and Simon and Schuster. To relieve "the mad pressure" that she felt writing in a cultivated "European" voice, she cooked up two rather racy literary alter egos and, until recently, kept them secret. Anne Rampling is a "contemporary American novelist" with an inclination toward erotica; A. N. Roquelaure is an S&M pornographer with a shocking penchant for leather collars, cock rings and other kinky bijoux.

Except for the elbow-length black hair, Anne Rice hardly looks like an author-dominatrix. Nor does she look like the literary sorceress *The Village Voice* credited with awakening "a subgenre of fiction" that began with Bram Stoker's *Dracula*. At forty-five, she is a small, pretty woman with the face of an Irish saint and the get-up of a parochial schoolgirl: running shoes, black tights, a pleated plaid skirt, white shirt, red cardigan, owlish black-framed glasses.

"I'm almost equally attracted to criminals and saints," she says, fingering the whip. "And I'm so much happier since I've become a pornographer. To be frank, it's harder to be Anne Rice. It's rendering the darker side of myself; it's dealing with whole areas of pain that I don't deal with as Anne Rampling or Roquelaure."

Flesh for Fantasy

Rice wrote *Interview with the Vampire* in 1974. She structured her first novel as the transcript of a tape-recorded interview with Louis, a chatty Un-Dead who unburdens himself about his life with Lestat, the vampire who created him. Louis and Lestat are masters of their human victims but slaves to the infernal thirst. Over two centuries, they mingle with swank mortals in Paris and New Orleans. They wear velvet and lace, drinking blood from crystal goblets. And they love each other with an exceedingly bloody passion.

The initial rejections of the manuscript were scathing. Anne had thought of publishing it herself until editor Vicky Wilson read it at a Squaw Valley writers' conference and bought it for Knopf.

"It was very strange and dark," Wilson remembers. "And it only got stranger and darker, and I couldn't put it down."

The book was not, Anne says, "a howling success in hard cover. I was bitter and angry at first. I thought they had slighted it, even the good reviews." . . .

What has made the vampire novels such unlikely bestsellers—and what forces stern literary sentinels like *The New York Times Book Review* to accord these eternal parasites serious consideration—is a combination of compelling narrative and guts. For better or for worse, Rice is a fearless writer. Call her the It Girl of contemporary fiction. Whatever the venue, she's never too squeamish to reach out and touch it: "Say there's a heart beating there, and you try to touch the heart." She points to a spot on the kitchen table. "When you write, you have to go through layers of stuff to touch it. I just call it *it*. I can go through a novel and pick out scenes where I touched it. Like the scene in which Lestat makes Gabrielle [his mother] into a vampire is it, sustained it for two pages." . . .

For its author, "the idea of fiction is to go through as little as possible to get to it." To that end, Anne's vampire cosmology has no truck with the stagy affectations of yore. There are no crucifixes or garlic necklaces; no wooden stakes. Her vampires can only perish by fire, sunlight or suffocating ennui. Blue vampires cry red tears. Louis, Lestat and other male bloodsuckers may not exchange bodily fluids in the customary fashion, but there is a startling homoerotic intensity to the way they love one another, stalk, suck and kill.

"She has an enormous gay following," says John Preston, a gay journalist and writer of erotica who became A. N. Roquelaure's pen pal and is now Anne Rice's close friend. "Her vampire books are metaphors for gay life and gay sex. She writes very well about it. There's so much there about being initiated into a secret world. *Lestat* is really the retelling of a gay story."

Having nearly been destroyed in *Interview*, Lestat awakens after a long and troubled sleep to the sounds of a rock band rehearsing. He makes a stunning comeback as—shazam—a rock star, playin' out his blood lust on the MTV. Her Lestat roars around on a big black Harley, Bach's Goldberg Variations pounding in his Walkman. The book is written as his autobiography, part of the rock star's fiendishly aggressive marketing campaign. "Sting is Lestat," young fans have told Anne.

Both vampire fans and S&M devotees ring the Rice home phone, which Anne keeps listed in order to hear from the "weird, wonderful human beings" who call from all over the country. Of the vampire fans she says, "One thing that causes them to write or call is the emotional impact the book had on them. They want the supernatural because it functions for them metaphorically. They want the supercharge of the fact that these characters are vampires. That's the heightened drama of life for them."

Grand passions can play in the affectless Eighties. Big stuff happens to Anne Rice characters. In *Cry to Heaven*, a novel about eighteenth-century opera castrati in Venice, the handsome Tonio becomes a star soprano only after losing his testicles. And if your knees involuntarily draw up while you're reading the clip-and-snip scene, well, that's what it's all about.

"I think I fell in love with the idea of the castrati," she says, because she saw their situation as "a magnification of all of us, of outsiders, people that feel individually maimed in some way."

Her vampires may be the ultimate outsiders; it was in keeping with that theme that Rice updated Lestat as a rock star. Rockers fascinate her "because they are these symbolic outsiders. There's nothing like them, no place else where anyone gets that kind of money and power and is still relied upon to be himself. I think it must be the most seductive thing in the world. And the most agonizing."

Referring to a favorite scene where Lestat rides on his big Harley, she says, "I'm very attracted to that image. Yet at the same time, I'm a very rational person who rarely ventures outside the house."

Clearly, her imagination does the adventuring. But its range and velocity can be stunning.

"How can a woman write so well about sex between men?" Sting wondered after reading *Cry to Heaven*. "How do you invent a believable vampire mind? What *do* you suppose this woman is like?"

"Whipped cream tonight?" Anne's husband, poet Stan Rice, poses the question with a smirk as he opens the refrigerator door.

"Sure, let's get wild."

Though Ms. Roquelaure's slave masters do some imaginative things with clotted cream, the Rices are talking dessert here.

Let it be understood that in the Rice household, only the dogs wear leather collars. Anne has been married to Stan, her high-school sweetheart, for twenty-five years. They live quietly with Anne's two pseudonyms, their son, Christopher, and Anne's sister Karen O'Brien, plus the bull mastiff, a Dalmatian, two birds and a white rat.

"We live like hermits here," Anne says. "We write all the time and spend the evenings at home with our son."

Stan, who is also the chairman of the creative-writing department at San Francisco State University, grabs a pile of papers and heads for the café across the street, where he does much of his writing.

The Rice home is a snug, lace-curtained cocoon of Victoriana and anthropological whimsy. The walls have many eyes, those of porcelain-faced antique dolls, macabre carnival masks, a deer head with fake buckteeth. A plaster Baby Jesus smiles on a Spielberg gremlin. Birds twitter; the mastiff snuffles in his sleep. Weekdays, from ten until six, the only sound is the muted click of the Tandy 2000 keyboard.

Ask what she does for fun, and she shrugs. She does have a shiny orange Vespa, but she hasn't ridden it since the first time she flicked on the engine and was terrified by the noise. She doesn't drive, period. She doesn't wear leather or frequent S&M boîtes. She went to a sex shop once with Stan and was horrified—not by the inflatable plastic vaginas but by the woeful hack quality of generic porn. She says she is a heavy VCR user, is afraid of the dark and will not go back to a restaurant where she is recognized as Anne Rice.

"I like mainly to be invisible," she says, "to sort of drift around unseen in the world." . . .

With her sisters, she has formed an ad hoc writers' collective. Alice O'Brien Borchardt, a nurse in Houston, has begun writing hard-boiled detective novels, which sister Karen inputs on Anne's spare Osborne computer. The fourth sister, Tamara O'Brien Tinker, is a Bay Area poet. Their father, Howard O'Brien, who is now retired, is working on his memoirs.

"It's not surprising to me that we should all write," she says. "We're all these loquacious Irish Catholics."

It follows, too, that as the formerly weird O'Brien sisters churn out their diverse forms of fiction, the bestselling O'Brien looks forward to working on a subject close to home.

"In this witchcraft novel, I'd like to deal with these sisters who have this sense of being weird and set apart." A dynasty of mothers, daughters and sisters will be the subject of *The Witching Hour*. . . . It will be about a family of psychic women who are visited, over generations, by a malicious male spirit named Lasher. The heroine and her mother are contemporary, but their roots will be explored backward through the witch persecutions of the sixteenth century.

Anne sees a clear parallel between these and the present-day witch hunts led by the redoubtable Tipper Gore and antiporn activists like Andrea Dworkin and Catherine MacKinnon.

"A great many of the feminists who are against porn and are pro-censorship seem to believe there is only one kind of female sexuality," she says, "and it's very limited. The only conclusion I can draw after twenty years of hearing women talk about sex is that the range embraces women who have never had an orgasm to women who say they had their first orgasm when they were eight years old masturbating with a Barbie doll. When you have that kind of range, how can you legislate what women are supposed to feel, what's normal, what's degrading?"

Of her own porn books she says, "They're meant to be good books to read while masturbating or fantasizing or wanting to simply enjoy sex."

Though she believes her porn sex is "safe"—no one is ever cut, burned, maimed or killed—she acknowledges her own lust for the lurid. "There's this tremendous capacity for violence in me. I love watching *The Untouchables*. I find it almost soothing to watch that kind of violence, and I'm not sure why. My characters are divided, these novels are divided, because I'm a divided person. The pen names are part of the division. It started when I was working on *Lestat* and I wasn't getting anywhere."

Frustrated, she slipped into disguise. A roquelaure is an eighteenth-century man's cloak, a romantic but concealing garment. The trilogy of Roquelaure books is a bare-assed parody of the Sleeping Beauty fairy tale. Beauty's Prince Charming wakes and claims her for the S&M theme park run by his mom, a cranky, off-with-their-clothes kind of Queen.

"It can be pretty silly," Anne admits. "There are a lot of paddling and spanking scenes, which on the surface are very tiresome. But to sado-masochists who share that fantasy, that is a very luscious kind of sexual contact to have."

For the writer, getting those fantasies onto a floppy disk was another obsession. "Before I die, I wanted to write my own brand of sadomasochism pornography and take it all the way—not have any fear of embarrassment to cause me to water it down."

Actually publishing the stuff brought its own delicious terrors. "I sent *The Claiming of Sleeping Beauty* off to my editor and my agent," she says, "and I woke up in the middle of the night in a mental sweat. It was a sense of exposure, of having gone so far out on a sexual limb that they would be horrified. And then I thought, 'This is fantastic. You haven't felt this way about anything you wrote for years.'"

Still, even when she began corresponding with John Preston through the office of one of her editors, it was as A. N. Roquelaure. At first, he didn't know who she really was. Once Anne revealed herself to Preston, he chided her for thinking she could share her secret with a select few. "She thought she could come out a *little* bit," he says. "Once it starts appearing in the gossip columns, as it did in her case before she owned up to it publicly, you might as well go for broke. You can't be a little bit of an erotic writer. Once you've done something like the Roquelaure books, you're an outlaw, and you may as well enjoy it."

So comfortable now is the outlaw with all her literary selves that the jacket of *Belinda* reads, "A novel by Anne Rice writing as Anne Rampling."

"The Rampling novels are about whatever's going on in my psychic life," she says. "They're novels of flight, of escape, with people busting loose. In the Rice novels I'm not into that. The vampires are never going to get out of their trap."

Not so for Lisa, heroine of Anne Rampling's *Exit to Eden.* She runs a triple-X-rated Caribbean sex club that's the antipode of civilization, even as Larry Flynt knows it. In the end, our dominatrix is tamed by one of her male sex slaves, and they escape this fleshy Fantasy Island for—*nawwwww*—reality: love, ballroom dancing and shopping at K-Mart. *Belinda* is about an illustrator of children's books who risks his respectable career when he begins painting nudes of the nubile sixteen-year-old Belinda. Anne says that she is the hero, Jeremy. She dedicated the book to herself, and it is Anne talking when Jeremy bemoans the confines of his respectable success: "But I wish something violent would happen, something unplanned and crazy. I wish I could just walk away from it all—you know, like one of those painters who fakes his suicide. . . . If I were a writer, I'd invent a pen name."

I ask if in owning up to her other names, the respected novelist isn't risking—even asking for—the same humiliation meted out to the sex slaves in her fantasies.

"I never thought about that," she says. "But that certainly isn't what happened."

In fact, nothing happened. Before Anne's dark secret was out, she wrote to her father telling him about the books and asking him not to read them. When people quizzed her about her three identities, she mumbled a lot, until she decided to resolve the issue in public. She accepted a local speaking engagement, and, with her husband and son in the audience, Sister Anne explained it all to them.

"I talked about the fact that I had grown up on the edge of this beautiful neighborhood called the Garden District that had these enormous antebellum mansions," she says, "and that every day I crossed that to go to school on the edge of the Irish Channel, that sunbaked neighborhood, with its shotgun houses, where reality was boiling cabbage and women in flowered dresses and people swinging at each other. The romance of the Garden District for me had been reality. All the Rice novels were an attempt to reinvoke that reality. The Rampling characters were trying to get out of the trap that the Rice characters are in, into contemporary life and into the mainstream—just as I was trying to get out of the historical and supernatural mode and write about contemporary life. Roquelaure is just upfront porn, an attempt to put down those fantasies. They're not gone, but I didn't want to go to the grave not telling that secret."

No one walked out on her.

"They told me they dug it," she says. In retrospect, she had a wonderful time getting it all out. "I felt like a burning bush up there." . . . Ultimately, her fondest wish is for the writer's special brand of immortality, Staying in Print. She says she saw a hopeful sign during a recent book party at an L.A. bookstore.

What critics might compartmentalize, faithful readers have united. They arrived at the autograph table with *all* of her books in their shopping bags and rucksacks. Anne Rampling Roquelaure Rice says her beating heart leaped.

"That was it," she says. "That was really *it*."

The Quotable Anne Rice

Actor Gary Oldman, who played Dracula in Coppola's *Bram Stoker's Dracula*, on *The Tale of the Body Thief*: "I got ideas from it. I don't know what it's like to be a vampire. *Clearly*, Anne Rice does. You read those books and you say to yourself, 'I believe that there are vampires in the world.'" (*Maclean's*, Nov. 16, 1992)

Film director Francis Ford Coppola on *Interview with the Vampire*: "I am the custodian of the Bram Stoker book, and I think it was worthwhile to do. But *Interview with the Vampire* is a much greater novel. I thought, 'Gee, this book really makes me *feel* like a vampire, like I'm in their community.' They drag somebody behind the garbage cans and just start sucking their blood, like drug addicts. My frustration is that the Anne Rice book has a more modern take." (*Maclean's*, Nov. 16, 1992)

Anne Rice on Hollywood: "My efforts with Hollywood are like things written in water." (*Maclean's*, Nov. 16, 1992)

New Orleans writer Poppy Z. Brite on Anne Rice, when asked, "Anne Rice lives in New Orleans. Do you two socialize?": "I've never met her, and to tell you the truth, I've barely read a word of her fiction. I started *Interview* but didn't get into it. I was so burnt out on vampires after writing *Lost Souls*—not to mention doing the publicity, during which people would sidle up to me at cocktail parties and book signings to tell me how they actually *were* vampires—that I haven't wanted to read much about them since." (*Horror* magazine)

Anne Rice on her mainstream appeal: "I've always thought my work was too extreme and eccentric to go mainstream." (*USA Today*, Nov. 16, 1994)

Anne Rice on vampires: "I've always been fascinated by the vampire, the elegant yet evil Byronic figure. It's easy to say it's a metaphor for the outsider, the predator, anyone who feels freakish or monstrous or out of step but appears normal." (*Omni*, Oct. 1989)

Anne Rice, when asked if she believed in vampires: "That depends on when you ask me and what mood I'm in. But seriously, sadly, they exist only in the imagination. Vampires are powerfully mythic. They confront our fear of the dead, our fear of being sucked dry by guilt. We also long for transcendence and immortality." (*Omni*, Oct. 1989)

Part Three: On Anne Rice

Anne Rice on her critics: "It puzzles me that there is such a gap between the critics' perception of my books and my readers' response to them. If someone from another planet were researching what humans read and only looked at the reviews, he couldn't possibly figure out why anybody reads my novels. He'd get a better idea if he just asked the readers." (*Omni*, Oct. 1989)

Anne Rice on her psychological imperative to write: "Writers write about what obsesses them. You draw those cards. I lost my mother when I was 14. My daughter died at the age of 6. I lost my faith as a Catholic. When I'm writing, the darkness is always there. I go where the pain is." (*People*, Dec. 5, 1988)

Anne Rice on New Orleans: "I love New Orleans. The twilight sky here is like no place on earth. It is violet and golden. New Orleans has all this lush beauty,

Statue at Norfolk, Virginia, cemetery

like Venice and Rome. I was born here, and I had been wanting to come back for years. I always remember the fantastic contrast of New Orleans in my childhood: the romance and gloom. Here were all these great big beautiful houses falling into gloom. If I begin a book elsewhere, my characters end up right back here." (*People*, Dec. 5, 1988)

Anne Rice on boxing: "I enjoy going to boxing matches—I am fascinated by performers of all kinds, and by sports which involve one man against another or against a force." (*Contemporary Authors*, New Revision Series, Volume 36)

Actress Dana Delany, who played Lisa in the film version of *Exit to Eden*, on Anne Rice: "We met her in New Orleans when we were shooting there and she couldn't have been nicer. She's been very supportive of the project. I read [*Exit to Eden*] after I got cast and I loved it. I think it's great. She knew that this [film] was not going to be the book. I don't think she has the emotional attachment to this [film] that she has to the 'Vampire' books." (from a 1994 interview on America Online)

Rice chronicler Katherine Ramsland on Anne Rice: ". . . I'm still completely amazed by her intelligence, the strength of her personality, and her generosity. I just find her so endlessly fascinating that I have never been disillusioned by her." (Princeton, N.J., newspaper, Nov. 16, 1994)

Anne Rice on anonymity: "I like mainly to be invisible, to sort of drift around unseen in the world." (*Rolling Stone*, Nov. 20, 1986)

Anne Rice on her literary voices: "The romance of the Garden District for me had been reality. All the Rice novels were an attempt to reinvoke that reality. The Rampling characters were trying to get out of the trap that the Rice characters are in, into contemporary life and into the mainstream—just as I was trying to get out of the historical and supernatural mode and write about contemporary life. Roquelaure is just upfront porn, an attempt to put down those fantasies." (*Rolling Stone*, Nov. 20, 1986)

Anne Rice on realizing her dream: "I didn't have a career or a job. Stan was a successful poet and a respected college professor, and it was perfectly okay with him if I just wrote. So I had nothing to sustain me but my dreams. And I have to admit I dreamed of great success and recognition. I had thrown in my lot with the most bohemian kind of life, and if I was going to be redeemed it had to be by great success. So I don't know if 'surprised' is

the right word. But I had the amazing thing happen: my dreams came true."
(*Publishers Weekly*, Oct. 28, 1988)

Anne Rice on why she made Lestat a rock star in *The Vampire Lestat*: "I felt that
was absolutely what he would do. Rock musicians are something new under
the sun . . . they are the epitome of the romantic artist in that they are expected
to surprise and change and remain independent all at the same time. It's the
perfect thing for Lestat to be, and the perfect way for him, in *The Queen of the
Damned*, to send out a call to all the immortals he's lost contact with, all over
the world." (*Publishers Weekly*, Oct. 28, 1988)

Anne Rice on *The Queen of the Damned*: "[It], for better or worse, is the first
book in which the vision is all there. Early on I had a vision that involved the
Twins and the dreams the immortals were having all over the world. My first
reaction was, 'You'll never get all that on paper. You'll get maybe half of it.' But
this time I decided I was going to write the dream book in its totality. And I
did. For me that was a tremendous leap forward, at least in terms of intention
and accomplishment." (*Publishers Weekly*, Oct. 28, 1988)

Anne Rice on *Memnoch the Devil*: "I wrote it before the movie [*Interview with
a Vampire*] ever broke because I was terrified that the movie would block me
and destroy my sanity and ruin my life, but it hasn't done that. . . ."
(Recorded phone message on Anne Rice's "hotline," Dec. 1994)

Anne Rice on *The Servant of the Bones*: "My heart right now is totally connected
to a book called *The Servant of the Bones*, which is not in any way connected
with vampires or witches. It's about a new hero, a ghost, who really doesn't
particularly like the job that he's been given. I'm in love with this hero and
in love with his dilemma." (Recorded phone message on Anne Rice's "hotline,"
Dec. 1994)

Anne Rice on New Orleans: "As Van Gogh found his inspiration in Arles, the
'lost generation' found theirs in Paris, I have found my aesthetic in New Orleans.
There is an atmosphere here different from any other city in the country.
People here live as individuals, the way they have lived for many years. I call
it vintage lifestyles as opposed to acquired lifestyles." (*New Orleans Magazine*,
date unknown)

Imagination Is Her Lifeblood

an interview conducted by Dale Rice
(October 15, 1993)

DALE RICE: How extensive is your research?

ANNE RICE: My research at this point never stops. I just continuously read history, archeology, anthropology, things like that. Not only do I find facts in these history books, I'm really being inspired by them. Good stories, whole novels come to life, say, as I read a book about Elizabethan England. It's all very unified right now. I don't break off and do research so much as I just read and study the whole time I'm writing.

D. RICE: What's your writing regimen like?

A. RICE: I have a longhand diary I carry with me everywhere, and I do quite a bit of jotting of ideas and notes in that. But I don't actually write except on the computer in my office at home. I generally write from 11 A.M. on in the day and then quite a bit in the evening if the house is quiet. When I work on a book, I look for a period of about three months where I don't have any distractions . . . and I live pretty much like a hermit during that period, only occasionally going out for a meal if dragged. That's how I get my work done.

D. RICE: Tell me about your imagination.

A. RICE: I would say it works nonstop. It's almost like having a chemical in the brain. Ideas, images, stories—they just come to me naturally. Right now, for example, I have several different projects I want to do. These projects grow, these ideas for novels, they grow and develop almost by themselves.

D. RICE: Who are your typical readers?

A. RICE: Boy, that's impossible to say. I just did a signing last night in Sacramento, California, and there were all kinds of people there. And that's my readership. I love that—the fact that it's almost impossible to classify.

D. RICE: It must make you feel good to have so many loyal fans.

A. RICE: It's very heartwarming. In some ways my readers have saved my life in that they have redeemed my life because they understand the books, they respond. When I go out on tour I see them and I talk to them. It may just be for a few seconds, but I love it. And they sustain me, and whatever else happens in life, I think, "Well, they understand. They got the book."

D. RICE: Is there a particular message you're trying to send readers?

A. RICE: I don't think of it that way. When I'm writing I definitely put everything I know in there. I'm almost obsessively concerned with certain moral issues and questions: How do we live a good life when it seems almost impossible? How do we go on when it seems meaningless? The novels to me have to mean a great deal or they're worthless. If they're not about us and they're not about everything that concerns us—if they're just about vampires and witches—then I've failed.

D. RICE: You once said you'd be proud to be called a southern writer. What sets southern writers apart?

A. RICE: I'm sure there are writers all over the world that could be likened to southern writers, but I think Eudora Welty, Tennessee Williams, William Faulkner, all of those people, they use language in a much more free way. They let it pour out. They're not afraid of it. They do not necessarily follow the minimalist path of other American writers. They also obviously seem to be at home with certain darkness and gloom in their work. They seem to enjoy describing that and finding that meaningful. I see that as something we share. Basically, I think southern writers are not afraid to be romantic in the very positive sense of the word.

D. RICE: What other authors do you admire?

A. RICE: A young author just came along, named Donna Tartt, who I think is absolutely marvelous. She wrote *The Secret History*, which I think is an incredible novel. Other authors that have influenced me powerfully would be people like Franz Kafka, Vladimir Nabokov. I answer this question differently, depending on whom I'm thinking about. I was influenced by the greats, certainly. I'm a slow reader and I came very late in adolescence to writers like Charles Dickens, Feodor Dostoevski and Leo Tolstoy, and I read them with great fervor. A writer that had a profound influence on me is Virginia Woolf. I loved the way she would weave the story, write about somebody walking through London, say, and then give the whole person's life and thoughts. I still strive to do things like that.

D. RICE: What's next?

A. RICE: I think my next novel will be about the Mayfair family again, and it will be about Lasher's species, but it's not really a sequel. I love the

Mayfair family. I'd love to write a whole book called *Mona*, just about Mona Mayfair, the 13-year-old heroine in *Lasher*. After that I'd like to get back to Lestat. There are many different things I want to do. I want to do completely new things that are in no way connected to the old work, yet I'd like to do another novel with Ramses the Damned, the character in *The Mummy*. This is a very rich, wonderful time for me. The battle is really to get the time, to sit down and let all this out. I don't think it will always be this way. I think there'll come a time when some of this dries up. It's bound to happen. It's like sports or dancing—you do it while you can do it and then there comes a time maybe when you can't do it.

A gravesite at the Lafayette cemetery

"Anne Rice:
Birth of the Vampire"

Anne Rice's first novel, *Interview with the Vampire*, has sold over
[6] million copies. It is the most widely read vampire story since
Bram Stoker's *Dracula*.

from "Anne Rice: Birth of a Vampire"

◆

Original airdate: October 30, 1994, on Lifetime. Produced and directed by
Anand Tucker. Edited by Peter Webber. Sound by Bob Briscoe. Photography
by Richard Numeroff. Reader, Neville Watchurst (for readings from *Interview
with the Vampire*). One hour, VHS format videocassette.

In a derogatory, let's-poke-fun-at-this profile, *USA Today's* television reviewer
Matt Roush wrote: "Rice, Krispy: Twice as ambitious as your average celebrity
bio . . . [it] is also four times as pretentious. Fans of her intense purple
prose—include me in—will initially be intrigued by this languid and stilted
mood piece of an oral biography. Rice, husband Stan and assorted family and
friends speak candidly of alcoholism and personal tragedy (the death by
leukemia of their daughter). Sautéed in New Orleans spiritualism, Rice's
murky psyche is exorcised through the writing of her bestsellers. . . ."

Truth be told, with the exception of two irrelevant moments—on spiritual
healing and parapsychology—this profile is a good, but not great, introduction
to the life of Anne Rice, not as a bestselling author but as a woman who has
seen her life permeated with darkness and illuminated with light.

"This is a film about what happened to Anne Rice before she became a
writer," we are told, and by and large it's an accurate description. Drawing on
voice-overs by Neville Watchurst, reading from *Interview with the Vampire*, in-
corporating MTV-style frenzied camera pans down Bourbon Street to simulate
how a vampire might see the world (brighter, more garish, more alive), the profile is highlighted with personal reminiscences: Anne Rice, Stan Rice, their son
Christopher, as well as her cousins Bill Murphy and Gertrude Helwig, her
younger sister Karen O'Brien, her older sister Alice Borchardt, and her friend
Michael Riley.

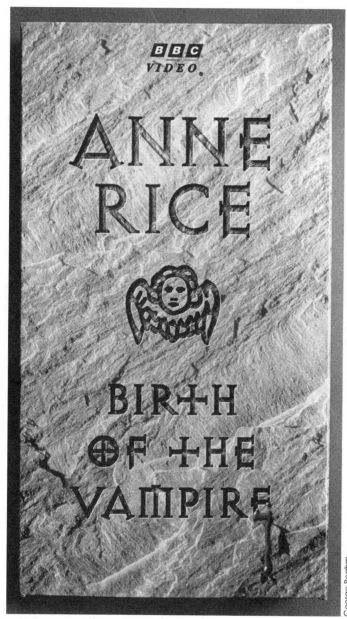

Video box for *Anne Rice: Birth of the Vampire*

George Beahm

Part Three: On Anne Rice

The profile opens with a shot of a single, brown eye staring at the viewer; the camera pans past New Orleans plantations, as the voice of Louis intones, "I was a twenty-five-year-old man when I became a vampire. . . ."

For Rice readers who have never been to New Orleans, this profile is a visual treat, showing the house in which she grew up on St. Charles Avenue, her current residence on First Street, the orphanage she is restoring (St. Elizabeth's), as well as interior shots of all three. In addition, we see Lafayette Cemetery—a few blocks from her house, and catercorner from the Garden District Book Shop, which is Vampire Central for Rice fans who go there to buy things Rice—and we also see shots of Rice's doll collection.

To its credit, the profile does not gloss over the family tragedies: the alcoholism that plagued her family, overshadowed by the loss of their daughter Michele.

Deliberately slow in pace and moody in tone, the profile is properly somber, the music sepulchral, and the photography haunting.

Louisiana cemetery

Scott Stewart

Interview with the Vampire Author

conducted by Merle Ginsberg
(October 1994)

TV GUIDE: You're normally quite protective of your private life. Why did you agree to do the documentary?

ANNE RICE: I was very taken with [*Birth of the Vampire* producer] Nick Kent and just trusted him. In the end, I was pleased, although I found it very wrenching to watch the whole segment about my daughter's death. If I had related *Interview with the Vampire* with that at the time, I couldn't have written it.

GUIDE: You've never really discussed your struggle with alcohol before.

RICE: I did so because I think drinking is really dangerous. I didn't see the end of my own dinner parties for ten years. Now, I haven't had a drink in fifteen years. My husband and I just quit, cold turkey, one day. I didn't want my son to have drunks for parents. I didn't want him to grow up with a drunken mother, as I did. At book signings, people come up to me and tell me *Interview* must be about coming off heroin. I didn't even think about the allegory of addiction while I was writing it, but it was obviously there.

GUIDE: How much do you think alcohol affected your early writing?

RICE: The writing eliminated the need for alcohol. I turned my pain into art. Alcohol helped me access the pain, but it kills your brain cells. The days of wine and roses are brief, I found out.

GUIDE: How do you feel about Prozac as a treatment for the kind of depression that led to your dependence on alcohol?

RICE: I think that Prozac is more helpful than Freud or Jung. It doesn't worry me as much as therapy—too much therapy can make people miserable.

GUIDE: When you start a new book, how do you decide if it will be part of the Vampire Chronicles, part of the Mayfair witches saga, or one of your erotic novels?

RICE: It's like these are people standing outside my door trying to get in—I see who makes it in. I slip into a dream state with the characters. The Mayfair witches novels are easier because there are people who win. The vampires are harder because they're darker.

Part Three: On Anne Rice

GUIDE: What do you do when you're not writing?

RICE: I'm pretty unhappy when I'm not writing. I write all the time.

GUIDE: A few weeks ago you took out full-page ads in *The New York Times, Variety,* and *The Advocate,* completely reversing your earlier criticism of the casting of Tom Cruise in the feature film of *Interview with the Vampire.* What brought that about?

RICE: [The movie's producer] David Geffen sent me a copy of the film on videocassette and I *loved* it! He took quite a risk, because the chances of me loving it were about a million to one. But [director] Neil Jordan has done a magnificent job. It's completely faithful to my book and my script. After seventeen years of developing this project, I can't believe it. My Lestat is there in Tom Cruise. He steps into a new realm. I never expected that.

GUIDE: Have you told him?

RICE: Yes, I called him after I saw the tape. He said, "Thank you." I also sent flowers to Kirsten Dunst, who plays Claudia. Every actor was exactly what I'd always imagined, including Brad Pitt as Louis. I am so relieved. I had surgery recently and I'm still sick, but now I feel as if I'm back. It could have sent me into the depths.

GUIDE: Does that happen often?

RICE: I have my black moments—when death seems so close, when not to kill myself seems such an effort. But I would never do that to my husband and son. I know my dark periods, and, as a writer, I've learned to ride them out. Darkness never really goes away once you've seen it. You learn to see the light in the darkness. In fact, once you've seen the darkness, the light is brighter. Writing is my way of working through it. It's what dancing is to a dancer.

GUIDE: Many people think there are a lot of allegorical references to AIDS in the vampire books, but given how much blood changes bodies, it's surprising you never refer to AIDS outright.

RICE: AIDS is already there. I refer to plagues, pestilence, disease. I respect it. I don't need to refer to it literally. Two years ago, my best friend, John Preston, a writer, died of AIDS. He lived in Portland, and we used to fax each other three or four times a day. I asked him why people with AIDS like these books, and—just before he died—he said, "They are a great bridge over."

Interview with the Vampire Author

GUIDE: You've admitted that you love violent movies, and violence figures prominently in your books.

RICE: The emotion, it speaks to me. Think of the violence in Greek dramas— it's part and parcel of Western art. My fans know that I use it as a metaphor. Vampires and witches are romantic figures. They're not real. My fans believe in the romance and so do I.

GUIDE: What are you working on now?

RICE: I'm going into my winter darkness now. I'm going right down to hell! I'm finishing up *The Servant of the Bones*, which isn't part of either the vampire or the witch cycles. It's about an extremely tempestuous ghost. And then I'm also working on *Memnoch the Devil*, which is about Lestat's darkest hour. I nearly collapsed over that one. The people who work for me started whispering to each other "Anne's contemplating death again—bring her bananas and milk!" *Memnoch* nearly killed me. But you have to fish the dark waters.

GUIDE: You actually seem quite happy right now.

RICE: Oh, yes, we're all happy around here. You know, the darkness comes and it goes. These are the things I'll never explain or know. Sometimes, I just feel like a receptacle. That's when the feeling is everywhere. There's the truth. Emotional truth. That's what counts. And that's what I loved about the movie of *Interview*. I called David Geffen at home and told him just that.

GUIDE: If Lestat found you in a dark alley, would you welcome his biting you? Would you want to become a vampire?

RICE: I don't think that I could resist Lestat—or immortality—if he walked in and said, "You've been channeling me all these years. Now I've arrived." I wouldn't have the strength. My husband says he'd resist, he'd kill him. Lestat is based on my husband, Stan, and his indomitable strength and will and faith I had when I was writing it. But in the end, the characters chose their personalities. They have freedom.

GUIDE: Will you be remembered as a popular bestselling author, or as an important one, do you think?

RICE: I hope and pray I'm remembered as both. A popular writer who wrote books that will last. But I would never be insulted to be called a popular writer again. My audience is brain surgeons and manicurists. My readers get me through the night. I'm blessed and I'm proud.

The Devil and Anne Rice

an interview conducted by Mikal Gilmore
(*Rolling Stone*, July 13–27, 1995)

I meet Anne Rice at her large, Greek revival–style home, which she shares with her husband, Stan, and their son, Christopher, in the aged Garden District of New Orleans. Rice was born and raised not far from this grand house. At fifteen she left New Orleans and eventually settled in the San Francisco Bay Area with Stan, a poet, painter and, at the time, professor at San Francisco State University. After some thirty years in California, Rice missed her hometown and extended family and, with her husband and son, moved back to New Orleans. In 1989 she purchased the First Street house where she now lives and writes. It is a richly atmospheric place, and it is little wonder that Rice has used it as the haunted central setting of *The Witching Hour*, *Lasher*, and *Taltos*—the first three volumes of her *Lives of the Mayfair Witches* series. The house is crammed with the stuff of Rice's obsessive imagination: showcases of valuable nineteenth-century French porcelain Bru dolls (utterly spooky with their human-like eyes), walls of books on ancient mythology and religious theory, rooms of religious statuary and even the odd skeleton or two, outfitted in century-old bridal or ballroom gowns and sporting flowing blond wigs. ("But they aren't real skeletons," says Rice as she gives me a tour of the upstairs. "I couldn't live with a real one.")

As we talk, Rice and I sit in a glassed-in side porch overlooking a large, lush lawn not far from the site where the fictional demon Lasher lies fictionally buried under a vast and ancient oak tree. Rice is dressed in a white, high-collared, billowy blouse with frilly cuffs and a long, black skirt, and she wears her trademark owlish glasses. At age 53, Rice is direct, plain-spoken and intellectually passionate. These days, she says, when she isn't sequestered in her upstairs office writing, she is busy researching matters related to religious history and mythology—the same subject matter that she says preoccupied her in *Memnoch the Devil* and will be at the thematic core of her next few books.

MIKAL GILMORE: *Memnoch the Devil* strikes me as perhaps your most passionate and inventive work since *Interview with the Vampire*. Obviously, you've taken considerable risks with this story—not only risks for your vampire characters and their secretive, immortal world but also risks that given the story's shock points might even affect your career. I also couldn't help wondering if the risks might run deeper—if perhaps there's something personal at stake for you in this parable about God and the devil.

ANNE RICE: If there was any book that ever beat me up, it was *Memnoch*. I had been thinking about it for more than two years—swimming in the ideas of it, going back and forth between its various scenes in my head. I had even made false starts and then thrown them away. Finally, early last year I sat down and thought, "I'm either going to write this, or it's going to kill me." So I took the month of February, wrote it and then collapsed. It nearly *did* kill me. I mean, there was something so dark in writing this book. I remember lying in bed one night thinking, "All right, Lestat's got to go to hell today. There's no putting this off any longer—it's time." And it was like . . . it was like going there with him, I guess. Toward the end, when he ran up the stairs of hell to escape, I was right with him. It was not a pleasure, writing those scenes. It was real agony, because I'm as close to Lestat as any character that I've been able to imagine and write.

GILMORE: Like *Interview with the Vampire*, much of *Memnoch* has a half-maddened, fever-pitch intensity to it, plus it takes some wildly unpredictable turns. Did you ever find yourself surprised by what you were writing?

RICE: Basically, I knew what I wanted: Lestat was going to meet the devil and God, and they were going to talk. And I knew that the devil was going to present certain arguments to Lestat, but I didn't know how *well* he was going to make them until I got into making them for him.

But you're right. This book was just as instinctively written as *Interview with the Vampire*, and there's been no book in between that's been that instinctively written. With all the others there was more thought, more doubt, more hesitation—some more so than others. Now I've come full circle. I write now as I did when I wrote *Interview*—all night long. *Interview with the Vampire* was written in five weeks; this was written in about four weeks, and it was the same sort of experience—just surrendering to the process. And I found myself asking the same kinds of questions. I kept saying, "How dare you write these things!"

GILMORE: Where did your interest in writing a novel about the argument between God and the devil come from?

Part Three: On Anne Rice

RICE: I had a teacher in comparative literature at San Francisco State back in the 1960s. I remember him once saying in a class on Goethe, "What would God and the devil have to talk about if it weren't for men?" I never forgot that, and I think that I have always been going at that idea in one form or another in my writing, though behind masks, you could say. I mean, when I wrote *The Vampire Lestat*, and I talked about ancient Egypt, I was going at it in a less direct way. Now I'm going right into my own heritage. I'm spending hours and hours reading every translation of the Bible that I can find as well as other religious histories and texts, and I'm fascinated by it all. It's an obsession, a passion. I see things now about my own religion and my own religious upbringing that I never could have seen in my 30s. I certainly couldn't have seen them in this way when I wrote *Interview with the Vampire* or *The Vampire Lestat*.

GILMORE: So how would you describe your view of religion now?

RICE: When I wrote *Interview with the Vampire*, I didn't think there was any question: There was no God. What was terribly important was to live in spite of that fact. Now I think it's terribly important that there *might* be. And it's not detached from life. It's right in the neutrinos and the atoms and the explosion in Oklahoma City.

A doll from the Rice collection

But my obsession is more than that. I'm trying to stand back and understand, as if I were one of my characters, why this age—which has come so far in so many ways—why is this age obsessed with near-death experiences and angels and gods, and why are movies showing people coming back from the dead over and over again as a common image? Why are the movies flooded with images of people who can fly? What does it all mean? What *does* it mean? Things are not getting simpler to me. They're getting more and more complicated, and the questions are multiplying. I was more sure there was no God when I was younger. I still suspect there isn't, that there isn't anything. That's my suspicion: that there is nothing. But I'm just not so *sure* anymore. It's all I want to talk about, all I want to think about, all I want to deal with—and I see this book and the next one as a new path for me.

GILMORE: By the end of *Memnoch the Devil*, Lestat would seem to have few questions about the matter: He's seen God and the devil face to face, and he's heard their debate.

RICE: Actually, I think that at the end, Lestat really hasn't been given any more direct sign from heaven than anybody is ever given. Maybe that's part of what I'm trying to say. That it can't make sense. You just can't have a God that cares that little. You *can't*. Either he doesn't know, or he's stupid, or he's a bad person. And if it is all true, then it certainly is a horror novel. That's part of what I'm trying to say.

GILMORE: The basic premise of *Memnoch* is so strong, it seems it could just as easily have been a non-vampire book—and may even have reached a different or broader audience than the Vampire Chronicles.

RICE: I *tried* to make it a non-vampire book. I tried to write it with immortal men, to take immortal men through the same experiences, and it simply could not get going. And I finally gave it back to Lestat. It's almost as if he laughed and said, "You know you need *me* to go there." And, of course, he was right: His going there did make quite a bit of difference. But I'm afraid my relationship with him is over. He left me when I finished reading the page proofs for this book. That same night, I put a message on my answering machine—I have a listed number for people to call—and I said: "Lestat is gone. He left me as he was standing in front of a Mercedes-Benz dealership on St. Charles Avenue, in New Orleans. This is a very strange feeling, but it's happened."

It was as if after all the things we'd gone through together—I'd survived Tom Cruise, I'd survived the [*Interview with the Vampire*] movie, even though *Memnoch* was written before the film was released—I'd gotten through all of that, and, *still*, he left me. It was like he was saying, "This is it—we've done it. You've done it. We've said what we have to say to each other. If you go on now, you've got to go on in another way."

GILMORE: What will you do next?

RICE: The current book I'm working on is called *Servant of the Bones*. The only thing I'd like to say about it is that it's about a very old ghost who is made for a particular purpose and decides after thousands of years just not to do what he's supposed to do. This book will be more similar to *Memnoch* than anything else. *Memnoch* put me right up against where I want to be— where I can write about ghosts and spiritual forces as something that may be real. I know I run a certain risk. My audience might say, "She's flipped out," you know? But it's very exciting to me to be writing about this ghost in the twentieth century and what he sees in something like the Oklahoma bombing.

GILMORE: You've written vampire and witch chronicles and a mummy yarn, and now you're undertaking an epic ghost series. In the course of writing these stories, you've become known as one of the preeminent authors of super-natural literature. What is it about that story form that has attracted you so?

RICE: I think all my writing has been part of a battle with my fears. When I write, I explore my worst fears and then take my protagonist right into awful situations that I myself am terrified by. And I think that the act of putting all that fear and terror and confusion into an orderly, plotted story has been very therapeutic for me. It definitely helps me to continue through life.

Obviously, I'm obsessed with death. I'm not obsessed, *per se*, with pain and suffering. I actually try not to write about it, surprisingly enough, and so even though my books are supposed to be bloody and horrible, there is a shrinking from this. Or at least there's a terrible moral dilemma there. I mean, I have to write about pain, obviously—the pain that other people have suffered and pain I'd be afraid to suffer myself. I feel very driven to do it, and it clearly helps me. I only hope that it's in such a framework that it does not simply add to the horror of someone else.

GILMORE: You mention your obsession with death. It has seemed that in some ways your best work has been a rage against death. Vampires achieving immortality and spirits seizing human life amount to a fantasized overcoming of death and all its sheer horrors and unfairness.

RICE: I think that since moving back here to New Orleans, I've begun to find some way I can accept the fact that we're going to die. But it is true that for a long time I found it just horrifying. I found it horrifying not so much because my life will be extinguished but because of the possibility that the Holocaust might mean nothing. Or the suffering of my daughter might mean nothing. That's the part that bothers me: the meaninglessness of it. The utter meaninglessness of it. And I'm still fascinated by the way people convince themselves that things have to have meaning. Every time you turn on a TV, you see a reporter talking to the parent of a retarded child or somebody who's been hit by a ton of bricks, and they say, "There *has* to be a meaning for this." And I'm always thinking: "No. There really doesn't have to be any at all." Despite that I now think atheism might be a bit naive and cocky, I still believe there is possibly no meaning to anything. There's *nothing* that can't be swept off the face of the earth. Nothing.

I remember going through that time when life was just unendurable. It lasted about three months. I was literally quivering. I would grab people and say, "Do you believe that there's a God? Do you believe we're all here for nothing?" I put it in *The Vampire Lestat*. I had Lestat do it, but actually it was I.

It's changed for me now. I just don't feel the same suffocating horror. I don't feel resigned. . . . It's hard to describe what I feel. Maybe what I feel is a capacity, finally, to enjoy everything, even though there may be no meaning. I was talking to a woman whose son recently committed suicide. He was a teen-ager here. I had lost a child, and this woman had lost a child. I was talking to her, and I said that what I honestly thought was, when the lights go out, and when that darkness comes, it never really goes away. The darkness never is really going to go away, but you just somehow learn to see the light also. And you know something other people don't know. You meet them, and you don't know whether they're better off or not, but you know something that they don't know. Because those lights have gone off for you.

GILMORE: Did you find that time provides a means of healing?

RICE: Well, it must, but I have a suspicion of that. I truly believe it's ruthless to be healed. You know what I mean?

Let me tell you a story. I've been scared of the dark all my life. I've been scared to be alone. I've spent very few nights of my life alone in any house—and I never stay in this house alone. But recently I have been losing my fear of the dark, and it is one of the most wonderful things. Just a week or so ago I was sitting up in my office. It was about 1:10 A.M., and I'd been thinking for a while about getting up and writing something on my wall. I write all over my office walls in felt pen. I was going to get up and write, "Someday

I will die, and it will all be over." But before I could do that the lights went out. There was a power shortage in the neighborhood, and it was as black as it is in the country. So I got up from my desk and woke my sister, because I knew she would have a lighter so that I could light a candle.

The lights were out for about 20 minutes, and it was *beautiful*. I remember walking through the house with my poor little sister, who was half-asleep. We came downstairs, and I thought: "This is what the house was like in 1857. It was this dark. This is a rare moment." I remember feeling absolutely euphoric, thinking how much I loved to walk through this house in the dark and how great it was not to be afraid anymore. At 1:30 the lights came back on, and I went upstairs. And then something occurred to me. I went and checked a memorial clipping on my bulletin board, and I realized it had been a year earlier to the day and hour that my best friend, John Preston, had died.

What lingered from that whole experience, more than anything else, was the *euphoria*. When I walked around in the dark, I didn't feel absolute horror that John Preston had died at 48 years of age, at the height of his talent, of AIDS, in a coma. I didn't feel a trembling horror. I felt a euphoria—an ability to tolerate *everything* at that moment. That was a great feeling, and so I'm calling that ruthless. Somehow, in spite of all the cruelty and absurdity of life, I was not afraid that night. I will die someday, and I will share that with everyone else. But I feel a fearlessness in those minutes, rather than the panic that used to clutch at me—for years—in the face of darkness and death.

That's the whole purpose, I think, of what people call fantasy writing. You can put the most horrible things into a frame, and you can go into that frame safely and talk about those things. You can go into the world of Louis and Lestat and Claudia and be able to talk about grief or loss or survival and then come back safely. That, to me, is the reason for all the artifice— the obvious high style of my books and their use of the supernatural. I would find it *much* harder to write a realistic novel about my life. I would find it too raw. I just wouldn't be able to get the doors open, I wouldn't be able to go deep enough.

GILMORE: Obviously, though, for many readers you have gone deep enough. Your books are not only terrifically popular, but they have also attracted the kind of fervent following more commonly associated with that of pop stars.

RICE: I did not expect books as eccentric as mine to have that kind of appeal or that kind of commercial momentum. I knew enough about publishing just to know what that meant, and I was astonished. I remember thinking that a book like *Interview with the Vampire* was just flat-out too weird. I thought at best it would become some sort of underground bestseller. I had no idea that it would have the great commercial life it's had as well.

But I've always had good luck, or good breaks, compared with many authors. And in the last few years the audience has spread out in an enormous way. If I lack any reader, if there's any audience I've failed to reach in America, it's the elite, literary audience. If there's been a failure to communicate, it's at the top—at the so-called top.

GILMORE: Well, judging from some of the reviews you've received over the years from literary quarters, that may well be true. What do you think accounts for much of the critical disdain that your work has received?

RICE: The subject matter. Scorn for the idea that anyone would write seriously about vampires. And then a secondary thing sets in once you become No. 1—that if you are the No. 1 bestseller, you must be an illiterate idiot. There are two prejudices that I fight.

I also think there's a cynical tendency in modern literary values to dismiss books that take on huge questions or issues, because nobody with any true sophistication could possibly do that. It's a sort of by-product of the post–World War II aesthetic of existential nihilism that says you cannot have heroes and heroines in novels. There are those who say that the great art of today is about nothing at all—that to be *about* something is pretentious and old-fashioned and limited. And my writing is filled with a kind of naive, dead seriousness about: Why are we here? How do we lead a good life? How do we keep believing fervently in love, and how do we make our lives not only good but heroic?

In a way I've been blessed in that I can ask those questions, and I'm blessed that I have the vision I have—a belief that one sensible person can study the world and learn something of God through the world.

GILMORE: Has that critical dismissal been hard for you?

RICE: Oh, yeah. In the very early days, definitely. People would practically come up to me and say, "I know you've written this calculated potboiler bestseller about a vampire. Well, it's not something I want to read." I wanted terribly to be taken seriously. I wanted to say, "Look, this is not about what you think. Give this a chance!" I was horrified by some of the reviews my work received.

But let me tell you something: I have a real problem with much of the so-called literary fiction of these times. I have not read John Updike or Anne Tyler.

I can't. I try. I just don't get into it. I think that there's a real arrogance to the pedestrian realism of the twentieth-century novel. Not only are books about ordinary people and ordinary lives and ordinary events and little-bitty epiphanies, not only are they *not* worth reading most of the time, they're simply garbage. I think our literature is at a low ebb right now, and there's a lot of reasons we came to this point where we turned away from the incredible power of Nathaniel Hawthorne or Herman Melville or Edgar Allan Poe and have chosen instead to write a diluted version of Henry James over and over again.

The reasons are, I think, more economic than the elite would like to face. It's an outgrowth of industrialization, really. It's the literature of quiet desperation or contentment—a literature that tells you that to try to attempt anything great in your life is unrealistic to the point of being irresponsible and dangerous. It tells you that any novel of substance is going to be about a normal couple in Connecticut or Berkeley and their quarrel over the custody of the children and how they both work it out, each in her or his own way.

The truth is, that is not the only story we have to tell. That is not even what our world is about. Our world is in fact filled with abnormal people and outrageous people and cataclysmic events and extremely romantic stories and acts of incredible heroism, and yet for some reason the upper-middle-class literary writers have decided that that's not worthy subject matter for their books. And they're dogmatic and nasty about it.

GILMORE: Clearly you're a writer who doesn't hedge your feelings. A couple of years ago that outspokenness landed you in a public controversy when you protested Neil Jordan's casting of Tom Cruise for the film version of *Interview with the Vampire*. Looking back on all that now, do you ever regret any of the things you said? Do you feel that possibly you were a bit too hasty in your criticisms?

RICE: My frank feeling is that it turned out so well that I can't think too much about doing anything differently. That's not to say that everything I did was wise or kind or constructive or that everything they did was wise or kind or constructive. I think they were very, very unkind to me and my readers in many respects—the people associated with the making of that movie—and they were very unwise. At the same time, I'm not sure that if I had been on the team whether anybody would have paid any attention to anything I had to say. Whereas when I wasn't on the team—when I was public enemy No. 1— there was a lot of attention paid to the things I said. I don't think people should be rewarded for saying angry and negative things, but in some ways I don't see how the movie could have turned out better. I think it's an absolutely unique film, and I'm very happy with it. I spend almost no time at all regretting anything that happened, and I don't want to hold any grudges, either.

GILMORE: Do you remember at which moment the film won you over?

RICE: When I saw Tom Cruise walking past the mosquito netting around the bed, and I heard his voice, and I saw that he *was* Lestat. I knew it instantly. He had gotten it. And I do credit him. That actor, for some reason, really made a contact with that character, and he produced a fabulous version of him. He made Lestat his own without taking my Lestat from me, and I feel tremendous love for Tom as a result. Now, to what degree I hurt him with my personal comments, or to what degree I spurred him on, that will always be open to debate. I don't want anyone to be hurt, especially not someone as nice as he is. In fact, I don't want anyone to be hurt, even if they're not nice [*laughs*]. But what I said, I said from my heart, and the feeling I got was that he understood. And in my conversations with him, I found him to be just a completely loving person, and I think his take on the books is right-on. He knows the character and understands the character perfectly. I'm not so sure about other people involved in the production, you know. I really don't know. I really don't know Brad Pitt at all. I'm not in any way connected with him. I know the readers loved him. They felt that he captured the guilt in Louis, and they were very pleased with him.

GILMORE: I couldn't help laughing when I read your statement: "I think we should nickname [Brad Pitt] the Barbie Doll from Hell because of the way he behaves toward us 'Vampire Chronicle' people."

RICE: Oh, yes, in my newsletter. Oh, I do think he looks like that [*laughs*], but I meant that lovingly. He's cute, you know? He is cute. But I have to confess, when he was declared the sexiest man in the world, I nearly fell over dead, because he does look to me like the Barbie Doll from Hell. He looks cute and young and like a kid. He looks as if he's about fourteen. That was a teasing comment.

GILMORE: It is possible, of course, that you may be in for a whole new round of controversy with *Memnoch the Devil*. You've written a book that questions the validity of God's ethos in a time when a powerful segment of American Christianity has become an increasingly intolerant, even violent, political force. Plus, the book has a couple of rather inflammatory scenes—

particularly the moment when the vampire Lestat meets Jesus Christ on the road to his Crucifixion.

RICE: It was inflaming to *me*. I didn't find it an easy thing to do, and yet it had the wonderful feeling of something absolutely inevitable and something that *should* happen. I was confronting there the Christ in whom I had believed totally as a young girl when I used to sit in church on Good Friday and imagine his wounds. I was really standing there with that Christ at that moment, and it was an excruciatingly difficult thing to write.

Yes, sometimes I'm afraid for this book. The public is very hard to inflame and very hard to wake up, but when they do notice or take offense at something, they can turn their fury with considerable bad effect, and I'm a bit afraid they may do that with this book. I never felt that way before. At the same time, I don't really think it's true. I think we'd be lucky if people notice that there's a book slated to be a bestseller that actually cares about God and the devil.

The book is so much about God, it's so much about compassion, it's so anti-violence and so anti-blood sacrifice that, to me, it's a wonderful book. I'm very proud of it. I don't really think it's going to draw to itself a lot of opposition, but I could be completely wrong. I'm certainly ready to defend it. I'm ready to stand there and talk about what I think is good in it and to defend it against people who would criticize it and defend the importance of us being able to talk about God and the devil in our work. I mean, we're living in the most amazing times. Amazing and horrible. It's a very exciting time to be a writer.

PART FOUR

Chiaroscuro—Anne Rice and the Cinema

Unlike a book, which is totally under the control of the writer, a film adaptation is usually divorced from the author and, sadly, far too often, divorced from the source material itself.

The stakes are high. A bad film adaptation can permanently cripple a writer's screen reputation. Witness, for instance, the case of *Stand by Me*, *The Shawshank Redemption*, and *Dolores Claiborne*—all are first-rate films based on Stephen King's fiction, though the flood of poorly adapted King works prejudiced moviegoers to the point that, in recent years, the advertising is careful *not* to mention his name, for fear of scaring his potential audience away. ("Aw, hell, it's just another bad King horror movie.") Or, alternately, people see the name King and associate it with horror movies only. ("King? He's that horror meister!")

A *good* film adaptation, on the other hand, has a salutary effect on the writer: Hollywood will want to develop other literary properties, thereby increasing the author's book audience.

The story behind the film adaptation of *Interview with the Vampire* would be, in itself, a book-length study—a book that Rice herself would want to read, as she explained to her fans in *Commotion Strange*. After years of effort, however, Rice's first book made it to the screen, but not without considerable controversy.

What was perceived as a bad casting call—Tom Cruise in the role of the vampire Lestat—became the rallying point for opposition against the movie, months before it was released. The controversy reminded me of a similar one that erupted in the "Star Trek" community when an English actor, Patrick Stewart, was cast as the captain of the *Enterprise* for "Star Trek: The Next Generation." (Today, of course, the fans can't imagine anyone else in that role.)

Just as Winston Groome (author of *Forrest Gump*) was initially unhappy when he heard that Tom Hanks had been cast in the title role, Anne Rice was similarly distressed when she learned that Cruise had been—in her mind— miscast.

Rice's fans and Rice herself expected the worst, but when the film was finally released, the very critics of Cruise have, in the main, become enthusiastic advocates, urging him to reprise his role in *The Vampire Lestat*, optioned by David Geffen.

Take a front-row seat in the cinematic world of movies as seen through Anne Rice's lens as a fan of the flicks. This section begins with Rice's perceptions of the horror film genre—her explication of what makes a horror film work—and ends with a multifaceted look at the first successfully adapted Rice film, *Interview with the Vampire*.

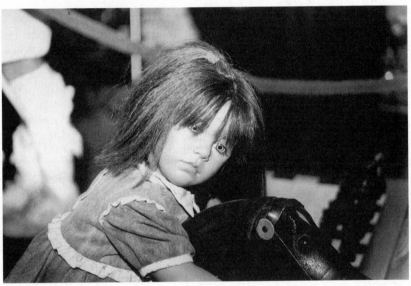

A doll from the Rice collection

Kat Frazier

Anne Rice:
The Art of Horror in Film

as told to Katherine Ramsland

What I like in horror movies are the ones that are heavily atmospheric, have some degree of elegance, and concern really tragic protagonists. Atmosphere has to do with the way the film looks and the way it's filmed, as well as the script and the character. For example, the scene in *The Bride of Frankenstein* where Dr. Pretorius is sitting in this crypt and the monster walks up and says, "Smoke," and he gives him a cigar. To me that's a fabulously elegant and atmospheric scene because of this lean, handsome, smiling doctor under these gorgeous stone arches with all these graves around him, simply taking the monster in stride. It's wonderful. *That* is atmosphere: building scenes carefully, lighting them so that you go into the mood of the scene and you share the mood of the people on the screen. I've seen horror movies where there was none of that. They're real failures.

The Wolf Man, Dracula, the first *Frankenstein*, and *The Bride of Franken-stein*—all of those movies are squarely in that tradition of having atmosphere and tragic characters. They present the monster tremendously sympathetically. In *Frankenstein*, when the monster visits the old blind man and becomes his friend, and when he "accidentally" throws the little girl into the water, he's presented as really capable of suffering, and at the end of *The Bride of Frankenstein*, when he says, "She dead, she belong with me. You go, you living," or whatever, it's a tragic moment. I love that stuff.

I don't really like horror that doesn't have that, but atmosphere and character don't necessarily exist in the same movie. I mean, you can have a wonderfully atmospheric movie but no character. To me, they have to include all those elements. It has to have atmosphere, some degree of elegance, and really great characters with a tragic dimension.

I feel that most of the Stephen King movies have been undistinguished—they have not had great atmosphere and they have not had great photography and that's been their tragedy. Now, I thought there was great atmosphere and photography in *The Shining*, but the characters didn't add up to anything. They weren't as good as in his books. So there's an example of where that just didn't work, as far as I'm concerned.

161

Part Four: Chiaroscuro—Anne Rice and the Cinema

Life-size Pumpkinhead model, on display at the Memnoch Ball 1995

Kat Frazier

Angel Heart is the modern horror classic. It's got atmosphere and there's dimension to the Mickey Rourke character in that film. I thought the suspense, the tension, the photography, the shots of the churches, the glimpses of things in his memory, and the use of New Orleans—it was very atmospheric. Terrific camera work.

Pumpkinhead was, I thought, a wonderful movie. It's what I call a B-movie, a fun B-movie, but it had great atmosphere—the witch's little hut out in the mountains was just fabulous and the mood created by Lance Henriksen's voice and tone and expression, the way he looked like a mountain man—all of that was wonderful. He's the greatest up-and-coming horror-movie actor that we have. He conveys horror. When he's on the screen, he's low-key and wonderful. He looks unique and has a unique voice. You've got to have people in horror movies that convey a believable response to what's going on. He delivers, emotionally. In *Pumpkinhead*, he really does seem terrified. He goes through all these scenes consumed with anger and rage when he wants revenge on the kids who killed his boy; then he seems consumed with guilt and moral conviction that the monster must be stopped. Those kinds of actors give it weight.

That's what we had in the old days when you go back to *The Bride of Frankenstein*—the people played it totally seriously. They went into the romantic vision and you've got to have that. *Rebecca* is really made by Joan Fontaine. The more I watch it, the more I realize her performance is what makes the entire movie work. I thought *Pumpkinhead* was a great combination of all of those elements.

I loved Cronenberg's *The Fly*. He's a gross-out director. *The Fly* to me was Jeff Goldblum—that's what made it. And *The Fly II*. I'd rank them with *Pumpkinhead* as B-movies. There was something that prevented them from being really great. There was some absurdity and comedy. I've been trying to define B-movie. It's a lighter touch, it's absurd things happening and being given very simple explanations. Now, you could say *Angel Heart* does that, too, but there's a way that *Angel Heart* is so psychologically deep and tense that it's making a demand on you that A-movies demand. In some way, *Pumpkinhead* doesn't do that, and neither does *The Fly* or *The Fly II*. There are moments when you can break up and laugh. It's comic-book fun, like *Re-Animator*—when he gets his head chopped off and he tells his head what to do, and he puts his head on that girl's breast—that's hilarious. It's hard to define B-movies because it doesn't have much to do with budget anymore. For me, the Bs are the ones that are sort of genre movies. They're great, but they're not really transcending. But a movie like *Angel Heart* transcends the genre—I don't think there's a comic moment in *Angel Heart*. There's never a moment when you laugh at the hokeyness of what you're watching. But there is in *The Fly*—the idea of him turning into a fly is preposterous.

I also love David Lynch. I loved *Blue Velvet* and *Eraserhead*. I felt I knew exactly what *Eraserhead* was about, awful as it is. There are moments when the world looks exactly like that. I've been through it.

People seem to be behaving like that, and things seem to be absolutely ghastly, and one thing after another is absurdly grotesque and you feel like hitting people around you and saying, "Don't you see it? Don't you see it? Don't you see how horrible this is?" And they don't. I felt *Eraserhead* was that vision, and *Blue Velvet*, too.

I honestly don't know why kids go for those slasher films. I cannot understand Freddy Krueger, Jason, or Michael Myers. They most resemble mummy movies. I did find *The Mummy* terrifying as a kid—that indefatigable force coming on to get you—and that's what those movies seem to be: they're like the stepchildren of *The Mummy*, but they have no moral sense. Good and bad are killed, it doesn't seem to matter. The force can't be stopped. Nothing protects people from it. Not cunning, not morality, not goodness, not deservingness, nothing. There's no depth at all to the monster himself and I just don't like it. To me it's just like a video game—who is he going to kill next?

I thought it was very sad that *Harvest Home* wasn't made into a magnificent film. The way it looks on videotape, it just doesn't have the dimension of beauty that so often happens on the big screen. It doesn't have the same cinematography. I think it could have been a magnificent film. I loved the idea of it. It's very scary, but I'm not sure it would scare me on film if I hadn't read the book. Unfortunately miniseries don't have integrity as a form right now. They jam four or six hours onto a two-hour tape. As long as that goes on, I don't think we can take them seriously. We can't really look at something like *Harvest Home* or *'Salem's Lot* and discuss it the way we can discuss a film. Even when a film is cut, it's not that bad.

The movies I could watch over and over would include *Rebecca*, which does not have a supernatural theme, but is certainly a dark gothic classic film. I've also watched every version of *Jane Eyre* that I can get my hands on—the Timothy Dalton one is magnificent. I've watched *Angel Heart* about five times. *Pumpkinhead* I've watched a number of times, but I think *Pumpkinhead* is more fun. Other B-movies I love are *Re-Animator*—I watch it all the time. I think it's a scream, an absolute howl. I watch *The Bride of Frankenstein* a couple of times a year. I think that is one of the greatest horror movies ever made. The guy playing Dr. Frankenstein is wonderful; everybody in it is great—it's the fullest, richest of the Frankenstein bunch. We really learn about the monster and his capacity for goodness and how he's been betrayed by his maker. I think that movie had the most of the book in it, although it has a silly introduction that ought to be thrown away.

I watch a movie like *The Bride of Frankenstein* over and over to be put in the mood of it. It's like listening to music for me. It's like, "Let's go put on Mahler's Ninth and sink down and listen to that." I want to revisit that mood, I want to be reminded of all of those elements if I'm going to write.

Another movie that I love is *The Thing* with Kurt Russell, for the tension, the suspense, and the interaction between the men as they confront the monster— the way in which macho courage keeps winning out. The most aggressive males survive. I love that. Also, there are no women in it, and to me that's very gutsy. Nowadays, they'd stick some muscular little broad in there, like in *Aliens*. It's gloomy and dark and I love that background music. I also love the theme that you don't know who is one of them.

The same thing in *The Invasion of the Body Snatchers*. That's another of my favorite movies—the Donald Sutherland remake by Kaufman. I think Brooke Adams did a wonderful job. The characters are so good and the photography is excellent—the way they use San Francisco, the way they make it seem claustrophobic and gloomy, and the terrific special effects when those things are growing in the pods. That, to me, is great.

But *The Bride of Frankenstein* is an infinitely greater movie even than those because it has a great theme—a magnificent philosophical theme—and the black-and-white photography was so masterly in that film that it surpasses anything made since.

Another film I really admire is *Frankenstein: The True Story*, written by Christopher Isherwood. I saw that right before I wrote *Interview with the Vampire* and it had an enormous impact on me—almost a frightening impact. I wrote *Interview* with those images from that Frankenstein swimming in my brain. When I created Armand, I was remembering Dr. Frankenstein and the monster going to the opera before he started to break out in bumps and began to decay. I was fascinated by all that, and I know that a lot of my writing was seminally influenced.

I love to be scared in these, too. *The Thing*, to me, was really scary. *Alien* is the scariest movie I've ever seen. I watched *Alien* twice with Stan at the Castro Theater sitting on the front row and both times nearly died. I was really crouching down, holding his arm, and I knew Sigourney Weaver was going to get into the shuttlecraft, but I was so terrified when she turned and looked around that corner and there was the alien standing there and she ran back and tried to disengage the exploding ship. Oh God! To me, that is one of the greatest masterpieces of all horror movies, Ridley Scott's *Alien*.

I don't think any movie is meant to be watched as many times as I watch movies. They almost all fall apart. I think it's deliberately made to have an impact on the first showing. It's not like a novel, where you can stop and go and stop and go. So when we subject these movies to laser disc and tape and we go over them and over them, we do see all kinds of weak links. Every link is perfect in *Alien*.

However, the only movie I would rank with *The Bride of Frankenstein* as a truly immortal horror flick would be *Blade Runner*—the fantastic Ridley Scott film about the replicants. The thing with *Blade Runner* that hits is when Sean Young goes to play the piano and Harrison Ford walks up and she says something like, "I didn't know whether or not I could play. I took lessons." She knows she's a replicant and she doesn't know whether she really took the lessons or the memories were implanted, and whether she has the skill—to me that's a great scene. It's dark. It's beautifully photographed, everything looks burnished, and there's wonderful Harrison Ford who can play anything. *Blade Runner* is pretty damn near perfect for me. In fact, you almost have to see *Blade Runner* about five times to get everything that's happening.

It's because of movies like *Blade Runner* and *Alien* that I think Ridley Scott is the only person who can make the Vampire Chronicles. He's far and away the greatest director to do it. I think our greatest directors are Scorsese, Woody Allen, and Ridley Scott, but Woody Allen and Scorsese wouldn't make this material. So that leaves the magnificent, the great, the untouchable, the incomparable, the inimitable Ridley.

He is the modern master. I wish he would do more horror movies. If Ridley Scott were to get some kind of gig where he could make horror movie after horror movie, like remake *Frankenstein*, remake *Dracula*, do the Vampire Chronicles, do *The Witching Hour*, he'd leave us a legacy that we'd be watching forever. It's very sad to me that the Stephen King movies have not, in the main, been given that kind of attention. I think *'Salem's Lot* could have been magnificent.

If I were coaching the making of the films from my books, I would say, first of all, they have to have someone who knows the horror-movie genre. People who don't know the genre tend to create clichés. The scripts I've seen from Hollywood over the years leave me very little hope that anything is going to be done with the Vampire Chronicles that will be any good. That's not to say that the present group of writers couldn't do something better, but in general, I think a number of things have to come together for those movies to work.

Number one, they have to be flawlessly conceived vampire films. It is absolutely integral to that work that these are cape-wearing creatures of the night and that they present all the accouterments of traditional vampires: they dress beautifully, they seduce their victims, they cannot go out in the sun. If the writers take away that romance and don't make a good vampire film, they are really misunderstanding the material.

Now the philosophical and psychological elements must be there because a vampire film alone isn't what this film is about. They have to create those characters, Lestat and Louis, and they have to get the tragic dimension and the questing nature of those characters because it's part of the imaginative concept of what a vampire is—that these people would learn something in the immortal state and they would have philosophical agonies. If that is taken out—and it's not present in most vampire movies—that's a terrible failure of imagination. So they must keep in those elements that have made the books work for people: the philosophy, the sense of a moral quest, the tragic ability to feel pain, to feel guilt—they must keep those dimensions to the characters.

The third element that I think is crucial, which has been absent in almost every script I've seen, is that they must keep the characters heroic. These are not stupid, bumbling, idiot characters, and it's amazing how scripts do that to them—make them stupid. This has happened to me all the time with Hollywood. I create a character and they depotentiate that character. They think that in order to make him sympathetic, they have to make him slightly stupid or pathetic. They particularly do this with the vampires, because the vampires are killers. So they feel that to make them sympathetic, they have to make them human. Yet these characters are heroic. My whole thesis is that if you're immortal, and you have preternatural strength, vision, and abilities to think, you're going to be a little bit quicker, faster, better, and smarter than human beings; you will have a greater capacity for pain, and you're going to realize the irony of your position very fast. When the writers take that out, it all falls apart.

There was a script of *The Vampire Lestat* that I saw, where he woke up in the twentieth century, climbed out of a hole wearing a cape, didn't know where he was, and was puzzled when people wouldn't take gold coins. That is *Love at First Bite* foolishness. Lestat decided to come up because of what he heard and he knew within twenty minutes where he was—before he even hit the surface. He was perfectly aware of the fact that people wouldn't be using gold coins. But you take away all that and you have another "stupid immortals" movie. To me, *Near Dark* was a "stupid immortals" movie. We're supposed to believe those people are immortal, yet they burn up on the highway because they forget about morning? That's really stupid. And we have a lot of those movies because of our inability to imagine how smart an immortal would have to be.

Those are the elements that would have to come together: get someone who could make a truly gripping vampire film that would include the elegance, the atmosphere, the scariness, and the seductive quality of the kill. They should go back and watch *Dracula's Daughter*—the moment when she seduces the young girl that she brings to her studio: they should watch the subtlety of that. They need that kind of subtlety, they need that kind of atmosphere, they need that kind of gracious touch to the scenes and characters, and then they need the philosophical depth and they need the heroic dimension.

The movie of *The Witching Hour* would have to transcend genre. If they don't do it with quality, it would just be a hokey mess. If I were coaching, I'd say go watch *The Innocents*, the movie based on *The Turn of the Screw*. Watch that for some of the greatest haunting scenes ever made. Get the dilemma of that tortured woman and her fear as she realizes she's in this haunted house, but also her courage—get that quality. Watch *Rebecca*. Try to get the atmosphere as close as the atmosphere of those two films. Try to show the heroic dimensions of the characters—don't make them weak to make them sympathetic. Make Rowan really strong. Don't decide that for her to be feminine and appealing to the audience she has to be a dingbat or a nurse; make her a brain surgeon and get someone like Julia Roberts to play her—someone who has a tremendous amount of inner strength and stature and a unique voice. Get Eric Roberts to play Lasher. Absolutely—that gaunt, haunted look, tremendous poise, that intensity. Get Tom Berenger to play Michael—he's the easiest part; he just has to be a very sweet, very likable, very indefatigable guy, but definitely show his strength and his attractiveness.

The Witching Hour would be so much easier than the vampires because the characters are human. You're showing humans against evil and evil wins. That is much easier to do. The vampires—it's difficult because everyone's a vampire. If you don't get that right, you've got something really disgusting. But even a middling director ought to be able to get some atmosphere in a haunted house, with an old woman and her oil lamp. And with what they can do with special effects today, like in *Ghost*, they ought to be able to do magnificent haunting scenes of Lasher. With the jars and the voices, and all that, they ought to be able to really get it first rate, and there are many quality older actors around who can play Carlotta and Aaron Lightner. The important thing would be to combine those classic elements—the philosophy, the struggle over good and evil, and the elegance, and the atmosphere. I wanted it to be the best, most haunting "old dark house" novel I could write. They have a story, they have a history to that haunting, and they ought to be able to get it right.

Part of my struggle at the machine is to get the words to describe what I can see. But you could convey those qualities with light and subtlety of expression. When Lasher appears and the scene is properly lighted, you can show a character that appears to be the utter embodiment of good and evil, beaming at you and yet terrifying you because he doesn't belong there. That is the big thing with all my books: I see them first very clearly and then I have to get that into words.

One of the reasons I don't protract a scene is because I can't do it. For example, in *The Queen of the Damned* when Mekare kills the queen, it's very quick. I think in a movie, that would be a much longer scene; they will probably convey the violence of that scene much better than I did. I don't mind. That's not my thrust. The same way with Michael's fight with Lasher. That fight can be much longer in film. It can be much more detailed and take more time on screen than it took to read as they fight around the pool and slide around and crash into the water. If they can get the quality of *Angel Heart* in those scenes—the glimpse of a smoldering horrible place, an inferno—it's all subtlety.

I think the core of successful horror films is subtlety. And that's why those scenes in *The Bride of Frankenstein* are so good: they take the time to show the monster's expressions; they let him speak and they develop tension. The camera lingers and the scene blossoms like an evil flower. That's what's needed. You have to show Stella in scene after scene where she appears to be good, and then in that hellish vision, she has to appear to be evil; there has to be a subtlety. That's how I think Lasher needs to be conveyed. Whoever plays that part has to show the capacity for cunning and deception, and yet this near-angelic appearance because he's trying to please the person to whom he's appearing. To me those are the most terrifying scenes I ever wrote. I would love to film the scene where he pushes Cortland down the steps, or where he appears to the doctor, right by him, or where he appears on the porch and he's not real—to me that's what that book is partially about.

Part Four: Chiaroscuro—Anne Rice and the Cinema

I don't think people in Hollywood honestly understand why these books are so popular. I don't think they understand the hold they have on the public imagination. This is the tragic flaw. *Presumed Innocent* is a very good case in point. I had reviewed that book for *The New York Times* and I'd read it with unusual care. I think they rendered that movie very well. In general, they used what the public had responded to in the book and it worked. *Gone with the Wind* did this, and *Jane Eyre* and *Rebecca*—these are amazingly faithful renderings, but in my conversations with some people in Hollywood, I have found that they don't know why my books are popular. They don't know

---

ANNE RICE AT THE (VAMPIRE) MOVIES

from New Orleans *Times-Picayune*
(October 30, 1988)

Nosferatu, the Vampire (1921): "Absolutely the most terrifying vampire I've glimpsed on the screen. Absolutely terrifying. Stan had a dream he met the Nosferatu figure in a field. It was going to kill him, and the way he managed to save his life was by flattering him."

Dracula (1931): "Quaint and wonderful fun. I love it. But it's not scary anymore. It's too old, too creaky, too boring, too slow. But Bela Lugosi is just a treat."

Dracula's Daughter (1936): "It has one of the most seductive kill scenes ever. A great victimization sequence. Very subtle."

'Salem's Lot (1979): "A pretty disappointing tele-movie. I think the book (by Stephen King) could have gone with a real theatrical motion picture treatment, a richer treatment. I thought it was a very good book."

Love at First Bite (1979): "I loved it. George Hamilton is the handsomest vampire on the screen. I get a lot of mileage out of that film, silly as it is. But the humor is just wonderful."

The Hunger (1983): "Very beautiful, very moving. Destined to be a classic. It handled the vampires in an interesting way. Catherine Deneuve's performance was wonderful and David Bowie was fabulous. Should be in everybody's vampire-flick library."

The Lost Boys (1987): "I thought it was fun. I got a kick out of it. The boys hanging upside down in the cave was terrific, a nice touch."

really what makes them work for the readers, and they're eager to gobble up the material for their own purposes.

I think we're in a wonderful period right now. There were about twenty or thirty years when no really good horror movies were made, not that I can think of. Hammer studios was making sort of schlocky ones in the sixties and seventies, but that situation began to change, maybe with *The Exorcist*, then *Ghost Story*. I thought *Ghost Story* accomplished a great deal. It wasn't as rich as the book, but it was very interesting, and then of course the popularity of Stephen King and Peter Straub caused more attention to the whole genre. That has produced a lot of bad movies, but it also has produced some wonderful ones. I think all kinds of things are happening. The public is obviously responding very strongly and people have gotten interested again in horror films on all levels, from the very schlocky to the very fine. So to me, this is a very rich and wonderful period. As usual, it's disappointing how unimaginative much of it is, and how imitative, but I have high hopes. I think it's a great time for horror-movie fans. When we go in the video store, we're more likely now than in the past to find something to see.

Horror is important to me and I enjoy it so much and feel so at home with it that I can't see it objectively. I just know that when I'm watching something like *Angel Heart* or *Blade Runner*, I feel an intensity that is several notches above that of a film without those elements. I can't explain it. Perhaps detective freaks love detective films in the same way. I just know that's what turns me on and I can't define it. Critics have written so much on that. I think one critic wrote something about there always being something extra in the horror movie. Someone else said that the horror movie is always erotic. I really don't feel that particularly. But certainly I'm a writer who is obsessed with the erotic and with horror, so perhaps they do work together. I'm so close to it that I can't really feel it. I've tried to analyze it and the explanations I think fall short: I feel like an outsider, I think most people do. I think when we're watching a horror movie, we're watching someone who's a monster, an outsider. We're watching him struggle with that dilemma and it's terrifying. But those explanations sound curiously academic and removed, and I just know that I love the stuff. I absolutely love it. The first movie I remember seeing was *Hamlet*, and the only scene I remember was the ghost scene and the scene with Ophelia floating downstream in the flowers. Those scenes would seem to be seminal in my life and in my work. I remember in high school when I had hardly read one novel in my whole life, I read *Great Expectations* and there was that wonderful gothic stuff with Miss Havisham. I don't think that's the answer, to say, "Well, she saw this and she was influenced by that." The truth is, other people saw those things and they were not influenced. So I don't know the real reason. I just know that it strikes some deep, deep chord in me.

I wrote a story once, called "Die, Die, My Darling," in which I tried to describe my sense of it. It was about a bunch of hippies watching TV, smoking grass. One of the hippie women complains about how her intensity puts everybody off. So they're watching this hokey movie called *Die! Die! My Darling!* with Tallulah Bankhead, and there's this scene where Tallulah Bankhead pauses on this gothic staircase and is about to try to murder her daughter-in-law. The hippie freaks out and says, "That's me. I am that woman and I am on that staircase forever and I am always trying, and I am the daughter being killed. I am all those people. That's it! That's it!" There have been many times when I have tried to write something that expresses that feeling of, "There I am, that's it!"

At moments like that, I know exactly what it's about and I know why I feel that I'm in it. Like to write the scene where Louis crawls into that crypt in the cemetery in Montmartre—that feels *so* normal to me, much more normal than sucking blood. Like with the Mayfairs in *The Witching Hour* when Rowan walked in the door of the house. I just loved it. I felt, "Okay, here it is at last. This is really it!" It's *that* feeling. And very few movies get it.

Commotion Strange #2

Extracts from Anne Rice's Zine

Why do you sell the rights to your books for movies?

The answer to this is simple. I love movies. I love them more than other peoples' books. I LOVE MOVIES! I watch movies constantly, I believe in them not only as entertainment but as an art form, and I am more inspired by them than by contemporary novels by other authors. The truth is I don't read anyone else's fiction these days. I used to, of course, and I still return all the time to Franz Kafka, Virginia Woolf, Nathaniel Hawthorne, Edgar Allan Poe, Dickens, Carson McCullers, Nabokov, Shakespeare, Hemingway, and a host of other writers whom I read frantically during my twenties and thirties and forties. They are my nourishment. I have their books all over my office.

But at some point, the writer in me took over from the reader, and as I pound away at the keyboard, turning my own dreams into narrative, I find that movies are my mainline to the contemporary culture.

When I knock off at night, exhausted, having finished a scene in a book, I sink down on the couch and turn on a laser disc of a film. My mind simply cannot relax into someone else's fiction.

Of course there will come again a season of reading. These things move in cycles. I know. But this right now is a season of film watching for me, and I feel I'm learning a great deal from film—about the world, about the souls of men and women, about life itself.

And having derived so much inspiration from films, having loved them so much, having grown up worshipping directors like Ingmar Bergman, and Frederico Fellini, Antonioni, and Truffaut, I dream of seeing my books made into great films. I see my books as films. They unreel before my eyes as films. I imagine them three dimensionally and in Technicolor as I write.

It's the love of film, the dream of great films, that keeps me connected with Hollywood—the dream that a genius director and an inspiring star will come together to make a movie of one of my books. It has happened once, and I'm dreaming it will happen again.

At the moment, David Geffen is my hero. I feel that he protected and sustained *Interview with the Vampire* until it became a film.

Part Four: Chiaroscuro—Anne Rice and the Cinema

Present plans for a movie that I would like to talk about now:

Belinda. This is a novel I wrote under the name Anne Rampling, but it was really a hybrid—a work done by me as the contemporary author Rampling, and also as the obsessed and somewhat dark writer, Rice. The point of the book was that Belinda was a heroine. She was good. She was seventeen, but she was a woman. She was trapped in childhood, and she had a right to seek out an older lover for herself, a man she felt was worthy of her, even though for him, making love to Belinda was breaking the law.

I am very excited about the fact that Tom Berenger, an actor I greatly love and admire, wants to make *Belinda*. I think the time is right for a story about a girl's love and desire for a man. And I can't think of a more desirable man, myself, than Tom Berenger. He will be perfect for the artist and writer, Jeremy Walker, in this novel, who loves Belinda, but knows he is risking his entire career by loving her because she is "under age."

Just yesterday I read in the news that a studio was contemplating a remake of *Lolita*. The article indicated the makers of the film planned to make it much more erotic than the Kubrick version of years ago in which Sue Lyon romped with James Mason. I couldn't be more thrilled!

I think this is one of many signs that the time is right for *Belinda*! I'm going to do anything I can to assist Tom Berenger in setting up *Belinda* and getting the project going. I hope to meet Mr. Berenger personally and discuss with him—as I have already done in writing—how important it is to me that Belinda be my heroine, that the movie be explicit and positive about her healthy and wholesome desire for Jeremy Walker, and her own dilemma as a young woman.

Belinda is no molested child. She is like Mona Mayfair in *Lasher* or *Taltos*—one of my heroines for this time.

For Berenger aficionados, let me recommend these films: *Someone to Watch over Me*, directed by Ridley Scott, a truly magical film; *Last Rites* in which T.B. plays a priest, an excellent and suspenseful film filled with delicious religious imagery both in New York and in Mexico, a film that deserved more attention than it got. Berenger was also in *Platoon* as everybody probably knows, and he has a great flair for comedy which came out marvelously in *Major League*. He has made other wonderful films. I'm still in the process of gathering them all on laser disc. Right now I'm looking for a film set in Ireland, called *The Field*.

I based Michael Curry physically on Tom Berenger when I wrote *The Witching Hour*. But I don't know if Berenger will ever play that role in the film. *The Witching Hour* is in development and, as I've said before, the whole question of influence or control is very, very hard to clarify for anyone, especially me.

Some films of the last two years I want to recommend to my readers.

I'm going now on instinct. I loved these films: I'm assuming that if you like my work you might enjoy these films too:

The Piano. Don't miss this one! It is genius. This is tragedy and romance in the deepest sense of those words. This is "serious." This is magnificent. Maybe one of the most important films ever.

True Romance with Christian Slater, Dennis Hopper, Christopher Walken, and numerous other wonderful actors. This is a brilliant film. Very crisp, very complex, very erotic, and very violent. It shows violence for what it is, and takes on the question of why violence is so romantic to us as Americans, why we are so obsessed with it in our entertainment. I would love to write more about this film later on. Bear with me. *True Romance* is worth seeing more than once.

Tombstone. Maybe one of the most fun westerns ever made. Worth it for watching Kurt Russell alone. Worth it for Val Kilmer's knock dead brilliant performance as Doc Holliday. I mean Kilmer in this film is beyond belief. There are some things in this film I don't understand, but if it's a mixed bag, it's a big delicious, luscious mixed bag. Check it out! Val Kilmer achieves so much here that it makes me lightheaded to think of his coming to us as Batman.

Stargate. I've recommended this one before and let me do it again. It's fun. It's light. In that I mean it does not take on the deep dark questions, and it is one of the few movies [recently] to which you could take a three-year-old child with no risk of that child being traumatized. It mixes the mythology of Ancient Egypt with the science fiction theories about the pyramid in a rather charming and very suspenseful way. The production values are high, the film is thrilling. It's good.

It was on the basis of a clip of this film, that I decided to sell the rights to *The Mummy* to Coralco. Roland Emmerich directed *Stargate*, and I hope he will do *The Mummy*. Emmerich, I think, is destined for greater and greater films. He knows how to do the fun action film superbly, but he brings to it a tenderness and compassion which you don't find in some of the other action directors. I felt his *Moon 44* was a very interesting film, too. This one's old. The tape I rented was wretched. Good luck.

Part Four: Chiaroscuro—Anne Rice and the Cinema

Dark Man. This is an older film. But if you enjoyed *The Crow*, if you went to see the *The Shadow*, if you liked *Dick Tracy*, you just may find your ultimate comic book masterpiece in *Dark Man.* It was made by Sam Rami, who seemed to understand how serious we want these movies to be. We don't want to be patted on the head, or exploited. If we enter the comic book milieu we want to take our brains and our hearts with us. *Dark Man* never insults us for an instant. It's mesmerizing. Liam Neeson is the star of *Dark Man.*

Now, thanks to *Schindler's List*, we all know what a genius Neeson is. So that confers a retroactive blessing on *Dark Man.* Like those of us who loved him as Dark Man can say, "See! We told you he was a great actor!" He never compromises in *Dark Man.* He plays the role as seriously as he played the role in *Schindler's List.*

That's the trick, I think, with our kind of films—fantasy, sci fi, speculative, imaginative, surreal—whatever we call them. We take the films seriously and we want the film makers to do that too. As a writer, I believe in my vampires. I am Lestat when we go out together. The only way to make films like *Interview with the Vampire* work is to do them straight, utterly straight.

---◆---

Interview with the Author of
Interview with the Vampire

conducted by Martha Frankel
(Jan/Feb 1994)

Over a Caesar salad at the St. Regis Hotel in New York, Anne Rice talks about the casting of *Interview with the Vampire*, about what actors turn her on, and about how she thinks up all the stuff that turns her readers on.

◆

MARTHA FRANKEL: So let me quote you: "You can't imagine how much I despise Hollywood producers and the studio system and many of the people there. I think they're awful, I can't warn writers enough to stay away from them. They will kill you."

ANNE RICE: [Laughter]

FRANKEL: Don't hold back, Anne. Tell us how you really feel.

RICE: Well, it's true, I've had a lot of different experiences in Hollywood, some I'm not really at liberty to talk about. I've been through a lot of bullshit and foolishness.

FRANKEL: Connected with *Interview with the Vampire*?

RICE: I've been involved with *Interview with the Vampire* for a long time. I've had a good relationship with [producer] David Geffen, although it's kind of iffy right now. When I was working on the script for *Interview*, I told him I wanted to do exactly what I wanted to do with it. And that's the way I wrote it. [Director] Neil Jordan has rewritten it, and they are putting his name on the credits, and I don't know if you know, but the WGA will only allow a director to share writing credit if he brings over 50 percent original material. I don't know if he's done that or not. Maybe he has.

FRANKEL: You haven't read the script?

RICE: No, I haven't. The last draft I did see was an in-progress draft that was extremely close to the book and my script. He actually put things back

177

from the book that I had left out, so it's possible that he can get credit for that as original material. I really can't evaluate until they shoot it.

FRANKEL: Do you think Neil Jordan is a good choice for director?

RICE: Well, I concurred in the choice, and was actually very excited about it. I had always loved *The Company of Wolves*. I mentioned it in the Vampire novels as one of the movies they watched. And I thought *The Crying Game* was amazing. My first choice would have been Ridley Scott, but he turned David Geffen down. David Cronenberg was also somebody I wanted badly, and I understand he turned it down. When I was presented with the idea of Neil Jordan, I thought, he's got courage, he isn't scared by gender, he loves to play with transcending gender and gender illusions and tricks. He'll know how to work with those characters without being afraid of their homoerotic quality. I still have faith in Neil Jordan. I just don't know. The Tom Cruise casting is so bizarre, it's almost impossible to imagine how it's going to work, and it's really almost impossible to imagine how Neil and David and Tom could have come up with it. I have one question: Does Tom Cruise have any idea of what he's getting into? I'm not sure he does. I'm not sure he's read any of the books other than the first one, and his comments on TV that he wanted to do something scary and he loved "creature features" as a kid, well, that didn't make me feel any better. I do think Tom Cruise is a fine actor. [But] you have to know what you can do and what you can't do.

FRANKEL: Let's talk about who would have made a good Lestat.

RICE: Well, Jeremy Irons would have been fabulous.

FRANKEL: Too old.

RICE: Oh, but he looked so good in *Damage*. When an actor's that great and he has a voice that's that great and a face that's that great . . . he could have done the role. He would have to have been made up to look younger, and he would have to have had wild blond hair, but he could have done it. All these characters are supposed to be immortal and they're supposed to be preternatural, so I'm not sure really young people can play them with the kind of depth that Jeremy Irons had in *Damage* and *Dead Ringers*.

FRANKEL: Who else?

RICE: I think John Malkovich could have done it. Peter Weller I thought could make an interesting Lestat. Alexander Godunov, who was in *Witness*. They needed an overpowering person like that, very blond, very tall, very athletic, very full. I think Brad Pitt would be a fabulous Lestat. I tried for a long time to tell them that they should just reverse these roles—have Brad Pitt [who is cast as Louis] play Lestat and have Tom Cruise play Louis. Of course, they don't listen to me.

FRANKEL: So it's not just a bad dream, huh? Tom Cruise is really going to play Lestat?

RICE: Oh, the choice is just so bizarre. Yes, he could do Louis, he could do that part, the brooding, dark, guilt-ridden, passive, reflective, reactive thing. But here's Brad Pitt, he did that wonderful thing with his hips in *Thelma & Louise*, remember that? I've watched that performance over and over again. And *A River Runs Through It*, you know, the grave, religious male romance about fly-fishing? This is a guy who could play Lestat.

FRANKEL: I think Christopher Walken would have made a good Lestat.

RICE: I think he could have done it, too. I think sometimes he plays parts a little cooler than I wish he would. But I thought he looked spectacular in *Batman Returns*. I was a big fan of that movie.

FRANKEL: So what about when they were talking about Cher and Anjelica Huston to be Lestat?

RICE: Oh, my editor, Vicky Wilson, really wanted Anjelica Huston to be Lestat. I wrote the script in which Cher was supposed to play Louis, not Lestat. Julia Phillips and I were developing that together, and the whole idea was that Louis would be a transvestite woman. At that time in history, you could own your own plantation and run things if you were a man, [but] you couldn't if you were a woman. It was the French law. So this was a woman who dressed like a man, and otherwise it was exactly the same as *Interview with the Vampire*.

FRANKEL: How'd you hook up with Julia Phillips?

RICE: Julia was trying to buy the rights to *The Vampire Lestat*, and Paramount still had *Interview*, and we hooked up. I called her and we started to talk about everything from there on, and we had a great friendship for a long time. Julia's very intense and I think her future as a writer is going to be spectacular. And I think she can do her novels and free herself from the whole Hollywood thing.

Well, *Interview* I sold in 1976 to Paramount, and then when it reverted back. Julia had *The Vampire Lestat*, and the contract that now exists was done for Julia. You know, it was us together. She was very much in communication with me, and would listen and run her ideas by me and vice versa. It was then inherited by Geffen. I always knew, theoretically, Julia could be fired, but Julia was the one that kept getting it together, so I never thought that would happen. But then she wrote things about Geffen [in her book, *You'll Never Eat Lunch in This Town Again*] that he perceived to be unkind and he fired her.

FRANKEL: What strikes me as funny is that Hollywood thinks of itself as so naughty, but there are things in your books that will never be shown on-screen.

RICE: Right. Unless I don't know what Neil Jordan is going to do with *Interview with the Vampire*.

FRANKEL: You've written some soft-core pornography . . .

RICE: It's hard-core.

FRANKEL: What's the difference?

RICE: By hard-core, I mean it is absolutely uncompromising. It contains the most detailed sex scenes that I knew how to write. I would imagine that soft porn means kind of blurring of the genitalia and stuff, and my stuff doesn't do that.

FRANKEL: No, it certainly doesn't. . . . You say you watch a lot of movies, so let's talk about the ones that you thought were erotic.

RICE: I've been influenced by films. I watch them so much because I'm a very slow reader, and when I want to unwind, I put a movie on. I find Tom Berenger and Kurt Russell just delightful to look at.

FRANKEL: Tom Berenger, huh?

RICE: Yeah, Tom Berenger has the greatest neck and chest. When I was writing *The Witching Hour*, I would take time off and watch *Someone to Watch over Me* just to base the character Michael on Tom Berenger. One of the sexiest things I ever saw was him walking around the apartment with the gun in *Someone to Watch over Me*. I just loved it. Another movie I loved is *Last Rites*, where he plays the priest from St. Patrick's Cathedral. That scene where he gets into bed with that Jezebel—I cannot sit still and watch that. I didn't think it was a great film, but I thought he did a fantastic job.

FRANKEL: Have you ever met him?

RICE: No, no. But when *The Witching Hour* came out, I asked CAA [Berenger's agency] to send him a copy and say, "These characters are based on you."

FRANKEL: And you never heard from him?
RICE: No.

FRANKEL: Did you go see *Sliver* because he was in it? That would show real devotion.
RICE: I saw it on disc. I thought it was very interesting. Again, it wasn't a great film. He's generally better than the films he's in.

FRANKEL: Did you watch him in *At Play in the Fields of the Lord?*
RICE: I was waiting for him to take his shirt off. I knew that would happen. But when he took off everything, I almost died. Kurt Russell is worth watching, just to see his arms. He was good in *Backdraft*. I thought that was a hilariously romantic film. You talk about male romance . . . *A River Runs Through It* was a fishing romance, *Backdraft* was a fireman's romance. As I get older I like looking at those kind of men. I just adore Arnold Schwarzenegger, I'll watch him in anything.

FRANKEL: Tom, Kurt . . . and Arnold?
RICE: I've written a book called *The Mummy*, and I wish—we have people interested in it and it's moving very slowly—but I wish Arnold Schwarzenegger would play that role. See, I think coming out of the wrappings as Ramses the Great with that terrific voice and that gorgeous physique, it'd be great. It would be something totally different for him. I've yet to see him in a film that I thought was really as good as he was. You know, he does films that I think are very easy for him. I'm sure he works extremely hard, but I would love to see him really have a juicy role.

FRANKEL: I'm sorry, but this Arnold thing, I can barely believe this.
RICE: Arnold's not what he seems. That's what I've been telling my mother-in-law. You've got to watch his films. The guy has this great sensitivity. The voice is beautiful. The mystery of that voice, and the compassion in his face, and the gentleness at the core . . . that's what does it. It's not what you think. The reason I wanted him so badly to play Ramses, too, is the voice. That's a very sexy thing to me, men's voices. I think Berenger's voice is just great. But to really refine this answer: Berenger is about the most erotic thing in film. I really do look at his films just to look at him. *Someone to Watch over Me* is almost hard to watch, it's so erotic . . . it's Berenger porn!

FRANKEL: What other movies do you find sexy?
RICE: I thought *Henry and June* was very sensuous, and I particularly liked

Uma Thurman. I thought *Last Tango in Paris* was wonderful. I think when you go back to *Last Tango* and films like that, the films of today seem very tame. That was a wild phase in film. *Pretty Baby* was a shocking film for me. I saw it again recently and left uneasy, because of the way it uses Brooke Shields. I thought the TV show "Beauty and the Beast" was tremendously sexy. Linda Hamilton was wonderful and Ron Perlman is great. I think he could play the Mummy, too.

FRANKEL: You like the oddest actors.

RICE: They're all hunks. To me, this is not a superficial thing. This is a very deep, sensuous thing. At this point in my life, in novels like *The Witching Hour*, I'm describing that kind of man. I never did it in my earlier novels. I was describing Eric Roberts—whom I also love, you know, some ethereal figure that is part angel, part male. I'm really enjoying expanding in this way. This is just the pornographer in me talking, but I would love to make a film with Berenger.

FRANKEL: So, you hate Hollywood, but you love movies.

RICE: I love film, and I think my feelings about Hollywood are pretty much the feelings of many, many writers. You know, you go there and you think so much can be done, and then you start to discover how many people are messing around who don't know anything.

FRANKEL: What about Daniel Day-Lewis? Would he have made a good Lestat?

RICE: If he had played Lestat we wouldn't be in this dilemma, but he turned it down. Even then, I suggested to Neil Jordan that it be reversed, that Daniel Day-Lewis play Louis and Brad Pitt play Lestat, but I don't think he agreed with me. I'm not even sure he understood me. Neil Jordan, by the way, is extraordinarily nice, one of the most gentle, kind human beings. In fact, I fear for him in Hollywood. I don't know how somebody decent can survive with those panthers out there. I don't know.

FRANKEL: You haven't mentioned *Bram Stoker's Dracula*. What did you think of it?

RICE: I didn't care for it. I didn't think it was sexy at all. But I love Francis Coppola. I thought *The Godfather* was great, and I was hoping he'd give us a Godfather of vampire movies. But I don't think he took it seriously. He thought it was a fun thing that he could do anything with. And he did anything. He'd show a great image, and then everything would go wild, and the power of the image would be lost. And then another great image would come up, and it would be lost, and I just didn't get it. And why he chose for Gary Oldman to look like Glenn Close, I have no idea.

FRANKEL: Was Tim Burton ever going to do *Interview with the Vampire*?

RICE: No, but I did write a script last year, a remake of *Frankenstein and Bride of Frankenstein*, and we wanted very badly for Tim Burton to do that. I did have one meeting with him. He was very charming. I think he later decided not to do the project, but I have tremendous admiration for him.

FRANKEL: So, just to make sure the record's straight, what's the biggest reason Tom Cruise is no good to play Lestat?

RICE: I don't think I've ever fallen under the spell of an actor when the voice wasn't a big component, and of course the very sad thing about Tom Cruise is he does not have that kind of distinct voice. How is he possibly going to say those lines? How is he gonna exert the power of Lestat? Over and over in the books, I say, you know, Lestat's voice was purring in my ear, or the voice was like toughened velvet, and here's this actor with no voice. I don't know how it's gonna work. Maybe he will drop out.

FRANKEL: Are you a loose cannon? Are they trying to tell you to shut up already?

RICE: No. I got one call in the very beginning. Actually, my readers had been screaming for several weeks before I started. Some people were blaming me. "How could you let this happen?" So finally, when I was contacted by the *L.A. Times*, I said what was on my mind. After about three weeks of trying to live with it, I was sitting at my desk and I realized I was just so angry at Neil Jordan that he'd let this happen, that I couldn't contain it any longer. I finally erupted in a conversation, but it had already blown like Vesuvius. It's not my doing. David Geffen doesn't know who Louis is or who Lestat is. Perhaps David's never even read *Interview with the Vampire*. I didn't ever get the impression that he had. Maybe at some point somebody read it to him, or he's heard the tape. They want you to believe in Hollywood that you need them, that they can change your life, and I think they're afraid of writers in some ways because they think they can't control us. There's a point where we can walk away. We don't need them, you know. If they say to me, you'll never eat lunch in this town again, my answer would be, "Do you promise?" I don't want to ever eat lunch in this town!

To My Readers:
A Personal Statement by Anne Rice
Regarding the Motion Picture
Interview with the Vampire

In Variety *(September 23, 1994) and in the* Advocate *(a gay magazine), Anne Rice took out ads that, as* Publishers Weekly *later explained, "described Rice's unequivocal pleasure and deep-felt gratitude for the film of that first novel. (It had been under development for 17 years.) Since she is concerned about being misquoted, her lengthy, passionate statement can be reprinted only in its entirety. Suffice it to say that her statement was a complete turnaround from earlier comments about her displeasure with the casting of the movie, especially Tom Cruise as the Vampire Lestat."*

The full text follows.

◆

On September 16, 1994, I saw a videocassette of the up and coming film *Interview with the Vampire*.

This film is directed by Neil Jordan, and stars Tom Cruise, Brad Pitt, Kirsten Dunst, Antonio Banderas, Stephen Rea and Christian Slater. It was produced by Stephen Woolley and David Geffen. It will be released this fall.

Unable to attend a recent sneak preview at the invitation of the producers, I was trusted with this tape by David Geffen so that I could have an early look at the film because it is based on my first novel, which was published in 1976—the first of the Vampire Chronicles.

This was for me an event of indescribable excitement. Living in a dramatic clutter of laserdiscs, and videotapes, I am nourished daily by movies, loving them as much as books. All my life I have looked to films for inspiration, consolation, amusement and enlightenment; and here at last was a tape of the film based on my own book.

I am making this personal statement now for my readers, and for myself.

If you have no interest in this, don't read it. It's not a news story. I paid for the space. I don't want to be misquoted; I don't want my statement cut to pieces. So I bought the page, and please feel free to turn it whenever you wish.

To My Readers: A Personal Statement

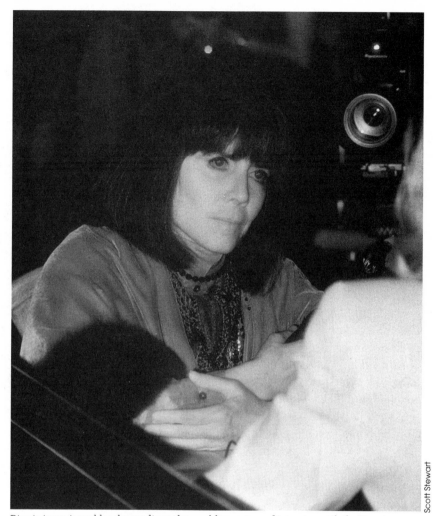

Rice is interviewed by the media at the world premiere of *Interview with the Vampire*.

What I have to say is this:

I loved the film. I simply loved it. I loved it from start to finish, and I found myself deeply impressed with every aspect of its making, including its heartfelt and often daring performances by all the actors and actresses, its exquisite set design and cinematography, and its masterly direction. But most personally, I was honored and stunned to discover how faithful this film was to the spirit, the content, and the ambience of the novel, *Interview with the Vampire*, and of the script for it which I wrote. I was shocked to discover that Neil Jordan had given this work a new and distinctive incarnation in film without destroying the aspects of it which I hold so dear.

I never dreamed it would turn out this way.

Never during seventeen years of development had I ever expected the film version of this book to emerge with so much of the heart and soul intact. Many scripts for *Interview with the Vampire* have crossed my desk over the years. In Hollywood restaurants, on Hollywood patios, at lunch tables at Le Dome and dinner tables at Morton's. I have talked and dreamed aloud about this film so many times I don't want to remember it all. And I have shed more tears over this process than I care to admit.

But this film surpassed my maddest expectations. Fearlessly it presented the love shared by the fictional characters, Lestat, Louis, Claudia and Armand; fearlessly it told the story of the making of the child Vampire Claudia; fearlessly it allowed my tormented vampire outsiders to transcend gender, and to speak from their souls about matters of life and death, love, loneliness, guilt and pain.

The charm, the humor, and the invincible innocence which I cherish in my beloved hero Lestat are all alive in Tom Cruise's courageous performance; the guilt and suffering of Louis are poignantly portrayed by Brad Pitt; the enigma of Armand is embodied in Antonio Banderas; the role of the Interviewer is handled perfectly by Christian Slater; Stephen Rea is delightfully sinister as Santiago; and Kirsten Dunst's mesmerizing performance as my tragic Claudia broke my heart.

In addition, the cinema maniac in me loved the pace of the movie, its tension, its suspense, its deep and spectacular sensuality. I loved its comic moments. I loved its stamina. I loved its relentless intensity, and its success as pure entertainment. I could not have hoped for anything better. I repeat, I never dared to hope for so much.

I thank everyone connected with this film—regardless of their motives or feelings—for attempting and accomplishing a unique work.

And I thank you, my readers—who wrote letters to me, the press, the studio, and the producers, who called to express your opinions, who came out in droves to my book signings to speak your hearts about this film, and about its casting and content.

Guys, you were great. You gave me to know that the book I'd written meant something to you. You gave me to know that Lestat, Louis and Claudia had a life in your minds, as well as in mine.

To My Readers: A Personal Statement

I wish every author could know the happiness you gave to me. I love you for it. And I hope and pray that I never let you down.

The recent development of the film has been an exquisitely painful process for me. Perhaps that's as it should be, given the nature of the book. But undoubtedly the process was painful or uncomfortable for others as well. I wish all of this could have been avoided. I wish that no one had been hurt, or insulted, or slighted or confused. But film making is an art, collaborative or not, and art can be vampiric; it can take all the tears and blood you have to give.

When you see this film, I think you will marvel, along with me, as to how something that developed with so many difficulties and so much controversy could turn out to give so many people what they want.

I think you will embrace the film as I do. I think you will find it spellbinding as I did. I think you will find it such a rich and sincere and unusual offering that if one part fails you, another will compensate for that disappointment; if one twist puts you off, another scene will engulf you; if any one incident doesn't please you, another will sweep you away.

If I'm wrong, if you don't like the picture—let me know. Laugh in my face. Write me letters. Come to the bookstores when I'm there and scream. I can take it. I've never been a cautious person. I have to stick my neck out now and say I think this film is great. I can't wait for Siskel and Ebert; I have to go on record immediately in my excessive and impulsive fashion.

I am proud to have my name connected with the screenplay and the film of *Interview with the Vampire*.

SEE THIS FILM, GUYS. SEE IT!

All my love to you,

Anne Rice

P.S. Be prepared to give the studio, the producers, the stars and everybody else just as much advice and help with the sequel as you did with this first film! By this time, perhaps they will be used to us.

PAID FOR BY ANNE RICE. PERMISSION IS GRANTED TO ANYONE TO REPRINT THIS STATEMENT AS LONG AS IT IS REPRINTED IN ITS ENTIRETY.

◆
Sucking Up

by Anthony Lane

I was honored and stunned to discover how faithful this film was to the spirit, the content, and the ambience of the novel, Interview with the Vampire, and of the script for it which I wrote.

Anne Rice, reassuring her readers, in a two-page ad in the *Times*

◆

To Anne Rice
A Personal Statement by
the Vampire Lestat
Regarding the Novel
Interview with the Vampire

On October 8, 1994, I finally got around to reading your novel *Interview with the Vampire.*

The book is, I am told, a worldwide success, but, as you know, the world has never interested me that much, and I have better things to do at bedtime than sit and read. When I think of all the novels recommended to me over the last two hundred years, I shudder at the hours that I wasted on Mr. Stoker, with his quaint "effects," or that vulgar little tramp Mary Shelley.

But a few days ago, still recovering from my exertions at Milan fashion week, I spent the night in the company of your prose.

I am making this personal statement now for my victims, and for myself. It's not a news story. I paid for the space. O.K., I had to rip a couple of throats along the way, but you know publishing.

What I have to say is this:

I loved your book. I simply loved it. I read it to a couple of naval recruits, and they loved it, too. It surpassed my maddest expectations, although personally I would have cut back on the adjectives a teeny bit. But I was honored and stunned to discover how faithful this novel was to the spirit, the content, and the ambience of my life. I was moved by your poignant sympathy, and touched by the good sense with which you banished the old mirror-and-garlic stuff. I mean, I have the sign of the cross on the front of my *car.* Having said hat, I notice you still buy all that crap about white faces, leeched lips, etc.

Sucking Up

Wake up, honey. Has Clinique not reached New Orleans, or what? And I know you think the books are "really" about guilt and suffering, and the plight of the outsider, but what did you expect me to do? Get married? Let me tell you, outside is a fun place to be. For one thing, I like to watch.

But these are just quibbles. Basically, I'm one lucky immortal. Anne, you are great. I wish every pansexual bloodsucker could know the happiness you gave to me. I love you for it. And I hope and pray, for your sake, that you never meet me.

And now I have a confession to make. I adored the book so much that I went and bought the sequels, and I loved them, too. I loved their stamina, their relentless intensity. And my undead friends in Hollywood tell me that a motion picture is on the way. At last! It must be *years* since I first made those polite inquiries. Never had much time for movies myself, not since von Stroheim died. But some while back, deep in my usher-and-bellhop phase, I spent an evening at the pictures, and there onscreen was this juicy little piece called Cruise, and I thought, *yes*. If anyone ever wanted to play me— no, to become me—it would be that boy. I'm so moved that somebody was kind enough to take an old vamp's advice.

So, did you see the movie? In a theatre, or only on tape? I hear you couldn't get to the screening because of a blood-related problem. Love it.

If I'm wrong, if you don't like the picture—let me know. Laugh in my face. Write me letters. Call me. I have to stick my neck out and say your book is great, and I'm sure the movie is great, too. Do forgive me if I skip the premiere; I have some travelling plans that can't be put off. As I always say, if you're destined to roam the earth for the rest of time, you might as well make a party of it—you know, really *roam*. It's so simple these days; who needs coffins in the hold when you can fly to Europe overnight and still arrive in the dark? I always travel Virgin myself. The stewards taste so fresh.

All my love to you,

Lestat

PAID FOR BY THE VAMPIRE LESTAT. PERMISSION IS GRANTED TO REPRINT THIS STATEMENT AS LONG AT IT IS REPRINTED IN THE BLOOD OF A RAT.

◆

A Review of
Interview with the Vampire

by Roger Ebert

Lestat ◆ Tom Cruise
Louis ◆ Brad Pitt
Armand ◆ Antonio Banderas
Santiago ◆ Stephen Rea
Molloy ◆ Christian Slater
Claudia ◆ Kirsten Dunst

Geffen presents a film directed by Neil Jordan. Produced by Stephen Woolley and David Geffen. Written by Anne Rice, based on her novel. Photographed by Philippe Rousselot. Edited by Mick Audsley. Music by Elliot Goldenthal. Running time: 115 minutes. Classified: R (for vampire violence and gore, and for sexuality). Rating: ★★★.

◆

Although one of the characters in *Interview with the Vampire* begs to be transformed into a vampire, and eagerly awaits the doom of immortality, the movie never makes vampirism look like anything but an endless sadness. That is its greatest strength. Vampires throughout movie history have often chortled as if they'd gotten away with something. But the first great vampire movie, *Nosferatu* (1922), knew better, and so does this one.

The movie is true to the detailed vision that has informed all of Anne Rice's novels, and which owes much to the greater taste for realism that has crept into modern horror fiction. It is a film about what it *might really be like* to be a vampire. The title sets the tone, and in the opening scenes, set in San Francisco, the 200-year-old vampire Louis de Pointe du Lac (Brad Pitt) submits to an interview by a modern journalist (Christian Slater), just as any serial killer or terrorist bomber might sit down to talk to *60 Minutes*.

His story begins in the late 1700s, in New Orleans, that peculiar city where even today all things seem possible, and where, after losing his wife and daughter, he threw himself into a life of grief and debauchery. His path

A Review of *Interview with the Vampire*

crossed that of the Vampire Lestat (Tom Cruise), who transformed him into a vampire, and ever since he has wandered the world's great cities, feeding on the blood of his victims.

The initial meeting between Louis and Lestat takes the form of a seduction; the Vampire seems to be courting the younger man, and there is a strong element of homoeroticism in the way the neck is bared and the blood is engorged. Parallels between vampirism and sex, both gay and straight, are always there in all of Rice's novels; the good news is that you can indulge your lusts night after night, but the bad news is that if you stop, you die.

Tom Cruise, who initially seemed to many people an unlikely choice to play Lestat, is never less than convincing, and his slight British accent, combined with makeup that is dramatic without being obtrusive, disguises the clean-cut star—makes him seem unwholesome in an odd, insinuating way. Brad Pitt, whose role is probably larger, and who has been at home as the depraved hero of films like *Kalifornia*, here seems more like an innocent, a young man who makes unwise choices, and lives (and lives, and lives) to regret them.

One of the creepier aspects of the story is the creation of the child vampire, Claudia, played by Kirsten Dunst, who is about 12 years old. The character

At the movie premiere of the film adaptation of *Interview with the Vampire* in New Orleans, from left to right: Karen Singer, Julie Champagne, Susie Miller, Kimberly Elizabeth, Melanie Scott, Sue Quiroz, Katherine Ramsland, and Beryl Bourgeois.

was 6 in the novel, but even twice as old she is disturbing, trapped in her child's body as she ages, decade after decade. Dunst, perhaps with the help of Stan Winston's subtle makeup, is somehow able to convey the notion of great age inside apparent youth.

The movie's unique glory is in its look, created by cinematographer Philippe Rousselot and production designer Dante Ferretti. Ferretti's credits include Scorsese's *The Age of Innocence* and Gilliam's *The Adventures of Baron Munchausen*, and here he combines the elegance of the former and the fantastic images of the latter into a vampire world of eerie beauty. The action, of course, largely takes place at night, in old Southern plantations and French Quarter dives, along gloomy back streets and in decadent boudoirs, and it truly takes flight after the action moves on board a trans-Atlantic sailing ship, and then into the catacombs of Paris. There are scenes set in a vast underground columbarium, where the Vampires sleep on shelves reaching up into the gloom, that is one of the great sets of movie history.

In Paris, Louis meets the Vampires Armand (Antonio Banderas) and Santiago (Stephen Rea), and begins to understand he is a member of an international clandestine society. Vampires, of course, need regular supplies of fresh blood, and the details involving its procurement are dismaying to the creatures, who, to live, must constantly feed off the lives of others. Their sadness is manifest in Rice's screenplay and the moody direction by Neil Jordan (*The Crying Game*), who take this subject, with its abundant possibilities for looking ridiculous, and play it as tragedy. Although much has been said about the film's level of violence (and although the R rating is quite correct), those who have seen other horror films will not be particularly shocked.

My complaint about the film is that not very much happens, in the plot sense. The movie is more about the history and reality of vampirism than about specific events, although some action does center around the fate(s) of Lestat. A stronger plot engine might have drawn us more quickly to the end, but on a scene-by-scene basis, *Interview with the Vampire* is a skillful exercise in macabre imagination.

Excerpts from "Anne Rice:
On the Film, *Interview with the Vampire*"

Feeling the need, perhaps, to clarify her position regarding the film version of
Interview with the Vampire, *Rice subsequently published a long opinion piece that*
was printed separately as an insert in Variety. *She also self-published the piece at*
a Kinko's in New Orleans, binding copies for free circulation through her offices and
at the Garden District Book Shop. (On the cover, a handwritten notation appears:
"From Vampire Central—a bit of concept art—Anne Rice/ January 3, 1995.")
Selected text from the insert follows.

◆

Dear Readers and Viewers,

As you may know, while the film *Interview with the Vampire* was in production with David Geffen, the author of the book had no legitimate contact
with him or with the studio or with anyone connected with the film.

When the announcement was made that Tom Cruise would star as Lestat,
I had deep reservations and severe criticisms. So did many of my readers. I
talked openly about this. A curtain thereafter divided me from the entire
production, and with reason. Nobody likes to be criticized, and that includes
movie people, too.

I understand and accept what happened. But to me, movies and books are
not like sports. There is no immediate consensus on whether a player had
scored a home run or a touchdown. So it was okay to speak my mind on the
casting, and I don't have any regrets.

But to continue. . . .

I saw no rough cuts of *Interview with the Vampire*; I saw no clips. I went
to no screenings. It wasn't until David Geffen himself took the unusual risk
of sending me a VHS tape of the movie, that I saw it. And I approached this
tape with a deep fear of being hurt, crushed, disappointed, destroyed by the
finished work.

When I saw the film on VHS, I came out at once in favor of it, declaring
that I loved it. I bought two pages in *Variety* to talk about it in a frank and

unedited announcement. No one controlled what I wrote, or had any opportunity to delete any part of it. I loved the film, I said so. . . .

What happened on opening weekend is now history as they say. The movie made about 35 million dollars, and broke all kinds of records to do with seasons and ratings, etc. I don't remember all the details but it was a luscious American success. And I marveled then and I marvel now. . . .

Well over a month has passed. I have had a listed number (1-504-522-8634) in New Orleans for weeks to receive by answering machine peoples' responses to the film. The film is now open all over the world.

Therefore, I think it's okay now to go into detail about how I saw this film. The film has established itself in the public consciousness. It's okay to talk about details. . . .

So here goes, point by point:

The look of *Interview with the Vampire* was for me perfect. Dante Ferretti knew exactly what he was doing with the sets. The costumes were impeccable. And the cinematography of Philippe Rousselot was extraordinary. Stan Winston's makeup achieved an eerie and effective otherworldly look. The score by Elliot Goldenthal I found to be quite wonderful.

Minor note: The hair of the characters in the film was eccentric—it was not in conformity with the descriptions in the book or my script, or with historical evidence. But it was very interesting, at times more than beautiful, and it worked.

The opening shots of San Francisco caught the grimness of the city, the urban mixture of desperation, poverty and affluent life. Though Brad Pitt did not appear as "beautiful" as I had wanted in the opening scene (the actor is incredibly beautiful actually) he was divinely otherworldly—the Stan Winston makeup had its own perfection and appeal with the blue veins beneath the skin, and Brad spoke his lines boldly and well.

As the film plunged into eighteenth century Louisiana, it had the atmosphere and feel of a pirate film—rugged, ragged, and full of rats and candles. Superb. This was infinitely better than the fussy *Dangerous Liaisons* look which worked beautifully for that film but which would never have caught the humid, friable, and doggedly makeshift life of the colony of New Orleans.

The shift to Paris was superb. In a few words and shots, the film caught the unmistakable vitality of a great capital city, and the contrast to the colony was splendid and thrilling.

The final New Orleans scenes had exactly the right pitch. They caught the shabbiness of New Orleans and the mysterious loveliness of its overgrown and neglected gardens.

Excerpts from "Anne Rice: On the Film, *Interview with the Vampire*"

The art direction, costumes, lighting, cinematography and craft of the film were sumptuous and thrillingly successful for me. I was grateful for the uncompromising lushness of the film, for its magnificent interiors and brutal exteriors, for its relentless attention to detail throughout in creating an immense and tantalizing and utterly convincing world, all of one fine and infinitely varying fabric. Bravo!

Now, I would like to discuss the actors and actresses. I'm using first names not because I know these people really well or anything, but because using last names always sounds cold to me. I don't like it. So. . . .

On Brad Pitt:

Brad Pitt immediately infused the despairing Louis with understandable feeling. He played it passive and quiet, and for me and for lots of viewers (they call me and tell me) he got what guilt is all about, a guilt sometimes that is unattached to any one death or loss. He captured the despair of someone who has fallen from grace, lost his faith, seen what he cannot abide. Brad's eyes, his manner, his soft voice throughout the film were magical.

Ironically, the Louis whom Brad played on the screen is more passive than the Louis of the novel or of my first draft screenplay (which was of course rewritten and changed and edited and enlarged by Neil Jordan). But Brad Pitt made this passive, suffering character totally appealing and sympathetic. His seemed to combine youth and patience, acceptance and conscience.

Favorite Brad Pitt moments for me:

Brad's soft voice saying the single syllable "No" when Lestat prepares to give the Dark Gift to Claudia.

Brad's last real scene with Claudia, their discussion on the balcony outside the hotel room—another contribution from Jordan which was never in my original script.

Brad's face when he finds the ashes in the airwell, and when he turns to confront those who have hurt him so deeply. Absolutely masterly acting. One of the most painful and exquisite moments in film that I have ever watched. Brad did it without a word. Magnificent.

Brad's soft conversation with Armand, especially the last conversation, which was not written by me, but represented, I thought, a wonderful dramatization of the parting of these two characters. The intimacy of this scene, its delicacy, the restraint and the love—were all glorious to behold.

Brad's anger with Christian Slater in their final moments. Excellent.

There were many other such moments with Brad Pitt.

I respect and am amused by Brad's recent redneck persona. I've been tempted to write a satire *Interview with the Redneck Vampire* just for him and probably will. (I loved Brad in *Kalifornia*. I've got the story all worked out and I think the Constitution protects satire. Who knows? Maybe "Saturday Night Live" will want it. One of my dreams for years has been to write for "Saturday Night Live.") The readers calling me really want Brad in the future Vampire Chronicle films. Well, Brad? Is a burrito really better than immortality? All jokes aside, you were a delicate and heartbreaking Louis; whatever you felt, you swept people off their feet.

On Tom Cruise:

From the moment he appeared Tom was Lestat for me. He has the immense physical and moral presence; he was defiant and yet never without conscience; he was beautiful beyond description yet compelled to do cruel things. The sheer beauty of Tom was dazzling, but the polish of his acting, his flawless plunge into the Lestat persona, his ability to speak rather boldly poetic lines, and speak them with seeming ease and conviction were exhilarating and uplifting. The guy is great.

I'm no good at modesty. I like to believe Tom's Lestat will be remembered the way Olivier's Hamlet is remembered. Others may play the role some day but no one will ever forget Tom's version of it.

(Let me say here that anyone who thinks I did an "about face" on Tom just doesn't know the facts. My objections to his casting were based on familiarity with his work, which I loved. Many great actors have been miscast in films and have failed to make it work. I don't have to mention them here. Why hurt anyone by mentioning the disaster of his career? But we've seen big stars stumble over and over when they attempt something beyond their reach.

(That Tom DID make Lestat work was something I could not see in a crystal ball. It's to his credit that he proved me wrong. But the general objections to the casting? They were made on solid ground. Enough on that subject. Tom is a great actor. Tom wants challenges. Tom has now transcended the label of biggest box office star in the world. He's better.)

Favorite moments with Tom:

Tom's initial attack on Louis, taking him up into the air, praised by Caryn James so well in the *New York Times*. Ah! An incredibly daring scene. The finest romantic scene in any film, and here please read the word romance as an old and venerable word for timeless artistic forms of poetry, novels and film.

Romance is a divine word which has never really been denigrated by the drugstore novels with the swooning ladies on the cover. Romance will be with us for all time. If you want to know more about Romance, put on a video of *The Fisher King* and listen to Robin Williams describe the deeper meaning of romance to his newfound girlfriend. It's worth it, believe me.

Back to Tom: other great moments.

Tom's bedside seduction of the dying Louis, in which he offers Louis the Dark Gift. Once again, Tom gave Lestat the virility and the androgyny that made both him and the offer irresistible. He was near blinding. I would have accepted the Dark Gift from him then and there. Only an actor with complete confidence and conviction could have done that scene or any of the others.

RICE ON THE VIDEOTAPE

As those of you know who did rent this tape, I am on it, recommending the film. I did this of my own free will and with great pleasure, and in my own living room.

If there is any doubt in anyone's mind, let me say again, I love this film and I do think it is about us, as well as about vampires. It's about outsiders, it's about those who feel deeply, who have lost faith in a meaningful universe and find an immoral or amoral existence impossible. It's about the desperate desire to live in spite of guilt. Claudia, as far as I'm concerned, is all children—when they reach the understanding that they will die, they want to know why they were ever brought into this world for that. Louis is my alter ego in this film. I didn't turn into Lestat until later on.

I went on the video very willingly to get some of this across, and had complete control over everything I said.

Though my books have long ago been taken seriously by a large audience (thank God and thank you), the movie went through some of the same snobbery that the book had experienced twenty years ago. Some people just didn't get it, they scorned it, they didn't give it a chance, they ignored the seriousness of it.

It was my desire to correct this impression that prompted me to go on the video with the blurb, which I spoke from the heart. We were absolutely amazed that Warner Home Video let us do it. It's a first for an author as far as I know, and we're proud to have broken a barrier here.

from Commotion Strange #3 by Anne Rice

Tom's angry outburst in the face of Louis' repeated questions. His stride, his voice both loud and soft, his frustration, his obvious discomfort, and inner conflict. Once again, Tom took over the screen, the theatre, the mind of the viewer. Immense power.

Tom riding his horse through the slaves' fire, and then turning the horse around so that he could face the suspicious mortals. That was on a par with Errol Flynn and Rudy Valentino. Maybe that scene buried Errol Flynn and Rudy Valentino. It was on a par with the opera greats who have played Mephistopheles. Only a genuine "star" can make a moment like that, and I'm as confused as to why . . . just as much as anyone in Hollywood. Let's close this one out with the one word: Grand! (No, can't stop talking about it.)

If I had to settle for one picture from this film, it would be that shot of Lestat on horseback looking back at the suspicious mortals.

That was and is my hero. That was and is my man. Lestat just won't be afraid of anybody. He won't stand for it. He hates what he is as much as Louis, but he cannot do anything but move forward, attempt to make existence worth it, attempt to create. He knows the formula for success, and has no patience with the formula for failure. That's Lestat.

Tom's rage and obvious pain in the scene with the bleeding wench and the coffin, one scene from the book which I did not include in my script. It was probably put in by Neil Jordan. If Tom had not given so much obvious depth to this scene, it might have been unwatchable. His desperation, his vulnerability, made it work, and he made himself in it the worthy object of compassion. No small feat! I found the scene, otherwise, to be disgusting.

The shot of Tom looking through the green shutters, and the falling rain, knowing that Louis is somewhere out in the night. This was a gorgeous and eloquent shot. Again, it was the actor who gave it the depth in all the subtle ways that only he can do.

Tom's making of Claudia, and here I want to praise the entire trio . . . Tom, Kirsten, Brad. . . . The scene is directed delicately and captures the intimacy, the blasphemy and the undeniable innocence and blundering of the human who has a supernatural gift to give and in his pain and confusion, chooses to give it, come what may. That's a scene for now, for our world of scientific and medical miracles, as much as any scene in Mary Shelley's *Frankenstein,* and Tom pulled it off right to the last second.

Later, Tom's confusion when after bringing Claudia a doll, he sees Claudia turn on him. About half of what I wrote for this scene in the script, or less, made it into the film, and I liked what I saw very much. I wish they'd gone

Excerpts from "Anne Rice: On the Film, *Interview with the Vampire*"

on with the version of this scene that is in *Queen of the Damned* (see Jesse's discovery of Claudia's diary, and the entry describing what happened), but alas, what they did was great.

Tom's manner and expression on the dangerous night that Claudia comes to him and offers him her "reconciling gift." Close in on those two at the harpsichord. Tom is seated, I believe. Kirsten is behind him. Close in on Tom's face after he deliberately torments Claudia, and as Claudia puts her arms around him and apparently offers him the acceptance he needs so desperately. Scenes like this, with Tom, make this film work.

Every humorous scene Tom attempted was a complete success. The rat and the glass, I adored it. The humor added apparently by Neil Jordan—the poodles, the piano teacher hitting the keyboard, the dressmaker biting the dust . . . well, I didn't adore all that, but Tom carried it off with true wit and style. And yes, it's all right to laugh at those parts. We do every time we go to see the movie.

There are many other great Tom Cruise moments throughout the film. Many. But these are the ones I cherish now.

The readers calling me desperately want Tom to play *The Vampire Lestat*. I hope he does. I hope I get to write the script for the movie. Tom's power, knowledge, skill, magnetism and artistic integrity are part and parcel of the success of *Interview with the Vampire*, and there is no doubt that Tom would bring power and magic to *The Vampire Lestat*.

(Let me digress again. For those of you who haven't read *The Vampire Lestat*, it is not really a sequel to *Interview with the Vampire*. It's a complete full novel on its own, beginning the Vampire Chronicles. *Interview with the Vampire* was the truly difficult film to make. *The Vampire Lestat* will take commitment, money and immense faith as well as talent, but compared to *Interview*, it is much, much easier to film. Lestat is the true hero of *The Vampire Lestat*. He is entirely sympathetic. The trick, I think, will be achieving a texture in that film that includes all of Lestat's adventures . . . from the snows of the Auvergne, to the boulevards of Paris, through the sands of Egypt, and through the visit to Marius' sanctuary, and on to the twentieth-century rock music stage. The tales of Armand and of Marius are also excursions for Lestat essentially. I hope Tom makes the journey.)

One point: I am puzzled by what seems to be a discrepancy between the way Tom played Lestat, and the way my hero, Producer David Geffen, and others have described Lestat as a character. Did Tom on his own make this role a little bigger, brighter and more complex than anyone else realized it could be?

I don't know. David Geffen called Lestat "nasty" when he was interviewed by Barbara Walters. Nasty? I don't get it. But David Geffen is my hero for getting this film made. No one else could have done it. So why quibble about what David said?

There is one problem created by the compelling charm of Tom's performance, obviously. Since he isn't all that nasty, why does Louis hate Lestat? How can he? Well, I'll take that problem any day over a more shallow solution. Tom hit the right note. And Louis was Louis. Nothing could comfort Louis. The film got it.

On Kirsten Dunst:

Magnificent and flawless as Claudia, shocking in her soft, perfectly paced shifts between adulthood and childish innocence. The role as she played it is far less sinister than the Claudia of the book, and perhaps even a little more innocent than my first draft script. But the change seemed to work wondrously to deliver the heartbreak of Claudia's dilemma to the audience. She was a woman, but she was in a child's body. The actress showed incredible intelligence and cunning, and yet a child's tragic vulnerability and heartrending capacity to be disappointed.

Anybody who doesn't see what this is about—all women are locked in the bodies of dolls; all self-contemplating human souls are locked in mortal and often confounding bodies—isn't perhaps asking enough of himself or herself as a viewer. To say this film contained only one idea or no ideas, as Janet Maslin said in the *New York Times*, is, I think, to severely underrate it.

The better part of the ideas of this film revolve around Claudia, and her dilemma is truly one shared by everyone. That the film arouses and sustains sympathy for her so that her inevitable fate is tragic is a great cinematic accomplishment.

What Kirsten did in this film has dealt a body blow to the rigid, stupid cliché of the demonic child. Kirsten blew *The Bad Seed* out of the water. She is utterly beyond the evil puppetlike child vampires of other movies. She drew us into her motives for violence and offered us a deeper understanding of all the moral rules given us, or created by us. That none of her gestures, words, or actions was prurient was a major achievement.

Favorite moments with Kirsten:

The entire transformation scene in the bed from suffering waif to glorious child killer.

Excerpts from "Anne Rice: On the Film, *Interview with the Vampire*"

Kat Frazier

Kirsten Dunst at the Memnoch Ball 1995

When she looks down from the balcony in the Rue Royale and says, "It means . . . I shall never grow up."

Her quiet voice in the scene where Lestat brings her the doll (again, about half of what I wrote survived there, maybe less, but I liked Jordan's changes except for one minor point which I'll make below).

Her seduction of Lestat and subsequent attack on him, especially the moment when she tumbles back on the couch next to the young boys and smiles up at Lestat. Perfection.

Her loving and intimate scenes with Louis in which she becomes a woman, remaining both a daughter and a mother.

The perfect pitch of prepubescent innocence throughout. The movie isn't about peephole sex, and nobody exemplifies that better than Claudia. It isn't about perversion at all. It never was. It is about the attempt of all of us to live in the light and with grace. Kirsten got the whole thing.

Her final scene.

Again, there are many other moments throughout the film with Kirsten.

Part Four: Chiaroscuro—Anne Rice and the Cinema

On Antonio Banderas:

As Armand, he gave the role an original interpretation, quite different from mine in the book or the script, but it worked for me as an intepretation of unique and spectacular charm. Antonio had the magnetism of a master vampire. He had the quiet confidence and the obvious power to spellbind. He redeemed the Theatre of the Vampires scene I think, with his sheer authority. He embodied the mystery of Armand and Armand's particular brand of utterly pragmatic evil. We know why he did what he did; we know it was bad; but in a way we can understand him.

I would have preferred to see his beautiful curly hair as it appears in *House of the Spirits*, or *Philadelphia*. But he was overwhelmingly successful as Armand, "the oldest surviving vampire in the world." The readers have totally embraced him in this part. I hope he will move into the next film and maybe without the black wig? But he can come on any terms as far as I'm concerned.

He was in the film so briefly that I can truly say my favorite moments with Antonio were all of his moments. But to those who have flipped over this actor, let me recommend again *House of the Spirits* and *Philadelphia*. There you will see more of our Armand than in *Interview with the Vampire*.

On Stephen Rea: This actor was quite marvelous as Santiago, which is not a sympathetic role at all, and in one scene Stephen makes cinema history. This is the scene where Brad Pitt steps out of the airwell, having seen the ashes collapse. Brad looks at Stephen. Stephen smiles. Who will ever forget the malice of that smile? (Or the pain in Brad's face.) Incredible. Truly one of the staggering moments of the film.

On Christian Slater: He was utterly convincing as the interviewer and he made the story all the more powerful by his entirely understandable reactions to the tale. For me, he was plenty young enough to be Daniel Molloy, and I hope we'll see him in *The Vampire Lestat* too, but again, I don't know. Like Antonio, Christian is in the film so briefly that I can truly say my favorite moments with him are all of his moments.

Minor Players: all flawless as far as I'm concerned. There was never a false word from anybody. Quite a back-up for the stars. The quadroon, Yvette, seemed real Louisiana. No simple thing. They were all good, really.

In sum, the cast of this film contained actors of undeniable talent, charisma and near enchanting manner. The performances alone are worth the price of admission as far as I'm concerned.

Excerpts from "Anne Rice: On the Film, *Interview with the Vampire*"

Another Digression: Beauty. Over and over again, I've said these stars were beautiful. I've talked about their physical gifts, but surely their beauty is the result of something infinitely deeper. These actors and actresses shape their own physical appearance with their educated brains and hearts. Beauty surrounds them and emanates from them. They walk in it, to quote Byron. If they had not expressed depth of soul in every word or gesture, their "beauty" would have been brittle, and not beautiful at all. I want to make this clear, because beauty is such a misused word.

I would also like to say that the beauty of the players seems to work for the audience nationwide, regardless of gender or age. The men calling my machine to voice their opinions are straight as well as gay. They are young and old. They were captivated by the spectacle. Lestat has fans among truck drivers as well as brain surgeons. They don't relate Lestat to gender or to sex necessarily.

Same with the women. They have responded wholeheartedly to what they have seen on the screen.

And even if I speak for this woman alone, allow me to say that a feast of gorgeous men is much appreciated, and rather long overdue. Women are starved for the sight of beautiful men. They are hungry for stylish and profound scenes with beautiful men. Before *Interview with the Vampire*, I had seen precious little of the male beauty I craved. Two examples are Tom Berenger in *Last Rites* when he takes off his Roman collar and makes love to the girl in the sacristy of St. Patrick's. Another would be the scene where Madeleine Stowe caresses Daniel Day-Lewis in *The Last of the Mohicans*, a scene largely focusing on her and her feelings about the man in her arms.

Let me add again that straight men are in no way turned off by such scenes. Why should they be? They watch Kurt Russell, Tom Cruise, Tom Berenger, Brad Pitt, Antonio Banderas, Jeremy Irons, Aiden Quinn and all the other beautiful men for their own reasons. And why not?

But it's a relief to have lived long enough to see movies begin to seriously consider the erotic taste of the female audience as well as the male. Men are highly romantic, and they crave romance and they always have. What could be more romantic than a Ludlum novel or a James Bond thriller or a film like *Backdraft*? Now Hollywood seems to get it—that this kind of romance and *Jane Eyre* are really the same. Maybe we're seeing the whole concept of the romantic film reexamined. We are seeing a renewed commitment to emotion, to heroism, a new abandonment to passion. Again, it's about time!

On the general direction by Neil Jordan, the cinematography, and the editing of this film: I'm lumping all this together because I truly don't know how to separate a director's contribution from that of the cinematographer and the editor. I don't know enough about film making. I don't know how much David Geffen influenced the film scene by scene. I wasn't there, and I don't have that experience on any film.

So, let's talk about the film as a film: Once again, the entire look of the film was perfection. It caught the dimness, the filth, the fragile handmade luxury and ornate aspirations of the eighteenth and nineteenth centuries; it caught the mud on the hem of the garment.

Over and over again, the viewer was brought in close to the faces of the characters, to hear them speak softly, to watch their eyes, their mouths. This was superbly and fearlessly intimate. Yet the camera moved back to give Lestat the room to be magnificent; Brad Pitt was mercilessly pursued by the camera in his despair, so that his misery became luminous. Claudia's prepubescent beauty and appeal were utterly respected. The handling of all players was masterly.

The pace of the film for me (and most readers calling in) was terrific. The film is genuinely thrilling. It is entertaining! You walk out exhilarated. You feel good and you want to go back. Many readers call me to say that they have seen the film over and over again. There is no lag for us in the second half of this film, and there is no conspicuous absence of human victims, in fact, no conspicuous absence of anything. It was an extraordinarily satisfying film.

The film achieved the Dickensian goal of being meaningful and fun; of being deep and interesting and fun. No small feat in an age in which "realism" has become synonymous with "serious" and we are told that films about every-day life should command our respect over everything else.

The film's moral themes came across to me as clearly realized: we can con-ceive of immortality, but we're mortal. Inside each of us, regardless of outward grace, there is a misfit. That misfit at times feels like a monster. That misfit may at times behave like a monster.

Whatever Neil Jordan's comments to the press, he seemed to believe in that and to make it work on the screen. The film is one which the audience starts talking about, discussing, arguing [over] before they ever leave the theatre. The film invites analysis. It invites a return viewing. It makes a difference to the people who see it.

The boldness of the scene with the whore and coffin is deeply disturbing in an excellent way. It makes you think about what you might do if you were Lestat. It makes you think about things you've done for entirely personal reasons. But it is disgusting.

The two panoramic scenes in Paris—Claudia dancing with Louis at a ball;

Excerpts from "Anne Rice: On the Film, *Interview with the Vampire*"

Claudia twirling in her new adult dress before the dressmakers—both were appropriately immense and unstinting. (Again, the hair of the characters is eccentric. Louis with that long flowing hair in a nineteenth-century Parisian ball room? It made me think of the wild west. But I loved it!)

Neil Jordan's humorous scenes were a true comic relief. Though I would never have recommended or written them—killing poodles, letting the piano teacher fall dead on the keyboard—I liked them and felt they were handled cleverly. They worked. And the shift between seriousness and humor worked.

The last scene involving Lestat: I was glad to see him, glad to have him back. When he said "I feel better already," I loved it. When he pulled the lace out from under his sleeves, I was overjoyed. So all that worked for me. It was enough in keeping with the ending of my script and the book for me to be happy, for me to see the possibilities of a sequel. But I didn't write it.

(I see no problem in moving from this Jordan created scene into *The Vampire Lestat*. None whatsoever. There are all kinds of ways to do it and be true to *The Vampire Lestat*, the book.)

Film choices made by Jordan and others, perhaps.

This movie obviously did not go into the heads of the Vampires. It really didn't go into the swoon as they experience it in my novel or script. It didn't really show the distortion of the senses of the Vampires. It made, however, a very interesting substitution.

In victimization scenes, the camera focused tightly on the eye of the attacking vampire; it gave us a portrait of the attack which had tremendous visual power. Jordan seemed utterly unintimidated by the plethora of bad vampire movies and vampire scenes that came before him. Perhaps this close-up on the eye of the Vampire, this attention to the choreography of the victimization scene, was trying to make us feel the swoon. I don't know. The film very successfully used a levitating scene as a substitute for the swoon in the first instance. Whatever the reason, over and over again, the film presented the moment of attack and submission as potent and worthy of serious treatment. I found these choices extremely satisfying.

There's no doubt in my mind that vampires are a metaphor for the predator in all of us, and that Louis and Lestat and Claudia speak directly to the ruthless part of us . . . especially to those of us who live in affluent twentieth-century America, surrounded by luxury and miracles, and yet painfully aware of what goes on in other parts of the world. The film never shied away from this. Again, I am confused by some of Jordan's statements about it. But I found these ideas to be eloquently embodied in the film.

I have only just begun to think about some of the questions the film posed: how far will we go not to be alone; how much will we sacrifice morally in order to attain our definition of magnificence, greatness or independence; the nature of dependency and love. The film isn't talking about mere survival; it's talking about the possibility of grand achievement as well as endurance— it's talking about reaching for the sublime.

These camera shots of killing over and over were rooted in these elements. I liked them.

The film's point of view: As far as I can tell, this film is shot from our point of view, the point of view of the reader of the book or the viewer of the movie. This is not a criticism. It is a comment on something I find very intriguing. What I mean is this: We are being told the tale by Louis, but the camera doesn't show us what Louis sees or how he sees it. The camera stays at the footlights of the stage, as though this were all a play—an acting out of the book.

Over and over the camera lets characters enter from left and from right as they would on a real stage; it brings them together for medium shots in which they speak their crucial lines. It draws back on panoramic scenes, well beyond the tactile sensations being experienced and described by Louis.

There are scenes in which Louis isn't present: Claudia's attack on Lestat, for instance.

There is as far as I can tell only one point of view shot in the whole film. This occurs when Claudia and Madeleine are being carried down a passage-way. You get one shot of the faces of those carrying them. I'm not sure whether or not it's from Claudia's point of view, or Madeleine's. If there are other such shots I missed them.

Again, this isn't a criticism. I find this an interesting approach on the part of the film makers. Perhaps it is most effective as showing the scope of the story, which is essentially small and gigantic simultaneously. It's several people talking about salvation and damnation amid spectacle that rivals the most high tech modern extravagance.

Whatever, I'm delightedly puzzled over it. It worked well, but why was it that way? What would have happened if we had seen things more consistently from Louis' point of view? For example, when Louis first comes upon Claudia, what would the scene have been like if we had drawn in close on her as he sees her, rather than in close on both of them? What if we had heard her heart the way Louis hears it? What if we had gone into his head for the swoon? What if the sudden entrance of Lestat had been hazy?

I'm not suggesting any of this. The film is immensely effective the way it

Excerpts from "Anne Rice: On the Film, *Interview with the Vampire*"

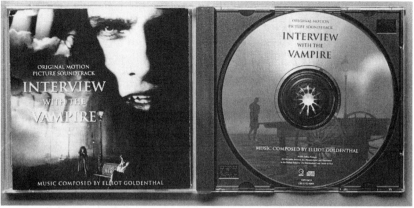

George Beahm

Soundtrack of *Interview with the Vampire*

is. I am simply pointing out that this was a choice that the film made, and one that worked, though I never expected it and can't fully explain it.

I suspect that the full impact of this "stage footlights point of view" was to make the contents of the film appear highly significant, which of course I believe it is. I liked it. There is something classical about making a film this way. The story is supposed to be subjective, but the drama is presented as though it has important meaning for us all.

Quibbles: Loving this film as I do, I hesitate to say anything critical really. But there are a few things that struck me as not so good. Mostly they had to do with editing, or with the unfolding of the story. They are the kinds of things that can be fixed.

The film watcher in me really wanted to know:

Why didn't the Vampires, Louis and Lestat, smell the decaying human body under Claudia's dolls? If I lived in that apartment, I would have smelled it. Certainly they would have. Why and how did the body remain undiscovered? Do these characters have powerful senses or not? I'm puzzled.

Why would dead blood affect a vampire? Why did Lestat get so hurt by drinking "dead blood"? I don't get it.

Did Lestat receive enough wounds from Claudia to really disable him? I don't think so. It should have been a much more violent attack with much more rents in the flesh. Lestat is a very strong guy. I don't get it.

How the hell did Lestat survive the fire in New Orleans?

Why wasn't Lestat in Paris? Shouldn't he have been there to show us

1) that he had survived and 2) to climax the dreadful kangaroo court trial of those who had attacked him? I missed him in Paris. I don't think the film lagged—I cherish the discussion between Brad and Antonio in this portion of the film—but Lestat's appearance would have been highly effective for me. This doesn't mar my enjoyment of the film. I just wish it had been different.

I thought the shot of Superman on the theatre screen, as seen by Louis, and the shot of the theatre marquee saying *Tequila Sunrise* as Louis walks off, were unforgivably indelicate and stupid. To throw up the words *Tequila Sunrise* at that moment blew the mood utterly. I winced. When I watch the film now, I close my eyes at that part!

Why did the Vampires break so many necks and spill so much blood? Aren't they too powerful to be so unskilled? Why were we treated to the scene of the prostitute with her legs sprawled apart with blood gushing down her dress? In the context of the film, does Lestat really go for that sort of thing? I know, I know, Janet Maslin thought this was the central image of the film. I didn't.

Why did the Vampires so brutally bully the girl on the stage of the Theatre of the Vampires? I don't get it. Why did they push her and shove her? They are immortals. They are very strong, and she is very weak. Why the indignity, the vulgarity? Why wasn't she thoroughly and mercifully enchanted at the end the way she was in the book? Why was the scene so gratuitously nasty?

Why was the final exchange between Louis and Lestat so brief? Good grief! Didn't Louis have a few questions? Didn't he have more to say to Lestat after all that time? I don't get it.

How could he just walk out of there? I couldn't have. Again, it was beautifully done, but I wish it had been different.

How did Lestat get to his position at the very end of the film? How? Couldn't there have been some indication of how he managed to be where he was in his last scene? The overall effect would have been stronger for me if there had been some clues. Again, I love the film, it worked. But I wonder. . . .

Once again, why didn't the Vampires cry blood tears!

My last question: why was this film an R rated film? Couldn't it have been just as profound, just as significant and just as thrilling without being an R rated film? I am assuming of course that the R rating had to do with the nudity and misogyny in the film, the sadism towards women with heavy sexual overtones. If I'm right, then why was that necessary?

Vampires don't have sex. They transcend gender. Vampire gore appears in comic books, cartoons, and PG movies, doesn't it? What's with the rating system? And what's with the gratuitous cruelty to women in this film? Why?

Excerpts from "Anne Rice: On the Film, *Interview with the Vampire*"

I think the film could have kept all of [the] philosophical and psychological complexity and been PG or PG-13.

I'm raising this point because the Vampire Chronicles have thousands of very young readers. For them, the books are extremely accessible. They read the books in school. They talk about them with their teachers. They write papers on the books. They call me with questions and write me wonderful letters. I've been asked to speak at schools about these books, and I have. I have spoken at an elementary school. I have spoken at a college. I have been interviewed in school newspapers as well.

Couldn't the film have been just as accessible to the young as the books are?

I hope kids and their families disregarded the R rating. I hope the young readers got to see the film, or that they will when it comes out on videotape. I think it says important moral things, and it is enchanting and spectacular. It's a banquet of images and words and colors and movement. I hope kids overlooked the vulgarity and brutality of some of the scenes. If they can overlook prime time TV and cable, why can't they see this film?

These nasty and mean scenes didn't ruin the movie for me, and I would let any child go to see it. The film has a redeeming moral context and undeniable splendor that kids are entitled to enjoy. But I don't like the handling of those anti-female sadistic parts. And I would have softened them, tried to transmute them with style, or—to put it bluntly—done them in such a way as to achieve a wider audience rating.

We cannot make only that art which is acceptable to children, but we must remember that *Moby Dick* and *The Old Man and the Sea*, and *Hamlet* can all be read or viewed by children without risk. Consider the appeal of *The Red Shoes* and *The Tales of Hoffmann*. Consider perhaps that the kids who did get to see *Interview with the Vampire* may remember it the way my generation remembers *The Red Shoes* and *The Tales of Hoffmann*.

There is a venerable tradition to making the most serious statement in a form that can be understood by an eight-year-old. I respect that tradition. That kids read my books gives me joy. I'm proud of all my readers, the very young, the very old, the seemingly mainstream, the eccentric, the cerebral, the whole crowd. I ought to be. I'd be a fool not to be proud of being a "popular" and "mainstream" writer. It feels great.

On other critics and the critical response to this film: To echo the offhand remarks of "Saturday Night Live"'s Brooklyn characters, "Forget about it!"

As for *Time* and *Newsweek*, I think we as readers and film lovers have to reconcile ourselves to the fact that these publications have become virtually worthless in covering books and film. The magazines are obviously fighting a losing battle with television and computer networks, but they aren't putting up much of a fight. Their reviewers seem shallow, stupid, and unforgivably uninformed. Let's kiss them goodbye.

Time and *Newsweek*, you no longer play a significant role in covering the news surrounding the arts, or in covering the arts themselves. You could turn this around. You could start writing reviews which are actually intelligent essays; you could return to commentary with perspective and validity; you could do your homework on the context of the films and books you review. Eh. I've given up on you.

The success of *Interview with the Vampire* is only one of many, many proofs that these magazines are no longer major cultural players. It is sad.

On the *New Yorker*: Pauline Kael, I miss you. Tina Brown, why don't you open up the *New Yorker* to teams of reviewers of films and movies? Give us a real controversy of criticism—review more books, more films and publish more reviewers. I'd love it, but I read the magazine every week no matter what.

On Janet Maslin in the *New York Times*: though I cherish her great praise of the film, I disagree, as already stated, with her dismissal of the ideas of the film and her dismissal of the underlying work. I think *Interview with the Vampire* is one of the richest, most complex and most thought provoking films I've ever seen. People will be viewing it and talking about it when we are no longer here.

On Caryn James: I treasure what you wrote in the *New York Times*.

On Liz Smith and her very frank and brave questions as to whether or not *Interview with the Vampire* was a gay allegory, and her question as to why people just don't make a gay film, and why do gays have be disguised as vampires—Here's my answer: Ms. Smith, the gays are us. That's all there is to it. There is no disguise. Gay allegory doesn't exist apart from moral allegory for everyone. This is now evident.

Philadelphia made the statement in a very direct way. Tom Hanks in that film played a man that could be any one of us for any number of reasons! Years and years ago, a gay allegory was made called *Bride of Frankenstein*. For most of its artistic life, people have been totally unaware that this film is a gay allegory, and with reason. IT DOESN'T MATTER. If it's about gays, it's about all of us, the secrets we carry, the traits which set us apart individually from others, the burdens we bear, the rage we feel, and the common condition that binds us.

The characters of *Interview with the Vampire* aren't gays disguised as vampires. They are us. They are us in our loneliness, in our fear, in our spiritual and

Excerpts from "Anne Rice: On the Film, *Interview with the Vampire*"

moral isolation. They are us in our ruthlessness, and in our desperate quest for companionship, warmth, love and reassurance in a world full of gorgeous temptations and very real horrors. They are fallible beings with the power of gods; and that is exactly what we are, all of us.

In sum, *Interview with the Vampire* is bigger than a gay allegory, and so is almost any gay allegory.

Gender influences everything but determines nothing! Vampires transcend gender. We as a modern people transcend gender, though we can never escape it. Ours is a time for which there are no precedents with regard to gender and freedom. Look in vain to ancient Rome. Look in vain to the Middle Ages. There has never been so much affluence, scientific knowledge and so much common awareness of violence and injustice. There has never been so much real wealth for so many, combined with instantaneous media confrontation of poverty and suffering. Some of us see life as a horror story, but a horror story with great, great meaning.

On the Horror Genre:

If we learn anything from this period in film history, let us learn this: that fantasy and horror can speak to the ordinary and the most eccentric; fantasy and horror can embody and reflect the most common and the most dreaded pain we all share; fantasy and horror can speak to the addict, to the celebrity, to the gay man, to the gay woman, to the housewife, to the working man or woman, to me, to you, to the truck driver, to the brain surgeon, to the monk, to the nun, and to the child. Poetry thrives in fantasy and horror books and films; so do great visions of truth. The ambition and the potential of these genres is limitless.

Finally, let me describe another aspect of this unique time. Today, what we share is more important than what sets us apart from one another. What we have in common is infinitely more important than what divides us. It has never been that way before, and the possibilities as well as the responsibilities are endless.

This is the full meaning of *Interview with the Vampire*. Kinked? Yeah. Weird? You got it. Universal? Most certainly.

Anne Rice
New Orleans, Louisiana, 1994

No rights reserved. Quote any, or all of it, anywhere, anytime you wish.

PART FIVE

A Look at the Books

In the course of a career that's spanned two decades, Anne Rice has, alternately, been praised and savaged in print. Her critics can't agree on what's right or wrong about her novels, but her fans speak with one voice: They love her books, period.

Unfortunately, bad reviews do have an impact: They turn the prospective reader away from Rice. Although her hard-core readership will buy each new novel and pass judgment after a reading, some newspaper reviewers have gleefully taken a hatchet to her books and merrily chopped away.

The numbers are more telling than the reviews. *Publishers Weekly* cites the following statistics on in-print figures: *Interview with the Vampire* (6 million, including 2 million of the movie tie-in edition), *The Tale of the Body Thief* (2.3 million), *The Vampire Lestat* (3.1 million), *The Witching Hour* (1.9 million in mass-market paperback and 425,000 in trade paper); and *Lasher* (400,000). The first printing of *Memnoch the Devil* set a new record: 750,000 copies.

Still, despite the numerous favorable reviews Rice has received over the years, she, like any other writer, will notice the negative reviews, because they are the ones that stick in the craw.

Rather than repeat what others have done, examining each book in detail— see *Prism of the Night* and *Anne Rice*—I've chosen instead to reprint key reviews principally from book trade journals. Unlike newspaper reviewers, the people who review for *Publishers Weekly* and *Library Journal* know that their recommendation will have an effect on book sales; and with that power comes responsibility, so the reviews are honest. They are not written to serve the author or the reader; they are written to serve the booksellers and librarians who must, on the basis of a review, decide whether or not to buy the book.

On the whole, Rice's books have reviewed well in the trade journals—the exception being *The Mummy*—whereas in newspaper reviews over the same period, the reviews are divergent.

The reviews are thematic: first, the Vampire Chronicles; second, the Lives of the Mayfair Witches; third, miscellany.

Note: *PW* reviews, unlike those in *LJ*, are published uncredited.

Interview with the Vampire

book review by Julia Parker from
Library Journal (May 1, 1976)

Surprise—that title belongs to a well-written fascinating first novel, not sub-way reader nonsense. In contemporary New Orleans a young reporter listens as Louis, a vampire, unfolds his tale. His story spans several hundred years (vampires are ageless and crosses do not bother them) of a Faustian search for some meaning to his life-in-death existence, an existence complicated by his relationship to three other vampires. Lestat, the Vampire who made him, is hated by Claudia, the five-year-old extraordinarily beautiful child-vampire Louis loves and helped create a vampire. After Claudia attempts to kill Lestat she and Louis go to Europe in search of other vampires. In Paris they find Armand, Master Vampire, and he and Louis fall in love, remaining together for a time after Claudia's death in a state of meaningless immortality. The small miracle here is that Rice's talents make Louis' story meaningful and moving.

Interview with the Vampire

audio review from
Publishers Weekly (July 3, 1987)

This production was one of five nominated for a Grammy Award in the Spoken Word category and it is easy to hear why. This lush, erotic and moving story of a 200-year-old vampire is read expertly by F. Murray Abraham. Following a brief but eerie opening musical passage, we listen to a mesmerizing story—"I was a 25-year-old when I became a vampire, and the year was 1791"—about an aristocrat from a Louisiana plantation who loses the will to live, only to have his blood sucked by the Vampire Lestat, who takes the suckee under his wing and schools him in the nuances of vampiracy. We hear of the young vampire's incipient physical changes—"my teeth had only just begun to change"—and psychic ones—"the sight and aroma of blood seduced me."

Certain passages are dizzyingly sensuous and sensual, and Abraham's voice and laugh are equal to the words. Like *Frankenstein, Interview with the Vampire* goes beyond the land of horror, thanks to the undeniable humanity of its monster-outcast. (With occasional, unobtrusive narrative bridges.)

The Vampire Lestat

audio review from
Publishers Weekly (November 3, 1989)

Michael York, who read last spring's *The Mummy*, has been enlisted again, and delivers with crisp intonation a genuine sense of chilling delight in the material at hand. York rises to fill his characterization of Lestat, bringing sincere melancholy and pathos to his story. And some story it is: the princely blood sucker here traces his somewhat peculiar genesis. Speaking from his present status as a 1980s rock star, Lestat recounts his indoctrination into the "order" while pursuing a theatrical career in 18th-century Paris. Next he is led on a quasi-mythical journey through ancient pagan rituals. With considerably fewer of the grisly killings that characterize the companion volumes, Lestat here comes across as vulnerable and appealing, always questioning the true meaning of his life among the undead.

The Queen of the Damned

book review from
Publishers Weekly (August 12, 1993)

The cult audience for Rice's two previous vampire novels, *Interview with the Vampire* and *The Vampire Lestat*, will undoubtedly broaden with this third book, which features the same characters and a more complex plot. As before, Rice tells her story in fine melodramatic style, overwriting with zest and exuberance: the text pulses with menace, mystery and violence, and with sensuality verging on erotica. Here Lestat and all other vampires pay the price for his obsessive need for fame, his reckless honesty in describing the "blood drinkers" among us, and his frenzied rock concert in San Francisco. Lestat's kiss has awakened Queen Akasha from her 6000-year sleep. She immediately begins a wholesale slaughter of most of the world's vampires, sparing only a small remnant (including Lestat) who she expects will join her in a crazed crusade against male mortals. Meanwhile, vampires and psychic humans around the globe are having the same terrifying dream in which twin red-haired women weep over the body of another woman, whose eyes and brains are on a plate nearby. As Rice gradually reveals the significance of the dream, she also focuses on Jesse, who works for the Talamasca, a secret society that collects data on those with paranormal powers. Though she ingeniously pulls together the various plot strands, Rice then almost loses the reader in philosophic overkill. She regains her verve in the final chapter, however, promising yet another mesmerizing installment of the Vampire Chronicles.

The Tale of the Body Thief

book review from
Publishers Weekly (August 24, 1992)

The fourth book of the Vampire Chronicles series . . . reconfirms Rice's power as a mesmerizing raconteur. In sensuous, fluid prose, she follows the tormented vampire Lestat as he struggles to integrate his bloodthirsty nature with his aspirations to achieve humanity. Desiring to see the sun, to love without taking blood, to seek God as mortals do, Lestat enters blindly into an unholy bargain. In order to experience mortality for one day and two nights, he agrees to switch bodies with the scoundrel Raglan James, a former member of the secret order of scholarly occultists called the Talamasca, and a "sinister being," according to David Talbot, the order's superior general and Lestat's longtime friend and advisor. But Lestat has given little thought to how James intends to use *his* body and its vampiric powers. Trapped in the mortal state, Lestat must overcome the human frailties of despair and physical pain to thwart James's evil intentions and, with Talbot's help, regain his immortal self.

Drawing on characters met in earlier novels as well as the lushly evoked settings of New Orleans, Miami and Paris, Rice once again deftly lures readers into the enchanting world of her anguished and deeply sympathetic hero.

The Tale of the Body Thief

audio review
by Barbara Valle from
Library Journal (December 1992)

This is the fourth installment of Rice's Vampire Chronicles, all available from Random Audio. The elegant, charming Lestat gets a chance to be human again for a couple of days when a scoundrel "body thief" offers to change places. Lestat's experiences and observations are a powerful, rich mixture of fun and gore as dramatized by reader Richard E. Grant. Musical bridges keep the complex narrative flowing, and Grant's voice is compelling and passionate. This presentation will surely add to Rice's legion of Vampire fans. Recommended for fiction collections.

Memnoch the Devil

book review from
Publishers Weekly (June 5, 1995)

Rice has made a career out of humanizing creatures of supernatural horror, and in this fifth book of her Vampire Chronicles she requests sympathy for the Devil. Having survived his near-fatal reacquaintance with human mortality in *The Tale of the Body Thief*, the world-weary vampire Lestat is recruited by the biblical Devil, Memnoch, to help fight a cruel and negligent God. The bulk of the novel is a retelling of the Creation story from the point of view of the fallen angel, who blames his damnation on his refusal to accept human suffering as part of God's divine plan. Rice grapples valiantly with weighty questions regarding the justification of God's ways to man, but their vast scope overwhelms the novel's human dimensions. God and the Devil periodically put on the flesh of mortals, and too often end up sounding like arguing philosophy majors. Meanwhile, the ever-fascinating Lestat, whose poignant personal crisis of faith is mirrored in Memnoch's travails, becomes a passive observer, dragged along on trips to Heaven and Hell before being returned to Earth to relate what he has witnessed. Though Rice boldly probes the significance of death, belief in the afterlife and other spiritual matters, one wishes that she had found a way to address them through the experiences of human and near-human characters, as she has done so brilliantly in the past.

Memnoch the Devil

audio review from
Publishers Weekly (July 31, 1995)

Rice has breathed new life into her Vampire Chronicles with this fifth installment, an unruly exploration of the metaphysics of the Devil. Vampire protagonist Lestat (it's okay, you can forget the movie's Tom Cruise now) is being stalked by Memnoch the Devil—Satan in disarming mortal form. To date, Lestat's philosophy has been: "You drink and kill because you cannot resist it." Now, he's asked by the Devil to stake his position on good and evil. In Dantesque form, Lestat is given a tour of purgatory and hell. He also gets to visit heaven and meet God. Rice then expostulates at length on "Eleven Revelations of Evolution," a bizarre version of creation. All this is plopped down amid a more standard plot structure, with Lestat up to his usual maudlin exercises. As always, Rice's crafty storytelling skills adapt nimbly to audio. The Anglo-sounding Roger Rees reads Lestat's role with the voice of a hopelessly weary aristocrat, making for a convincing air of Victorian decadence and moral decay.

The Witching Hour

book review from
Publishers Weekly (September 21, 1990)

"We watch and we are always here" is the motto of the Talamasca, a saintly group with extrasensory powers which has for centuries chronicled the lives of the Mayfairs—a dynasty of witches that brought down a shower of flames in 17th-century Scotland, fled to the plantations of Haiti and on to the New World, where they settled in the haunted city of New Orleans. Rice plumbs a rich vein of witchcraft lore, conjuring in her overheated, florid prose the decayed antebellum mansion where incest rules, dolls are made of human bone and hair, and violent storms sweep the skies each time a witch dies and the power passes on. Newly anointed is Rowan Mayfair, a brilliant California neurosurgeon kept in ignorance of her heritage by her adoptive parents. She returns to the fold after bringing back Michael Curry from the dead; he, too, has unwanted extrasensory gifts and, like Rowan and the 12 Mayfairs before her, has beheld Lasher: devil, seducer, spirit. Now Lasher wants to come through to this world forever and Rowan is the Mayfair who can open the door. This massive tome repeatedly slows, then speeds when Rice casts off the pretentious, scholarly tones and goes for the jugular with morbid delights, sexually charged passages and wicked, wild tragedy.

The Witching Hour

audio review from
Publishers Weekly (November 2, 1990)

Rice's previous horror-literary novels have all been adapted for audio, so the arrival of the newest, *The Witching Hour*, should find a ready audience. The plot centers on Rowan Mayfair, of the 13th generation in a family of witches. Having been put up for adoption as an infant, she remains unapprised of her ominous fate and is working as a successful San Francisco Bay Area doctor. One day she saves a man from drowning, and he returns from death's grasp with heightened psychic abilities. Together the two are drawn back to Mayfair's ancestral home in New Orleans, tempted and coerced along the way by the devil himself. Once there, the uncovering of family secrets (heads floating in jars and so forth) leads to a crescendo of terrifying effects. In all, this is a wide-ranging multigenerational story that is forcibly compressed to satisfy abridgment requirements. And while tension remains high and a healthy gothic spirit prevails, the drama and love story sometimes stoop to conventional formula.

Lasher

book review from
Publishers Weekly (August 9, 1992)

Returning to the Mayfair clan she introduced in *The Witching Hour,* Rice offers another vast, transcontinental saga of withcraft and demonism in the tradition of Gothic melodrama. The eponymous Lasher is a demon spirit who preys on female Mayfairs in his attempt to procreate. Rowan Mayfair, queen of the coven who has borne Lasher's child, has now disappeared. At times this main narrative is lost as the story moves from the Louisiana Mayfairs to the Scottish Donnelaiths and the clandestine London Talamasca society, with copious personal histories and myriad characters. Long sections ramble without a compelling point of view, and are dampened by stock elements: clichéd wind storms, sexy witches, the endless supply of money the Talamasca has at its disposal. At times, Lasher is too much in evidence (rattling the china, gnashing his teeth) to be frightening. But embedded in this antique demonism is a contemporary tale of incest and family abuse that achieves resonance. It is maintained through the character of Lasher, both child and man at the same time, who manipulates his victims with his own pain. At their best, Rice's characters rise above the more wooden plot machinations with an ironic and modern complexity: Mona, the young feminist witch with shark-like business instincts; Julien, the dead patriarch, who movingly recalls his male lovers; Yuri, the clever Serbian orphan. Despite lapses into uninspired language, ultimately the novel is compelling through its exhaustive monumentality.

Taltos

book review from
Publishers Weekly (July 4, 1994)

Cutting-edge gene mapping intertwines with ancient mysteries in this continuation of Rice's series of novels about witches and the supernatural. A "taltos"
is the superhuman result of the crossbreeding of two human witches who
possess an extra chromosome; almost a monster, the creature is capable of
beastly behavior fueled by an extraordinary sex drive. In *Lasher*, the eponymous offspring of Michael Curry and Rowan Mayfair of the New Orleans
Mayfair witch clan proved to be just such a mutant; before he was slain, he
repeatedly raped his own mother, siring a little "goblin" daughter, Emaleth.
This new novel features a second taltos, also fathered by Curry, but mothered
by a 13-year-old sexpot niece of Rowan's named Mona, who is herself the most
powerful witch of the Mayfair clan. Other plot elements involve renegade
members of the secret order of Talamasca, who want to kidnap and cross-
breed two taltoses; a 200-year-old taltos from New York named Ashlar, who
is posing as a toy-industry magnate specializing in dolls; and a dwarf called
Samuel from the witches' holy glen in Donnelaith, Scotland. Pulsing with a
persistent sense of foreboding, the novel is soggy with meandering, atmospheric prose that verges on softcore porn. And, as usual, what happens in the
book is clearly less important to the author than the number of chills she can
send down readers' spines. She has not lost her touch.

The Mummy, or Ramses the Damned

book review from
Publishers Weekly (May 5, 1989)

An uneasy marriage of romance and horror, this potboiler, first of a projected series, is marinated in sentimentality, melodrama and absurdity. In 1914, Lawrence Stratford, a shipping mogul-turned-archeologist, discovers the tomb of an ancient Egyptian ruler whose mummy supposedly already graces the Cairo Museum. The mummy witnesses the murder of Lawrence by his greedy nephew, Henry, and, back in England, where it's on display in the Stratford mansion, the mummy intervenes when Henry tries to kill Lawrence's beautiful daughter, Julie. The mummy turns out to be Ramses the Second, of superior looks, brains and virility despite his advanced years (3000), rendered immortal by an elixir. Julie falls madly in love, dresses Ramses in her late father's clothes and finally—after too many pages—succumbs ("Batter down the door . . . the virgin door. Open it, I am yours forever.") But Ramses pines for Cleopatra, with whom he dallied a thousand years after his own reign; he immortalizes her mummy and unleashes a killer-monster. Missing a ripe opportunity to skewer 20th-century values and sexual mores, the prolific, bestselling Rice, ever-fascinated with the undead, avoids character and plot development, larding largely lifeless, sloppy prose with a surfeit of epiphanies and calamities.

The Mummy, or Ramses the Damned

audio review from
Publishers Weekly (June 2, 1989)

In this audiotape, released simultaneously with the Ballantine original trade paperback, Rice has diverted herself from her wildly popular vampire fare to explore alternative heroes of the deliciously undead variety. Here, ancient

Egyptian royalty Ramses and Cleopatra are summoned back to life following long rests in their cozy sarcophagi. York, in his crisply British, starched-collar reading, presents the tale like a wonderful Hollywood serial adventure. The setting: Egypt and Great Britain, 1914. While the plot line is problematical (certainly more farcical than the Lestat vampire series), it may well be better heard than read, coveying its cinematic charms. And the tape version misses none of Rice's signature tricks, solidly delivering a love story with bones and flesh exposed, blood trickling. Strains from Verdi's *Aida* are used to heighten the effect as the story reaches its conclusion.

♦
Appendices

This section provides detailed information on material published in various media, both in print and out of print.

Current through September 1995, the appendices that follow cover not only the supernatural material—the bulk of her work to date—but also the *non*supernatural material.

Keep in mind that addresses change, as will prices, so it's best to write or phone to confirm availability before sending a personal check or money order for payment.

Appendix 1: Books, lists both in print and out-of-print titles by Anne Rice, as well as notes on forthcoming projects as announced by Rice in her newsletter. (The prices listed are the publisher's suggested retail price.)

Appendix 2: Books About Anne Rice.

Appendix 3: Audiography, lists audiotape recordings.

Appendix 4: Filmography, Videography, and Discography, lists, respectively, films, videotapes, and compact discs (music).

Appendix 5: Graphic Novel Adaptations, lists material published in comic-book format.

Appendix 6: Resources, lists mail-order sources from which virtually anything by Rice can be ordered.

APPENDIX ONE
Books

Note: The following lists only U.S. first editions.

Beauty's Punishment, by A. N. Roquelaure. New York: E .P. Dutton, 1984; trade hardback, novel. This is the second book in the "Beauty" trilogy.

Beauty's Release, by A. N. Roquelaure. New York: E. P. Dutton, 1985; trade hardback, novel. This is the third book in the "Beauty" trilogy.

Belinda, by Anne Rampling. New York: Arbor House (a Belvedere Book), 1986; trade hardback, novel.

The Claiming of Sleeping Beauty, by A. N. Roquelaure. New York: E. P. Dutton, 1983; trade hardback, novel.

Cry to Heaven. New York: Alfred A. Knopf, 1982; trade hardback, novel.

Exit to Eden, by Anne Rampling. New York: Arbor House, 1985; trade hardback, novel.

The Feast of All Saints. New York: Simon & Schuster, 1979; 570 pages, trade hardback, novel.

Interview with the Vampire. New York: Alfred A. Knopf, 1976; trade hardback, novel. This is the first book of the Vampire Chronicles.

Lasher. New York: Alfred A. Knopf, 1993; trade hardback, novel. This is the second book of Lives of the Mayfair Witches.

Memnoch the Devil. New York: Alfred A. Knopf, 1995; 354 pages, trade hardback, novel. This is the fifth book of the Vampire Chronicles.

The Mummy, or Ramses the Damned. New York: Ballantine Books, 1989; 436 pages, trade paperback, novel.

The Queen of the Damned. New York: Alfred A. Knopf, 1988; trade hardback, novel. This is the third book of the Vampire Chronicles.

The Tale of the Body Thief. New York: Alfred A. Knopf, 1992; 430 pages, trade hardback, novel. This is the fourth book of the Vampire Chronicles.

Taltos: Lives of the Mayfair Witches. New York: Alfred A. Knopf, 1994; trade hardback, novel. This is the third book of Lives of the Mayfair Witches.

The Vampire Lestat. New York: Alfred A. Knopf, 1985; hardback, novel. This is the second book in the Vampire Chronicles.

The Witching Hour. New York: Alfred A. Knopf, 1990; trade hardback, novel. This is the first book of Lives of the Mayfair Witches.

Forthcoming

In 1996 Rice will publish the first novel in a new series about ghosts, *Servant of the Bones*.

From her telephone hotline message in January 1996: There is currently a work in progress, a novel tentatively titled *Symphonie for Mary Anne*, which originally started out as the sixth Vampire Chronicle.

But, as Rice said, "It has been completely taken over by the heroine and her passion for the violin, and it's not a vampire novel any longer—it's a ghost novel.

"I'm very excited by this novel. I feel as passionate about it as any vampire novel I've written or any of the Mayfair Witches novels, and I hope my readers will understand my need to do things that are totally new and not sequels to the other series.

"This novel is not in any way a sequel to *Servant of the Bones,* which is also a ghost novel.

"That's what I'd like to do right now—things that are completely new and have nothing to do with what I've done before."

APPENDIX TWO

◆

Books About Anne Rice

Anne Rice by Bette B. Roberts. New York: Twayne Publishers: Simon & Schuster Macmillan, 1994; 173 pages, hardback. A scholarly study of Rice's canon, written by the author of *The Gothic Romance: Its Appeal to Female Writers and Readers in Late-Eighteenth-Century England.*

The Anne Rice Trivia Book by Katherine Ramsland. New York: Ballantine, 1995; 242 pages, paperback. Drawing from the wealth of research material assembled as a result of the research for her books on Rice, Ramsland noted in the introduction to this book that the extensive detail in Rice's fiction provided "more than enough trivia . . . to fill at least one book." Short answer, multiple choice, fill-in-the-blank, and matching questions cover the Rice canon with over 1,000 queries. (Note: Material based on Rice's "Beauty" novels are not included in this first collection of Rice trivia.)

Haunted City: An Unauthorized Guide to the Magical, Magnificent New Orleans of Anne Rice by Joy Dickinson. Carol Publishing, trade paperback, $14.95, 256 pages.

Prism of the Night: A Biography of Anne Rice by Katherine Ramsland. New York: Dutton, 1991; 385 pages, cloth. Nonfiction. Indexed. A critically acclaimed biography on Rice, this groundbreaking work is indispensable reading for any Rice fan. Written with the consent and cooperation of Anne Rice, *Prism of the Night* is a thoughtful and illuminating biography that sheds light on the author and her canon as well. To the publisher's credit, the book is updated with each new edition; a chapter is added to the end of the biography proper.

The Roquelaure Reader: A Companion to Anne Rice's Erotica by Katherine Ramsland. An authorized companion book from Plume, a $12.95 trade paperback. This book focuses on Rice's erotica and pornography. The book contains a concordance, a long biographical essay with numerous quotes from Rice on her erotic imagination, and a trivia section. It also contains excerpts cut from *Exit to Eden.*

The Vampire Companion: The Official Guide to Anne Rice's "The Vampire Chronicles." New York: Ballantine Books, 1993; 508 pages, hardback. Nonfiction. An insider's look at the first four novels in the Vampire Chronicles, this "interpretive guide" to Rice's world was written with the consent and cooperation of Anne Rice. As Ramsland put it:

> This book is intended as a supplement to *The Vampire Chronicles*, and even though parts of plots are summarized in places, the *Companion* should not be seen as a substitute for reading the novels. Consisting of over one thousand entries, the *Companion* also includes a chronology of events that begin with the Vampire origins; maps of significant locations; cross-references; and over one hundred drawings and photographs. I organized the entries in encyclopedic fashion and added background material, expanding the significance of key events and ideas. I categorized the contents of Rice's novels according to characters, places, themes, literary allusions and devices, symbols, famous quotes, and vampire-related terminology. . . .

The Witches' Companion: The Official Guide to Anne Rice's "Lives of the Mayfair Witches." New York: Ballantine, 1994; 522 pages, hardback. Nonfiction. Similar in scope, layout, and design to her previous companion book, *The Vampire Companion*, this covers in exhaustive detail the three novels that make up the Lives of the Mayfair Witches.

Forthcoming Projects

The Anne Rice Reader, edited by Katherine Ramsland, is principally a collection of scholarly essays on Rice's fiction, plus a section discussing the film *Interview with the Vampire*, two Rice short stories, and an interview with Rice. Scheduled for publication as a trade paperback in the spring of 1997, the book will appear under a Knopf imprint.

Conversations with Anne Rice by Michael Riley. Ballantine Books, trade paperback, $12.

The Gothic World of Anne Rice [tentative title, price not yet determined], edited by Ray Browne and Gary Hoppenstand. Bowling Green University Press, 1996; 280 pages, hardback and trade paperback. The book will consist of approximately fifteen scholarly essays about Rice's fiction.

APPENDIX THREE
◆
Audiography

Note: Unless otherwised noted, the recording is unabridged.

Anne Rice's "The Vampire Chronicles." Random House Audiobooks. Six cassettes, running time of 9 hours. $39.95. The first three books (*Interview with the Vampire, The Vampire Lestat, The Queen of the Damned*) in a coffin-shaped box with inserts showing a vampire in a coffin (presumably Lestat) and a young blond child (presumably Claudia).

Beauty's Release (third of three novels in the "Beauty" trilogy). Simon and Schuster Audioworks. Two cassettes, running time of 3 hours. $17. Read by Elizabeth Montgomery, with Christian Keiber as Laurent.

Beauty's Punishment (second of three books in the "Beauty" trilogy). Simon and Schuster Audioworks. Two cassettes, running time of 3 hours. $17. Read by Elizabeth Montgomery.

Belinda. Random House Audiobooks. Two cassettes, running time of 2 hours. $16. Read by Al Mohrmann.

The Claiming of Sleeping Beauty (first of three novels in the "Beauty" trilogy). Simon and Schuster Audioworks. Two cassettes, running time of 3 hours. $17. Read by Amy Brenneman.

Cry to Heaven. Random House Audiobooks. Two cassettes, running time of 3 hours. $16. Read by Tim Curry.

Exit to Eden. Random House Audiobooks. Running time of 2 hours. $16.

The Feast of All Saints. Random House Audiobooks. Abridged. Two cassettes, running time of 3 hours. $8.99. Read by Courtney B. Vance. (Note: This, according to Random House, is "a price-less audio.")

Interview with the Vampire. Random House Audiobooks. Two cassettes, running time of approximately 3 hours. $16. Read by F. Murray Abraham. An unabridged recording, read by Abraham, on three compact discs is also available from Random House. An unabridged recording read by Frank Muller on 10 cassettes (running time, 14.75 hours). Rental, $17.50; purchase, $83. Recorded Books.

Lasher. Random House Audiobooks. Two cassettes, running time of 3 hours. $17. Read by Joe Morton.

Memnoch the Devil. Random House Audiobooks. Four cassettes, running time of 4 hours. $23.50. Read by Roger Rees.

The Mummy, or Ramses the Damned. Random House Audiobooks. Two cassettes, running time of 3 hours. $16. Read by Michael York.

The Queen of the Damned. Random House Audiobooks. Two cassettes, running time of 3 hours. $16. Read by Kate Nelligan; the character of Louis is read by David Purdham. An unabridged recording read by Frank Muller on 15 cassettes (running time, 21.75 hours). Rental, $20.50; purchase, $109. Recorded Books.

The Tale of the Body Thief. Random House Audiobooks. Two cassettes, running time of 3 hours. $16. Read by Richard E. Grant. An unabridged recording read by Frank Muller on 14 cassettes (running time, 19.25 hours). Rental, $19.50; purchase, $104.

Taltos. Random House Audiobooks. Abridged. Four cassettes, running time of 4 hours. $22.50. Read by Tim Curry.

The Vampire Lestat. Random House Audiobooks. Abridged. Two cassettes, running time of 3 hours. $16. Read by Michael York. An unabridged recording read by Frank Muller on 16 cassettes (running time, 23.5 hours). Rental, $21.50; purchase, $115. Recorded Books.

The Witching Hour. Random House Audiobooks. Abridged. Two cassettes, running time of approximately 3 hours. $15.95. Read by Lindsay Crouse.

Note: Recorded Books, Inc., distributes its own line of unabridged books on tape directly to its customers, who normally rent the tapes. You can use a credit card and place an order by phone (1-800-638-1304) or mail a check to Recorded Books at: 270 Skipjack Road, Prince Frederick, MD 20678.

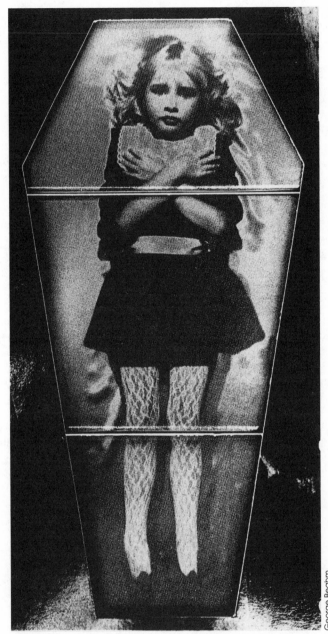

George Beahm

Triptych design for the audio collection, *Anne Rice's "The Vampire Chronicles"*

APPENDIX FOUR

◆

Filmography, Videography, Discography

Filmography

Exit to Eden. October 1994. Savoy Pictures. Directed by Garry Marshall. Produced by Alexandra Rose and Garry Marshall. Written by Deborah Amelon and Bob Brunner. Photographed by Theo Van De Sande. Edited by David Finfer. Music by Patrick Doyle. Running time: 113 minutes. Rating: R (for nudity and sex-related scenes). ◆ Cast: Lisa (played by Dana Delany), Elliot (Paul Mercurio), Sheila (Rosie O'Donnell), Fred (Dan Aykroyd), Martin (Hector Elizondo), Omar (Stuart Wilson), Nina (Iman), Tommy (Sean O'Bryan). ◆ Comments: The critical consensus is that this movie is light fluff. "It's adequately entertaining and instantly forgettable," observed R. Scott Bolton of *Hollywood Hotline*. "To sit through the S&M comedy . . . it helps to be in pain—the pain of an excruciatingly wrongheaded blend of broad farce and sex-fantasy fluff," wrote Susan Wloszczyna for *USA Today*. Roger Ebert: "On the first page of my notes, I wrote 'Starts slow.' On the second page, I wrote 'Boring.' On the third page, I wrote 'Endless!' "

Interview with the Vampire. November 1994. Geffen Productions. Directed by Neil Jordan. Produced by Stephen Woolley and David Geffen. Written by Anne Rice. Photographed by Philippe Rousselot. Edited by Mick Audsley. Music by Elliot Goldenthal. Running time: 115 minutes. Rating: R (for violence, gore, and sexuality). ◆ Cast: Lestat (played by Tom Cruise), Louis (Brad Pitt), Armand (Antonio Banderas), Santiago (Stephen Rea), Molloy (Christian Slater), Claudia (Kirsten Dunst).

Videography

Anne Rice: Birth of the Vampire. Running time, 45 minutes. CBS Fox Video. 1994.

Exit to Eden. Running time, 120 minutes. HBO/Savoy Video. 1994.

Interview with the Vampire. 123 minutes. Warner Home Video. 1995.

Discography

Interview with the Vampire. Geffen Records, Inc., 1994. Music composed by Elliot Goldenthal. Music produced by Matthias Gohl. Orchestrations by Robert Elhai and Elliot Goldenthal. Conducted by Jonathan Sheffer. Recorded and mixed by Steve McLaughlin and Joel Iwataki. Electronic music produced by Richard Martinez. Orchestra contracted by Emile Charlap. Recorded and mixed at Manhattan Center Studios, New York. Music editors: Michael Connell and Chris Brooks. Soundtrack editor: Todd Kasow. Mastered by Vlado Meller at Sony Music, New York. ◆ "Libera Me," "Born to Darkness, Part I," "Lestat's Tarantella," "Madeleine's Lament," "Claudia's Allegro Agitato," "Escape to Paris," "Marche Furnebre," "Lestat's Recitative," "Santiago's Waltz," "Théâtre des Vampires," "Armand's Seduction," "Plantation Pyre," "Forgotten Lore," "Scent of Death," "Abduction & Absolution," "Armand Rescues Louis," "Louis' Revenge," "Born to Darkness, Part II," "Sympathy for the Devil" (performed by Guns N' Roses).

◆

Graphic Novel Adaptations

Unless you've gone into a specialty store—one that caters to comic-book fans—you've probably never seen any of the graphic novel adaptations of Rice's work. To the Rice purist who doesn't want interpretive editions, graphic novels will seem superfluous, especially since they are adapted from in-print texts. Still, for the Rice completist, these adaptations are, at the least, visual variants worthy of your attention.

Note: Innovation, which has published the majority of the graphic novel adaptations, is no longer in business. Your best bet is to check at comic-book specialty stores for individual issues, and bookstores for the book compilation, *The Vampire Lestat*.

Interview with the Vampire (Innovation). A twelve-issue series. Full color covers and full color interior pages. Trim size: approximately 6.75 x 10.25 inches. Page count: 32. Cover price, $2.50; mail order, $3.50; 12-issue subscription, $42.

The Master of Rampling Gate (Innovation, June 1991). Trade paperback; page count: 64 pages. Credits: adapted by James Schlosser, painted by Colleen Doran, lettered by Vickie Williams, edited by David Campiti. Cover painting by John Bolton; book design by David Campiti; logo design by George Broderick Jr. ◆ This graphic adaptation is based on a revised version of the short story of the same name that appeared in *Redbook* magazine.

The Queen of the Damned (Innovation). A twelve-issue series. Full color covers and full color interior pages. Trim size: approximately 6.75 x 10.25 inches. Page count: 32. Cover price, $2.50; mail order, $3.50; 12-issue subscription, $36.

The Vampire Companion (Innovation). A three-issue series. Full color covers and full color interior pages. Trim size: approximately 6.75 x 10.25 inches. Page count: 32 pages. $6.95.

#1 (1991): Introduction by Renee Nard; "Interview with the Vampire Writer," conducted by Renee Nard; article, "The 'Queen of the Damned' Switches to Witches" by Steve Garbarino; Interview with Faye Perozich (adapter and designer of "Anne Rice's *The Vampire Lestat*"), "Queen of the Adapters," conducted by Renee Nard, illustrated with page-by-page breakdowns to show how a comic-book adaptation is done; Interview with Joseph Lieaneaus Phillips (character designer and penciller on part of "Anne Rice's *The Vampire Lestat #1*"), "The Penciller Phillips," conducted by Renee Nard; Interview with Michael Okamoto (penciller for "Anne Rice's *The Vampire Lestat #3 and #4*), "The Master of Pencilling Great," conducted by Renee Nard; two pages from *The Vampire Lestat #4* (art by Daerick Gross and Mike Okamoto); Interview with Daerick Gross (penciller-painter for "Anne Rice's *The Vampire Lestat*"), "The Feast of All Saints," conducted by Renee Nard; Interview with David Campiti (editor and publisher of Innovation Publishing), "The Claiming & Release of the Editor," conducted by Renee Nard; and an article, "The Anne Rice Vampire Lestat Fan Club" by Teresa Simmons (one of the founding members of the Vampire Lestat Fan Club).

#2 (1991): introduction, "The Thirst Continues" by David Campiti; "An Interview with Anne Rice," conducted by Katherine Ramsland; article, "*Prism of the Night*: First Look Behind the Scenes of Anne Rice's Authorized Biography" by Katherine Ramsland; Interview with John Bolton (cover painter for "Anne Rice's *The Vampire Lestat*, *The Master of Rampling Gate*, and *Interview with the Vampire*), "Bolton Across the Atlantic," conducted by Diana Light; Interview with Sandy Collora, "The Collora of (Creature Effects) Magic," conducted by Diana Light; article, "Coven Party II: Honoring Anne Amidst the Madness" by Teresa Simmons (one of the founding members of the Vampire Lestat Fan Club); cover reproduction of *The Master of Rampling Gate* by John Bolton; article, "Special Previews" by Jim Elliott, updating the readers on forthcoming Innovation projects, illustrated with 12 pages of art.

#3 (1992): introduction, "It's Nice to Have a Companion . . ." by David Campiti; Interview with Anne Rice, "The Queen of the Chroniclers," conducted by Teresa Simmons; article, "Biographical Reflections: A Look at *Prism of the Night*" by Katherine Ramsland; Interview with Daerick Gross, "Words of Wisdom by the Gross," conducted by Diana Light; Interview with Christopher Moeller, "Mulling It Over with Moeller," conducted by

Diana Light; Interview with Cynthy J. Wood, "A Writer Out of the Wood Work," conducted by Diana Light; a one-page photo gallery; an Interview with Vickie Williams, "A Woman of Letters," conducted by David Campiti; an article, "Coven Party III: Le Bal Des Vampires" by Teresa Simmons; a profile of Michael Walker, "A Sculptor You Can Sink Your Teeth Into," by David Campiti.

The Vampire Lestat (Innovation). A twelve-issue series. Full color covers and full color interior pages. Trim size: approximately 6.75 x 10.25 inches. Page count: 32. (Note: in the compilation, the page count is 384 pages.) Cover price, $2.50; mail order, $3.50; 12-issue subscription, $42. Exclusive of the individual issues as published, there are five editions of the compilations:

- a trade paperback from Ballantine, with a cover by Daerick Gross.
- a trade paperback from Innovation, with a cover by John Bolton; $28.
- a hardback from Innovation; $45.
- a limited edition of 500 copies in hardback, signed by Faye Perozich (adapter of the series), Daerick Gross (artist/painter), and David Campiti (editor/publisher); $59.95.
- An edition of 2,000 collated sets of *The Vampire Lestat* 1 through 12 and *The Vampire Companion* 1 and 2, laid in a plastic tray case, accompanied with a certificate of authenticity signed by David Campiti; $49.95.

The Witching Hour (Millennium Publications, 105 Edgewater Road, Narragansett, RI 02882). A thirteen-issue series; issue #5 is due out in January 1996. Full color covers and full color interior pages. Trim size: approximately 6.75 x 10.25 inches. Page count: 32 pages. Cover price, $2.50. (Note: The first three issues have been collected as a graphic album, *Anne Rice's THE WITCHING HOUR: The Beginning*, 108 pages, $10.95.)

APPENDIX SIX
◆
Resources

1. Mainstream Bookstores

A prolific author, Anne Rice is not only a bestselling author but a celebrity in her own right. To her credit, she has not succumbed to the cult of the celebrity, preferring to avoid the limelight and focusing on that which brought her the fame: the writing itself.

Rice's major books are published by Alfred A. Knopf, usually in the fall, in time for the Christmas trade. Released in hardback, the first editions are so noted at the bottom of the copyright page with the notation "First Edition." (Rice collectors should ensure that this notice is on their copies, since advance orders can sometimes generate additional printings *before* the official publication date; for instance, there are copies of *The Queen of the Damned* in which the publishing information states: "Published October 31, 1988/ Second Printing Before Publication.")

Typically, most independent bookstores charge full retail, though discounted copies can usually be found at the chains through their frequent buyer programs, and stores like Sam's Club and the Price Club typically stock each new Rice novel at discounts ranging up to 45 percent.

For the Rice collector who wants to round out his collection, the trade bookstore is a good place to special-order items like books and audiotapes, though one may be in for a wait; if a regional wholesaler or distributor does not have the item in stock, it may take four to six weeks to order from the publisher. (Note: Do not expect the retailer to be knowledgeable about the graphic novel adaptations; chances are good he's familiar with—if anything—the trade editions.)

2. Mail-order Specialty Booksellers

Unlike their trade counterparts, mail-order booksellers usually specialize and are more knowledgeable about availability of product from specific authors. For

Anne Rice readers, for instance, mail-order dealers that specialize in horror and fantasy usually stock not only the trade books but the more exotic material too, like the signed, limited editions that are usually not in trade bookstores.

For the Rice reader wanting first editions, these dealers are the preferred sources; they not only take care meticulously to grade the books, but also pack and ship carefully, ensuring that your order arrives in good condition.

Based on personal dealings, I recommend the following mail-order booksellers:

Barry R. Levin Science Fiction & Fantasy Literature, 720 Santa Monica Boulevard, Santa Monica, CA 90401. Proprietor, Barry R. Levin. Phone: (310) 458-6111. ◆ Barry rightly bills himself as a "premier purveyor of science fiction & fantasy rarities." If, for instance, there existed a copy of *Memnoch the Devil* bound in the relatively scarce skin of long pig, signed in red ink with a decidedly red-rust color, accompanied by a stench when the book was opened, then Barry could locate it for you. My recommendation: If you are looking for proofs or advance copies of Rice's books, this is a good place to start.

The Garden District Book Shop, 2727 Prytania Street, New Orleans, LA 70130. Proprietor, Britton E. Trice. Phone: (504) 895-2266; electronic mail on America Online: BETbooks. ◆ Located a few blocks from Anne Rice's home, Trice's bookstore has the good fortune to have affiliated with Rice. In addition to hosting several signings, Trice also offers signed Rice books by mail and, for collectors, publishes limited, signed editions of each new Rice novel. (Although these are rebound copies of the Knopf editions, these are still the only signed editions available of the more recent titles, with small print runs: 500 copies, $150; and 26 lettered copies, $350.) *The* bookstore of choice for Rice fans, Trice's is well worth your time at which to stop and shop if you're in New Orleans; otherwise, drop him a note and ask to be put on his mailing list, and let him know what specifically you are looking for, and he'll find it.

The Overlook Connection, PO Box 526, Woodstock, GA 30188. Proprietor, Dave Hinchberger. Phone: (404) 926-1762; fax, (404) 516-1469; electronic mail on America Online: Overlookcn. Accepts Visa, Mastercard, personal or business check, money orders. ◆ In business since 1987, the Overlook Connection caters to fantasy, science fiction, and horror fans. Publishes an illustrated newsletter with an emphasis on new books, though some collector's items are available.

Robert and Phyllis Weinberg, 15145 Oxford Drive, Oak Forest, IL 60452.

• A highly regarded company that caters to collectors, the Weinbergs are collectors themselves and have their fingers on the pulse of small-press publishing. They publish a monthly newsletter that features new, in-stock titles. (Note: Depending on the publisher and the project, in the small-press field, it is routine to accept advance payment for books that may be months away from publication. The Weinbergs do *not* list anything in their catalog unless it is in print and ready to ship.)

3. Meeting Anne Rice Fans

By mail: If you're a member of the official Anne Rice's Vampire Lestat Fan Club, the club will provide an updated correspondence list of members.

By electronic mail:

• On America Online (AOL), look under the keyword SCIENCE FICTION, where you will find several discussion groups organized by topic.

• On the Internet, check out the following mailing lists:

1. ANNERICE
2. ARBOOKS

Both have the same site address: PSUVM.PSU.EDU

The site ANNERICE is more general and focuses on the writer, whereas ARBOOKS focuses only on her books.

Also, check out the following usenet newsgroup: alt.books.annerice

Finally, use a web browser to look for Anne Rice web site pages; several are available, and updated periodically.

There has been at least one Anne Rice hoax perpetrated online; a discussion group on America Online, purporting to have been started by Rice herself, generated dozens of queries from readers asking questions. In *Commotion Strange #3*, Rice sets the record straight: "Regarding E-mail, Internet, etc.: I'm not hooked up to anything, and have no modem. . . . I speak sometimes through my friend Britton Trice on the Internet. Anyone else claiming to be me or to speak for me is not telling the truth. Britton Trice is my sole connection."

In person: Attend the Annual Gathering of the Coven, which is sponsored by Anne Rice's Vampire Lestat Fan Club, where she may make an appearance. (You may also catch her on a nationwide book tour, where she gives interviews to the media and attends book signings at stores, as she did for *Memnoch the Devil*.)

4. Touring New Orleans

For Rice fans, a trip to New Orleans is literary nirvana. For basic information on New Orleans, contact The Greater New Orleans Tourist and Convention Commission, Inc., 1520 Sugar Bowl Drive, New Orleans, LA 70112; telephone (504) 566-5011.

Perhaps the best time to make the trip is in October in time for the Annual Gathering of the Coven, but be forewarned: lodging, I'm told, is hard to come by in October due to tourists and conventioneers, so make reservations early.

When you contact the Tourist and Convention Commission, it will send you a packet of information: a calendar of events, an accommodations brochure, and a visitor's guide which has excellent full color maps providing detailed information. (Additionally, you'll get mailings from hotels separately, since the commission makes its mailing list available to local businesses.)

Obviously, no trip to New Orleans is complete without seeing Anne Rice's home in the Garden District—one of many sights to see on the Gray Line Tour; located at 2 Canal Street, #1300, New Orleans, LA 70130; telephone (504) 587-0861; FAX (504) 5587-0708. "Enjoy a walk through New Orleans' elegant Garden District, well known for its beautiful, luxurious homes off of St. Charles Avenue. View the oldest house in the area, built in 1838, the home where Jefferson Davis died in 1889, and the home of celebrated author Anne Rice. Visiting Lafayette Cemetery, one of our 'Cities of the Dead.' Takes approximately two hours."

If your taste runs toward the macabre, there is a three-hour tour of the "Cities of the Dead," available through Cukie's Travels, Inc.; located at 1229 St. Thomas Street, New Orleans, LA 70130; telephone (504) 244-9679. "Take a trip back in time through our unique 'Cities of the Dead' Cemetery Tour. Hear about the history & background while walking through two and walking and riding through the third one. By reservation only. A unique, interesting and informative tour you shouldn't miss."

An alternative to the walking tours above: Magic Walking Tours; telephone (504) 593-9693. Unlike the other companies, this one doesn't require reservations. "Join us at point of departure 10 minutes before tour!" Tours include: St. Louis Cemetery #1; French Quarter; Garden District; VooDoo; and Haunted House, Vampire & Ghost Hunt. (A note to the wise: bring your own fire-hardened wooden stakes . . .)

For the Rice purist, wanting to see how reality has influenced her fantasy worlds, a careful reading of Ramsland's two companion books (*The Vampire Companion* and *The Witches' Companion*) will provide a wealth of Rice sites. (For instance, in *The Vampire Companion*, the entry for the Café du Monde in New Orleans: "Here, Lestat ponders his situation after Marius and Louis reject him for becoming mortal.")

On guidebooks: There are plenty to choose from, updated annually. My recommendation: *New Orleans* by Bethany Ewald Bultman, with photographs by Richard Sexon; a trade paperback, 300 pages, $16.95. Another good choice, more Rice-specific: *Haunted City* by Joy Dickinson; a trade paperback, 256 pages, $14.95.

5. Contacting Rice Directly

Anne Rice is readily accessible. With the most famous address in New Orleans—not unlike Stephen King's address in Bangor, Maine—Rice, predictably, gets a lot of fan mail at 1239 First Street, New Orleans, LA 70130.

"Answering personal letters: Can't do it anymore. Just downright impossible. Occasionally I have a minute, but my life now is a desperate fight to find a few hours to be alone with this machine, writing on my work. What distracts me is not only continuous requests for publicity, but my great and loving family whom I enjoy and want to spend time with, and wouldn't give up for the world. But I have become overbooked, there is no doubt about it," she wrote in *Commotion Strange #3*.

In November, after the movie release of *Interview with the Vampire*, she relisted one of her phone numbers and urged her readers to call, to hear her updated recorded message on current projects, and to leave messages for her, which she may answer in *Commotion Strange* or through the fan club newsletter. Anne Rice's hotline: (504) 522-8634.

With Undying Thanks

I first met Anne Rice at an American Booksellers Association convention, where she patiently and graciously signed books for two hours nonstop. Taking the time to talk to each bookseller, she gave each her undivided attention and, for those few moments, made each person feel special.

I was in that line, getting a book signed for a friend of mine, and her charm and genuine honesty won me over—a sharp contrast to some of the others who had somehow been cajoled or forced into attending, to sign books, and who gave the distinct impression that time spent in a penal colony would have been preferable.

When I got home, I headed to the bookstore and bought the first book by her I could find. It was *Interview with the Vampire*. After reading the first few pages, I was hooked. The last time I had been so captivated by a writer was when I had picked up a copy of *'Salem's Lot*, another book about vampires, by a then little-known writer named Stephen King.

On this book, a small army of people helped out in many ways, both minor and major, and a lengthy recitation would run, like the end credits of a movie, far too long. Instead, let me thank the key people who were instrumental in helping shape this book.

♦ Colleen Doran, whose enthusiasm for Anne Rice prompted my interest in Rice. In addition to providing an interview, writing the preface, and combing her considerable book collection to find every Rice book she could find, she kept her eyes open and gave me clippings from various magazines that featured interviews, profile material, or articles. Thanks, Colleen. I am in your debt.

♦ Katherine Ramsland, who with her first book on Rice established herself as *the* Anne Rice expert. Her phone calls, faxes, and photocopies of her published material were of immeasurable help.

♦ Michael Collings, who once again dropped everything in order to write a new piece for this book. (Guardian angels are all the rage these days; I believe in the earthbound variety, like Michael.)

♦ Britton E. Trice, who has his hands full running a retail bookstore and mail-order bookstore operation, always found the time to answer questions, send resources, and keep me updated on Rice news on the publishing front.

With Undying Thanks

♦ The folks at the New Orleans *Times-Picayune*, who sent copies of photos, photocopies of articles and profiles about Rice, and bibliographic information about Rice that, otherwise, would have been impossible to locate.

♦ Earl Perry, Scott Stewart, Kat Frazier, and Bob Beamer for photographs of New Orleans and Anne Rice.

♦ The fine folks at Andrews and McMeel, who once again proved that business and friendship are not mutually exclusive: Donna Martin, my book editor, who with each manuscript has worked wonders—and, often, miracles; JuJu Johnson, who kept the lines of communication open; Katie Mace, who is an absolute joy to work with; and Matt Lombardi and Carol Coe.

♦ Others who must be mentioned: Sascha Mabus-Vosper, Mel Graziano, Rusty and Maria Wornom, Stephen Spignesi, Charlie Fried, and Lori Zuccaro.

♦ Finally, I am as always indebted to my wife, Mary, who has been my sounding board on everything that went into the book—text, photography, design—and helped out in other ways, far too numerous to mention.

◆
Acknowledgments

"Foreword," written especially for this book, is © 1995 by Colleen Doran. All Rights Reserved.

Part One

"The House at 1239 First Streeet," by Martha Ann Brett Samuel and Ray Samuel, originally appeared in *The Great Days of the Garden District*, and was published in 1978 by the Parents' League of the Louis S. McGehee School.

"Novel End for Landmark: Rices Purchase St. Elizabeth's for New Home," by Ronette King, originally appeared in the New Orleans *Times-Picayune* (May 29, 1993).

"Rice Plans Museum for Dolls at Home," by Coleman Warner, originally appeared in the New Orleans *Times-Picayune* (April 26, 1995).

"An Interview with Anne: The New Orleans Experience," conducted by Ronnie Virgets, originally appeared in *New Orleans Magazine.*

Part Two

From the "Playboy Interview: Anne Rice," *Playboy* magazine (March 1993). Copyright © 1993 by Playboy. All Rights Reserved. Used with permission.

"A Hell of a Good Time: the Memnoch Ball 1995," written especially for this book, is copyright © 1995 by Sascha Mabus-Vosper.

The liner note for *Tableaux de Lestat* originally appeared in a separate handout accompanying the recording. Copyright © 1994 by Mel Graziano.

Part Three

"Why I Wrote a Biography of Anne Rice" originally appeared in *Footsteps* (Summer 1990), and is reprinted with the permission of the author.

"Rice on *Prism of the Night*" is an excerpt from Anne Rice's Zine, *Commotion Strange #3* (1995). No rights reserved.

Acknowledgments

Part Four

Acknowledgments

"To My Readers: A Personal Statement by Anne Rice Regarding the Motion Picture *Interview with the Vampire*" was originally published in *Variety* (Sept. 23, 1994). No rights reserved.

"Sucking Up" by Anthony Lane. Reprinted by permission; © 1994 by Anthony Lane. Originally in *The New Yorker*. All rights reserved.

"A Review of *Interview with the Vampire*," by Roger Ebert is copyright © 1994 by The Ebert Co. Ltd., and reprinted with the permission of the author.

Excerpts from "Anne Rice: On the Film, *Interview with the Vampire*," originally appeared in a booklet bound in *Variety*. No rights reserved.

Part Five

Julia Parker's book review of *Interview with the Vampire*. Reprinted from *Library Journal*, May 1, 1976. Copyright © 1976 by Reed Publishing, USA.

Audio review of *Interview with the Vampire*. Reprinted from *Publishers Weekly*, July 3, 1987. Copyright © 1987 by Reed Publishing, USA.

Audio review of *The Vampire Lestat*. Reprinted from *Publishers Weekly*, July 3, 1987. Copyright © 1987 by Reed Publishing, USA.

Book review of *The Queen of the Damned*. Reprinted from *Publishers Weekly*, August 12, 1993. Copyright © 1993 by Reed Publishing, USA.

Book review of *The Tale of the Body Thief*. Reprinted from *Publishers Weekly*, August 24, 1992. Copyright © 1992 by Reed Publishing, USA.

Audio review by Barbara Valle of *The Tale of the Body Thief*. Reprinted from *Library Journal*, December 1992. Copyright © 1992 by Reed Publishing, USA.

Book review of *Memnoch the Devil*. Reprinted from *Publishers Weekly*, June 5, 1995. Copyright © 1995 by Reed Publishing, USA.

Book review of *The Witching Hour*. Reprinted from *Publishers Weekly*, September 21, 1990. Copyright © 1990 by Reed Publishing, USA.

Audio review of *The Witching Hour*. Reprinted from *Publishers Weekly*, November 2, 1990. Copyright © 1990 by Reed Publishing, USA.

Acknowledgments

Book review of *Lasher*. Reprinted from *Publishers Weekly*, August 9, 1992. Copyright © 1992 by Reed Publishing, USA.

Book review of *Taltos*. Reprinted from *Publishers Weekly*, July 4, 1994. Copyright © 1994 by Reed Publishing, USA.

Book review of *The Mummy*. Reprinted from *Publishers Weekly*, May 5, 1989. Copyright © 1989 by Reed Publishing, USA.

Audio review of *The Mummy*. Reprinted from *Publishers Weekly*, June 2, 1989. Copyright © 1989 by Reed Publishing, USA.

Photos

All photos by George Beahm © 1995 by George Beahm. All rights reserved.

All photos by Kat Frazier © 1995 by Kat Frazier. All rights reserved.

All photos by Earl Perry, Jr., © 1995 by Earl Perry, Jr. All rights reserved.

Photo by Bob Beamer © 1995 by Bob Beamer. All rights reserved.

All photos by Scott Stewart © 1995 by Scott Stewart. All rights reserved.